IMAGES
of America

HUNTINGTON BEACH LIFEGUARDS

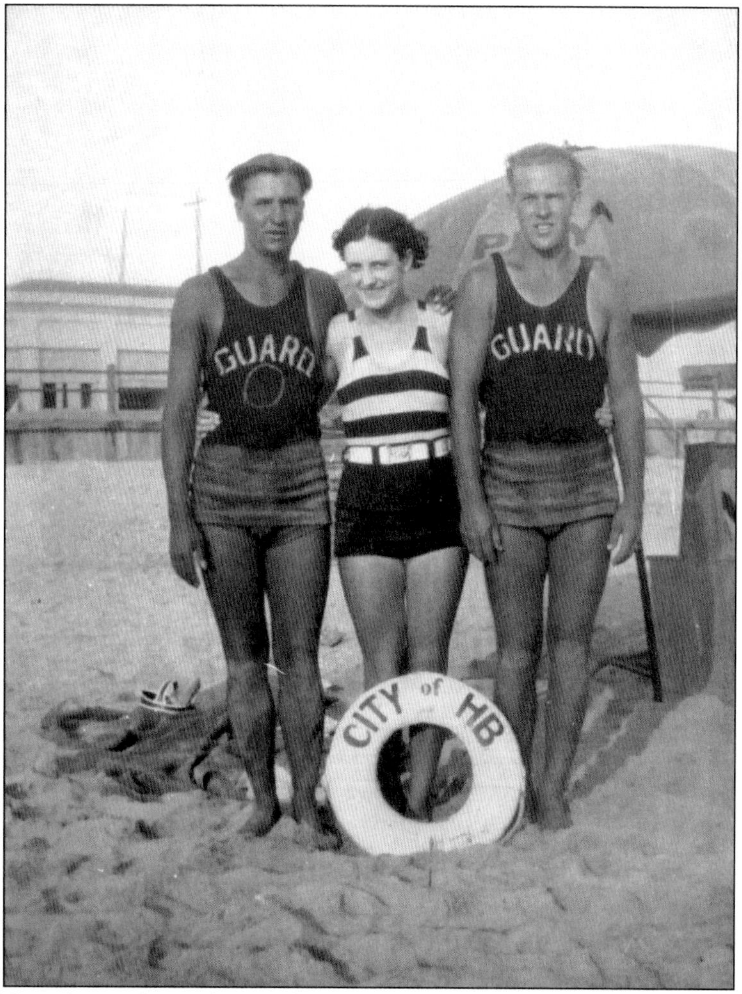

The best of friends stand together in the summer of 1928. From left to right are Gene and Johnie Belshe and Bud Higgins. Gene Belshe was the Huntington Beach lifeguard chief from 1928 to 1931, then a recent U.S. Navy veteran and champion swimmer. Bud Higgins was the lifeguard chief from 1932 to 1950 and later served as the Huntington Beach fire chief. Both led outstanding public safety careers. Gene, a police officer and later motor officer, ultimately became the Huntington Beach assistant chief of police. In 1942, during World War II, Gene, his wife, Johnie, and their young son, Buddy, together set up a bullet manufacturing shop in the cellar of city hall. They produced 1,000 rounds per week for the war effort and police department. Johnie was a swim instructor for decades, starting at the Salt Water Plunge. In 1950, the first Huntington Beach Pier Swim (the 57th annual occurred in 2007) was organized by Gene and Johnie. Buddy Belshe retired in 2007 after 57 years of lifeguard service: 47 years at Newport Beach and 10 years at Huntington Beach. He is pictured on page 121.

ON THE COVER: The year is 1938, when Huntington Beach's lifeguards were then in their fourth decade of a great tradition. Today's edition of the Huntington Beach lifeguards provides a wide variety of marine safety services using highly skilled staff, as well as specialized training and equipment. The beach is internationally recognized as one of the safest, busiest, and best in the world. For the identification of these lifeguards, whose status as cover models came seven decades after the fact, please see page 23.

IMAGES
of America

HUNTINGTON BEACH LIFEGUARDS

Kai Weisser

ARCADIA
PUBLISHING

ISBN 978-0-7385-5605-5

Published by Arcadia Publishing
Charleston, South Carolina

Printed in the United States of America

Library of Congress Catalog Card Number: 2007935823

For all general information contact Arcadia Publishing at:
Telephone 843-853-2070
Fax 843-853-0044
E-mail sales@arcadiapublishing.com
For customer service and orders:
Toll-Free 1-888-313-2665

Visit us on the Internet at www.arcadiapublishing.com

This book is dedicated to Raymond Bray as well as all the lifeguard heroes of the past and to all the lifeguard heroes of today and tomorrow.

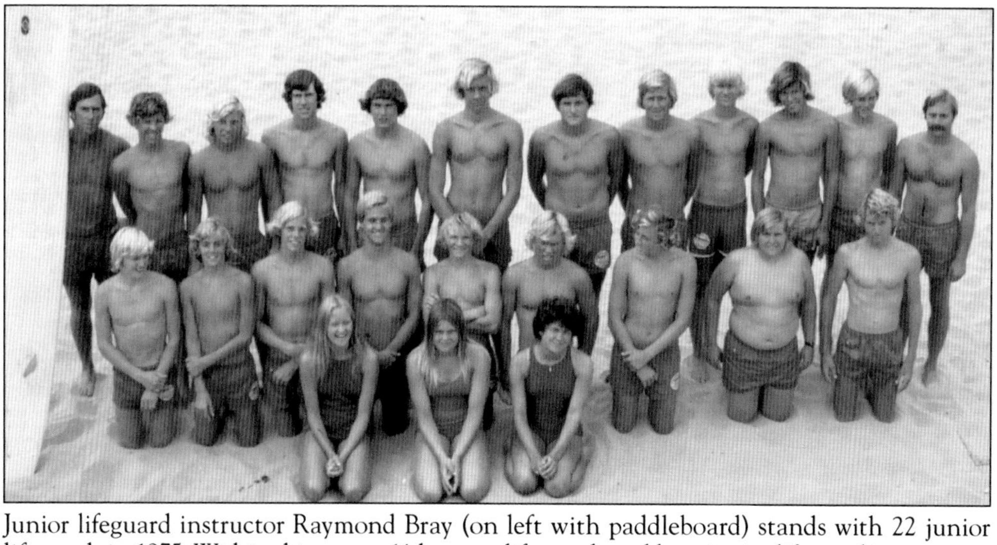

Junior lifeguard instructor Raymond Bray (on left with paddleboard) stands with 22 junior lifeguards in 1975. Within this group, 11 became lifeguards and later junior lifeguard instructors, and three became Huntington Beach Marine Safety Officers. Bray was a legendary lifeguard, competitor, junior lifeguard instructor, teacher, Fountain Valley High School swim and water polo coach, and incredible person.

Contents

Acknowledgments

This book was an incredible journey that led, in sometimes funny ways, to a wide variety of locations in Orange, Los Angeles, San Diego, and Riverside Counties. I thank everyone for their contributions and support. The Huntington Beach Marine Safety Division was the original source for this book; therefore, I am most grateful to marine safety chief Kyle Lindo, Mike Bartlett, Matt Karl, Claude Panis, Mike Eich, Kristina Eich, Doug Leach, and Eric Rex. From the lifeguard alumni, I must also thank Max Bowman, Doug D'Arnall, and Bill Richardson for placing so many names to unidentified faces. I also thank Bob "Knis" Knisley (1937 crew), Jack Cockrell and Lewis Ross (both 1942 crew), Harlo LeBard and Elmer Combs (1944 crew), and Frank Ciarelli and Chuck Linnen. From Huntington State Beach, thanks go to Mike Brusard, Bill Kramer, Lonnie Graham, Steve Hicks, John Rodgers, John Hernandez, the Deboer brothers, Alex Peabody, and Mike Martino. Newport Beach Marine Safety officers John Blauer and Brent Jacobson also deserve thanks. References for this book include Diann Marsh's *Huntington Beach: The Gem of the South Coast*; Lt. Michael Biggs's *The First 80 Years: History of the Huntington Beach Police Department*; Harry Henslick's *Huntington Beach: An Oral History* (California State University, Fullerton); archived issues of the *HB News*; the personal notes of Bud Higgins, shared by his granddaughter, Gae Treece; several old issues of *Ocean Lifeguard* and *American Lifeguard Magazine*; and, of course, the Internet. Retired Los Angeles County lifeguard chief Bob Burnside was my archivist mentor from my first photograph collected in 1991 to the last. I am even more grateful for the photographs and information collected from the late Johnie Belshie in 1991 and, interestingly, from Los Angeles County lifeguard lieutenant Bud Bohn. In 1978, Bohn interviewed Bud Higgins on cassette tape as they were parked in front of HB lifeguard headquarters in Bohn's VW van, while Pacific Coast Highway (PCH) traffic sometimes muffled the recording. Priceless! Photographic credits go to Huntington Beach Marine Safety Division, Huntington Beach Surf Life Saving Association, Huntington State Beach, Office of the Huntington Beach City Clerk, Huntington Beach Public Information Office, Huntington Beach Police Officers Association, Amateur Athletic Foundation of Los Angeles (AAFLA), First American Title, Old Courthouse Museum, Orange County archivists Phil Brigandi and Chris Jepson, Jerry Person, Tom Mays, Dennis Masuda, National Dorymen's Association (NDA), Peggy O'Donnell, Aaron Pai, Alice Gustafson, Marylin Noth, Cris Catell, Marty Armstrong, Steve Reuter, Triduo.com, and myself (personal photographs). Finally, I give thanks, gratitude, hugs, and much more to my wife, Tara, and children, Lauren and Nolan.

INTRODUCTION

Huntington Beach (HB) is located in Orange County, California, and is recognized internationally for its nine miles of wide sandy beaches, surfing, municipal pier, sporting events, and a host of other activities, including the filming of movies and television commercials. Huntington Beach, Surf City USA®, a registered trademark of the HB Conference and Visitors Bureau, is a true coastal playground destination.

Likewise, the tradition and history of the HB lifeguards is internationally recognized for its marine safety professionalism, public education, aquatic rescue, lifeguard Tower Zero, junior lifeguards, and capability to protect the millions of diverse beach visitors each year. During the summer of 2007, the reality television series *Beach Patrol* filmed the HB lifeguards and, after compiling heroic footage, made the dramatic documentary *Ocean Force: Huntington Beach, OC* in 2008. Within the documentary, possibly the only one of its kind in the United States, the HB lifeguards revived and saved a 14-year-old boy with an Automatic External Defibrillator (AED) within two to three minutes of cardiac arrest and collapsing in the ocean. The photograph of this event with CPR in progress can be seen on page 122.

The history and story of the HB lifeguards is an interesting one, and this book includes the California State Parks, Huntington Beach, in Chapter Four and the Junior Lifeguard Program in Chapter Five. In addition, early HB lifeguard archival material is presented for the first time with photographs and history that have been awaiting discovery.

For the first HB lifeguards, the world-famous Huntington Beach Pier was a focal point, and that same tradition continues today. On July 4, 1904, the celebrated Henry Huntington Pacific Electric (PE) "Red Car" arrived at the pier with the first of many passengers, tourists, and bathers. These early visitors may have met George A. Reynolds, HB's first lifeguard (without pay), who served from 1904 to 1907. According to Delbert "Bud" Higgins, an 1888 law required at least one lifeboat, or dory, be stationed at bather beaches; the last dory at the HB Pier was stationed there about 1940, and the first lifeguard, George A. Reynolds, was an excellent doryman.

Beach patrons in the early part of the century swam slowly and awkwardly using the sidestroke, breaststroke, or even the dog paddle. Unfortunately, drownings at Huntington Beach and along the Southern California coast were not unusual. Common sense inspired early HB lifeguard rescue techniques, including throwing a life ring from the pier (with line attached and stationed every 75 feet) or providing a "swim line" in the water secured by heavy posts perpendicular to shore. A third and inherently more dangerous rescue alternative was the use of the lifeboat.

Sometime after Reynolds's tenure, the HB lifeguards selection and pay was equally shared with the Huntington Beach Company and the City of Huntington Beach. In 1920, two World War I veterans and HB High School graduates Charles "Chas" Robert Nutt Jr. and Henry Brooks were hired as ocean lifeguards. Nutt was likely born in Pacific City (renamed Huntington Beach in 1903). Brooks was an outstanding athlete who was born in Williston, North Dakota, and became Huntington Beach's first black lifeguard and later a distinguished artist. In 1921, early in the HB oil boom, police chief Jack Tinsley controlled both the fire and lifeguard departments and appointed Harry Lee the head lifeguard. Junior lifeguard Bud Higgins, who turned 14 the same year, began lifeguarding in 1924, and served as lifeguard chief from 1932 to 1950.

Gene Belshe (lifeguard chief from 1928 to 1931) and Higgins, the city's first full-time lifeguards, emerged as lifesaving and surfing pioneers and together built HB's first surfboards. Higgins would later recall when he and Belshe invited the "Father of Surfing," Duke Kahanamoku, to surf the HB Pier, as well as when "the Duke" made a heroic 1925 rescue, reported by the Newport police chief as "the most superhuman surfboard rescue act the world has ever seen." Lifeguard chief Higgins watched the city reorganize the police and fire departments in 1934, separating the lifeguards and establishing their own department. The years to follow were full of change and innovation, including the relocation of the municipal lifeguard headquarters from the beach onto the pier; the acquisition of four-wheel-drive vehicles with sirens, radio, and telephone communications; and the joint effort with Newport Beach lifeguard chief Frank Crocker to produce the first lifeguard training and general orders manuals.

In 1950, Huntington Beach welcomed the new lifeguard service in the California State Park (and Bolsa Chica in 1960), Bud Higgins became HB's new fire chief, the HB city lifeguards were quickly placed under the fire department, and Elmer Combs became the new lifeguard chief. That same year, lifeguard Frank Ciarelli rescued a 17-year-old Rosemead boy who broke his neck diving off the HB Pier into shallow water. After a lawsuit, the city prohibited pier jumping and the pier ladder was removed from the beach. In 1953, Combs embarked upon a lengthy teaching and basketball-coaching career at HB High School, leaving Higgins to appoint Fred Swartz the lifeguard chief to work with Capt. Rocky Freeman. In 1955, Higgins placed Capt. Robert "Hammerhead" Gravage (later to find fame in the television series *Gunsmoke*) in charge, followed by Capt. Vincent G. Moorhouse in 1956.

Moorhouse, an elite U.S. Navy Underwater Demolition Team (UDT) instructor and combat veteran, was appointed the HB lifeguard chief in 1957. He quickly reestablished the lifeguard's autonomy, separating it from the fire department, and shared his rigid semi-military leadership of "like it or not," which once again led to widespread changes and innovation for the HB lifeguards. The most obvious changes were the new khaki lifeguard uniforms, CPO caps, and badges visible in the annual crew photographs. The first rescue boats (*Sentinel* and *Guardian*) appeared, the first lifeguard Underwater Search and Recovery Team was created, and training was increased to include Emergency Medical Technician (EMT) certifications and lifeguard officers deputized by the chief of police. With the Southern California population growth and surfing boom, the staff of full-time lifeguards increased from 2 to 13 and the number of seasonal lifeguards increased from 32 to 72. In possibly the organization's finest hour, the HB Junior Lifeguard Program was created in 1964, and today more than 1,000 boys and girls participate each summer.

Also in 1964, the HB Surf Life Saving Association (HBSLSA), the HB State Beach Lifeguard Association (HSBLA), and the National SLSA organizations were formed—similar to the Australia lifesaving structure. The first National SLSA officers were Bob Burnside, president; Dick Hazard, vice president; Max Bowman, secretary; Don Rohrer, treasurer; and Tim Dorsey, sergeant in arms. In 1971, World Life Saving (WLS) was founded in Australia with Moorhouse serving as the first international liaison, the NSLSA president in 1974, and the WLS president in 1976. The first lifeguard exchange program between California and New Zealand began in Huntington Beach and continues today with annual representatives selected by the California SLSA. The HB lifeguards continued their lifesaving association support at the highest levels with the 1988 election of Max Bowman as WLS president and Doug D'Arnall as secretary general, and the 1992 election of Bill Richardson as U.S. Lifesaving Association president.

In 2008, marine safety chief Kyle Lindo supports 3 lieutenants; 10 marine safety officers; and more than 120 seasonal lifeguards, 29 of which are junior lifeguard instructors. Huntington Beach provides a wide variety of marine safety services utilizing highly skilled staff, as well as specialized training and equipment, and is recognized internationally as one of the safest, busiest, and finest beaches in the world.

One

THE EARLY YEARS 1904–1949

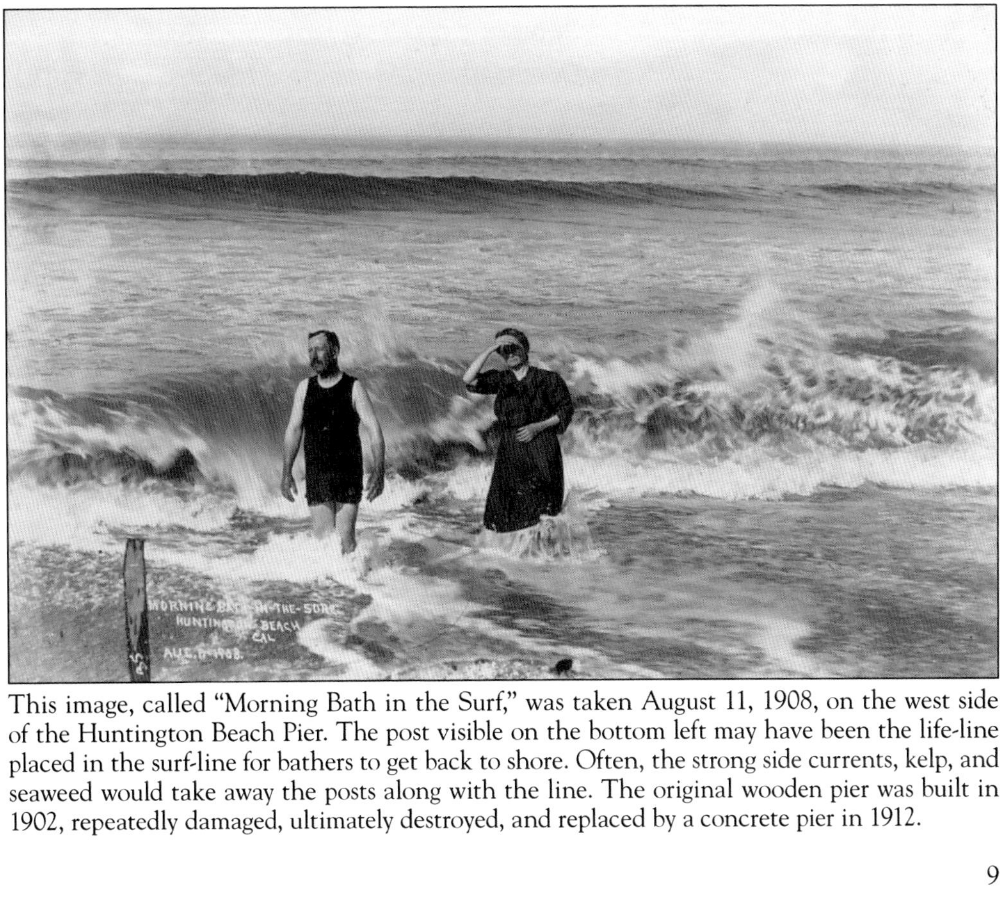

This image, called "Morning Bath in the Surf," was taken August 11, 1908, on the west side of the Huntington Beach Pier. The post visible on the bottom left may have been the life-line placed in the surf-line for bathers to get back to shore. Often, the strong side currents, kelp, and seaweed would take away the posts along with the line. The original wooden pier was built in 1902, repeatedly damaged, ultimately destroyed, and replaced by a concrete pier in 1912.

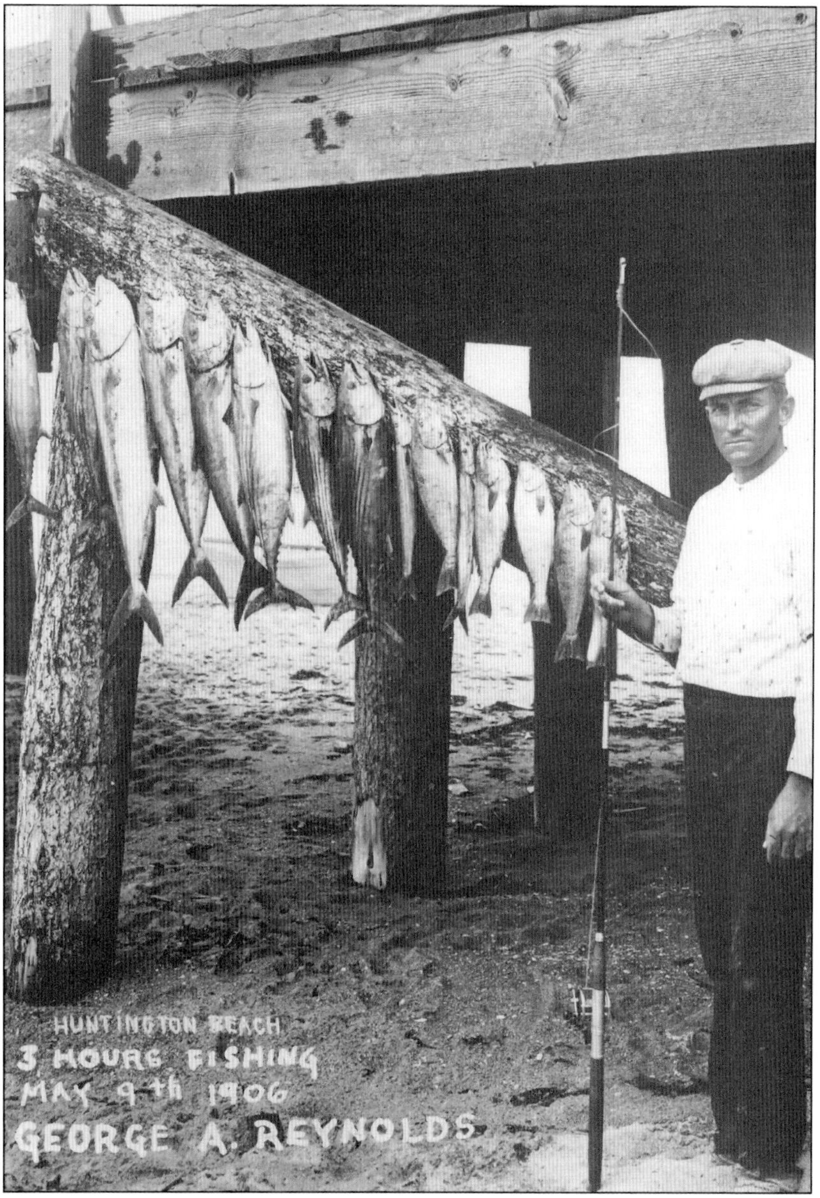

George A Reynolds, an excellent fisherman and doryman, was the first Huntington Beach lifeguard from 1904 to 1907. In 1906, next to the original wooden pier, he wrote "fishing from the lifeboat about ½ mile from shore, early one morning—using a 6B Wilson spoon for lure." He caught five bonita, three yellowtail, two barracuda, and five yellowfin croaker. Reynolds was the first pier area manager in 1904, was town constable in 1905, patrolled the dirt streets of Ocean Boulevard and Main Street on bicycle, and was the first volunteer community bandleader. He became a real estate agent and later an engineer, and in 1908, George and his older brother Alva obtained a U.S. patent and investors, and built the Reynolds Wave Motor. "The Reynolds Invention Will Soon Revolution the World's Power Supply," proclaimed an advertisement in the *Huntington Beach News*. The wave motor was built on the Twenty-First Street Wharf and harnessed just enough energy to light the bulbs on the wharf. Because it was unable to harness more energy, the last *HB News* report on the wave motor was in 1913.

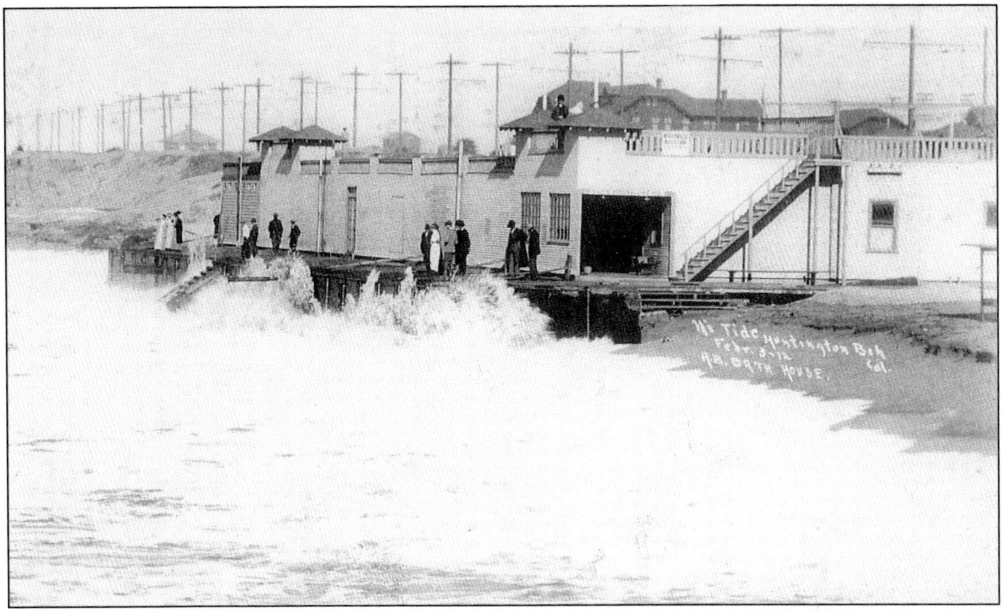

The high tide and surf pounds the west side of the pier Bath House in this February 3, 1912, photograph. The Bath House, also known as the Salt Water Plunge, first opened in 1911. The Plunge in later years was a major attraction and held summer swim meets often attended by the Los Angeles Athletic Club.

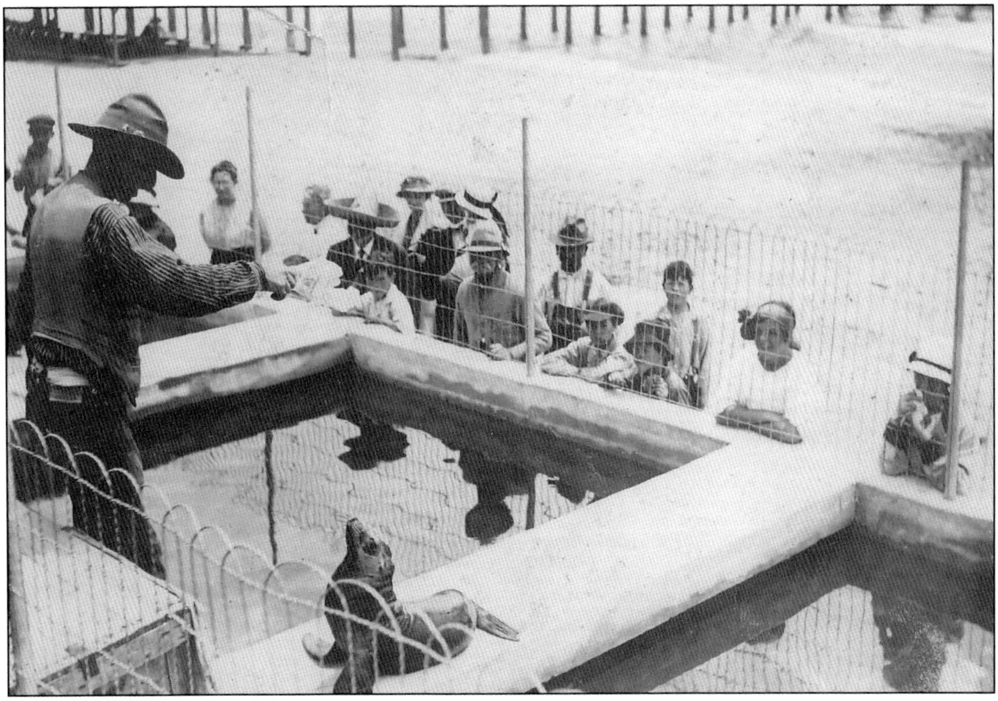

Ben the seal was a favorite attraction for locals and visitors to the pier in 1915. Ben was not the first or the last rescued seal to call the small concrete saltwater pool home. At the time, it was a relatively great expense for the city to feed Ben—a cost of $227 for the year. The new, 1,000-foot concrete pier was built in 1912.

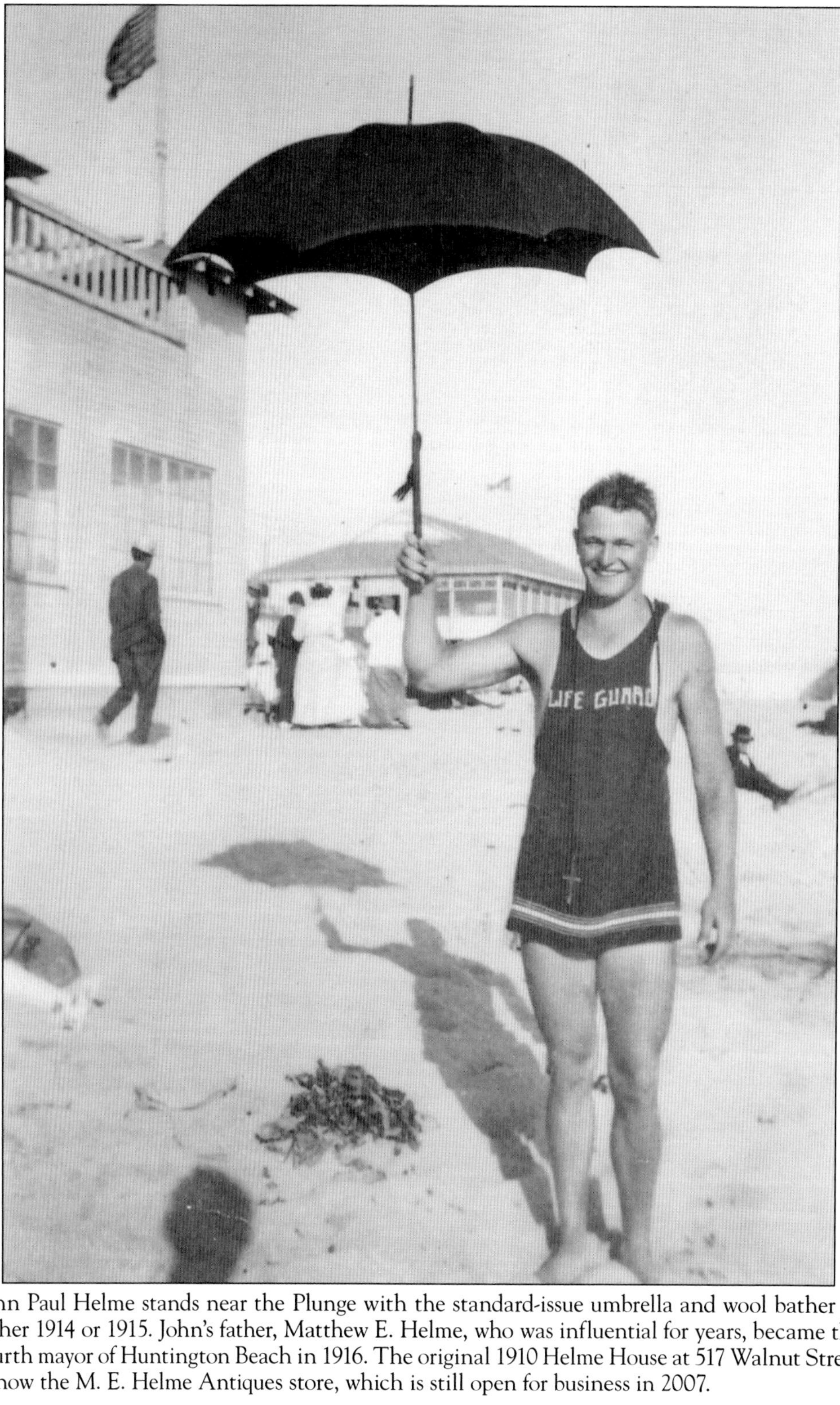

John Paul Helme stands near the Plunge with the standard-issue umbrella and wool bather in either 1914 or 1915. John's father, Matthew E. Helme, who was influential for years, became the fourth mayor of Huntington Beach in 1916. The original 1910 Helme House at 517 Walnut Street is now the M. E. Helme Antiques store, which is still open for business in 2007.

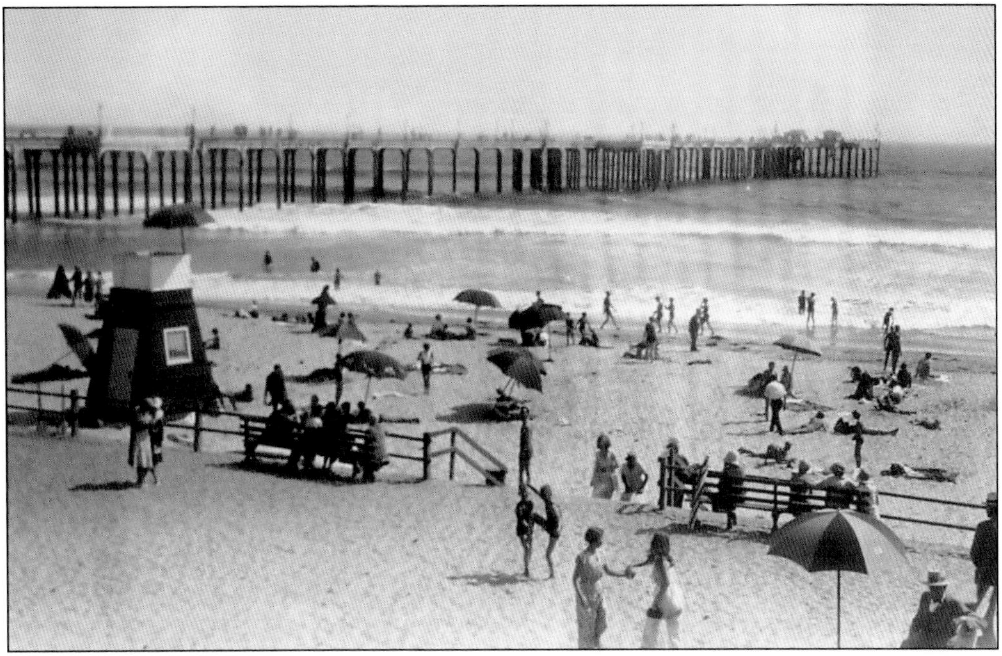

This early-1920s beach photograph, likely taken from the Plunge, shows the west side of the pier and the only lifeguard tower at the time. In 1921, the chief of police Jack Tinsley was given the responsibility of the fire department and to hire lifeguards as needed. Prior to Tinsley, the selection and hiring of lifeguards was shared equally between the Huntington Beach Company and the City of Huntington Beach.

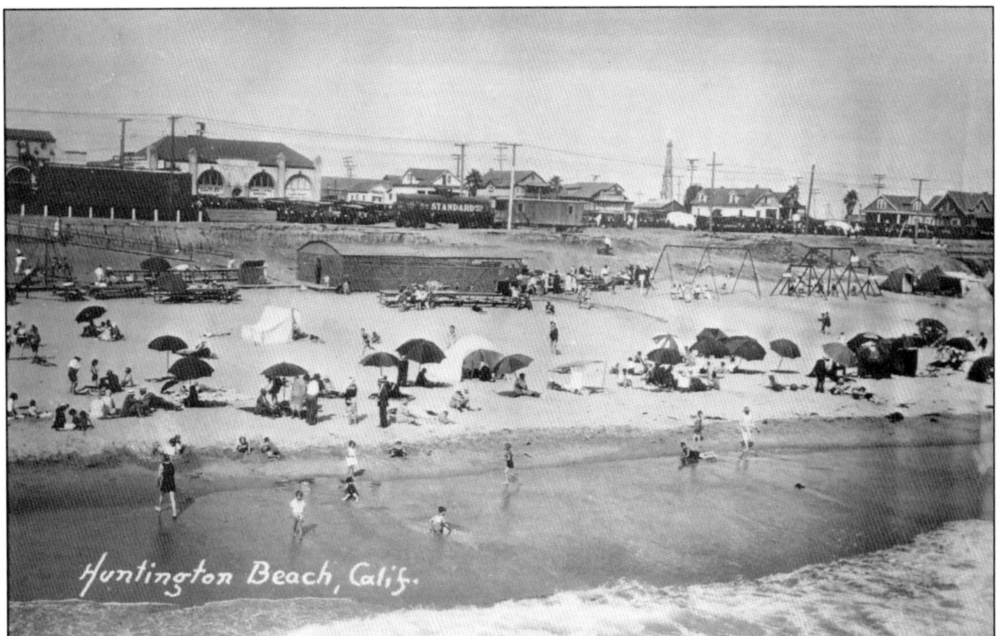

This early-1920s pier photograph of the east side—called the south side now—shows the swings and playground area, plenty of tents, and an oil well in the distance. The east side of the pier was not yet protected by lifeguards and was still owned by the Huntington Beach Company.

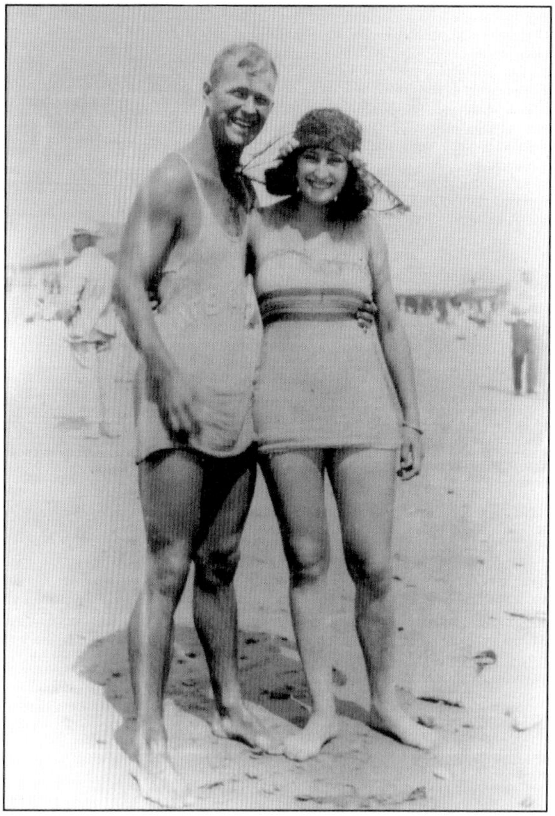

This photograph, recognized for decades and labeled "August 1920, Charles Robert Nutt Jr. and wife," is somewhat of an enigma. Robert Nutt Jr. and Henry Brooks were the 1920 Huntington Beach lifeguards, but the man seen here is not wearing a lifeguard logo or swimsuit. Perhaps the subject of this photograph is Charles "Chas" Robert Nutt Sr., who was the Huntington Beach city clerk for many years prior to and including 1920. The search for an image of lifeguards Nutt Jr. and Brooks continues.

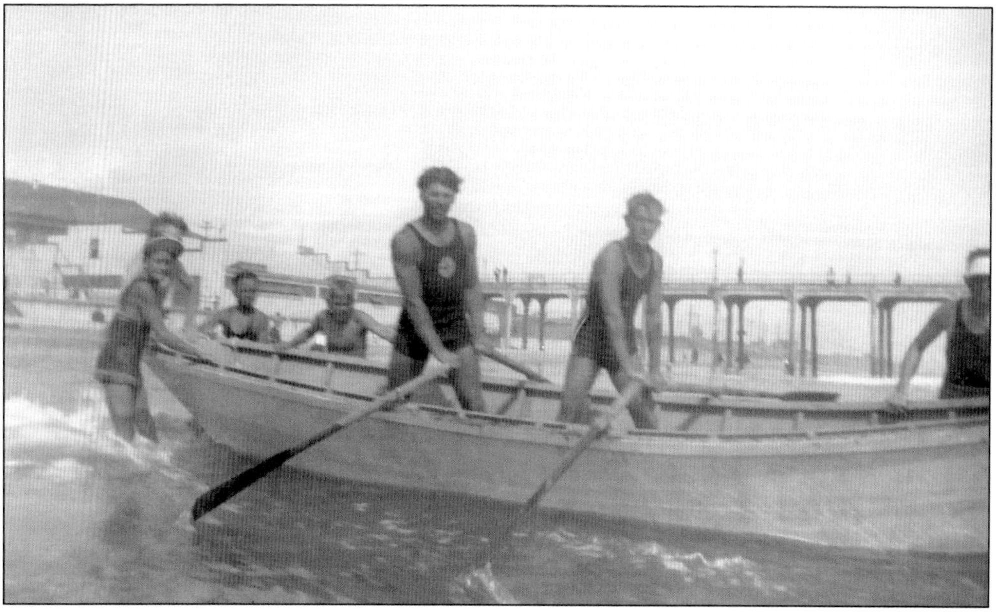

This great 1924 photograph of Harry Lee (left) and a young Bud Higgins in the lifeboat came from Johnie Belshe. Lee was the head lifeguard from 1921 to 1926 and was previously a Long Beach lifeguard, oil worker, boxer, and an early mentor of Higgins. At age 14, Higgins was a junior lifeguard in 1921 under the tutelage of Lee, and he started lifeguarding in 1924.

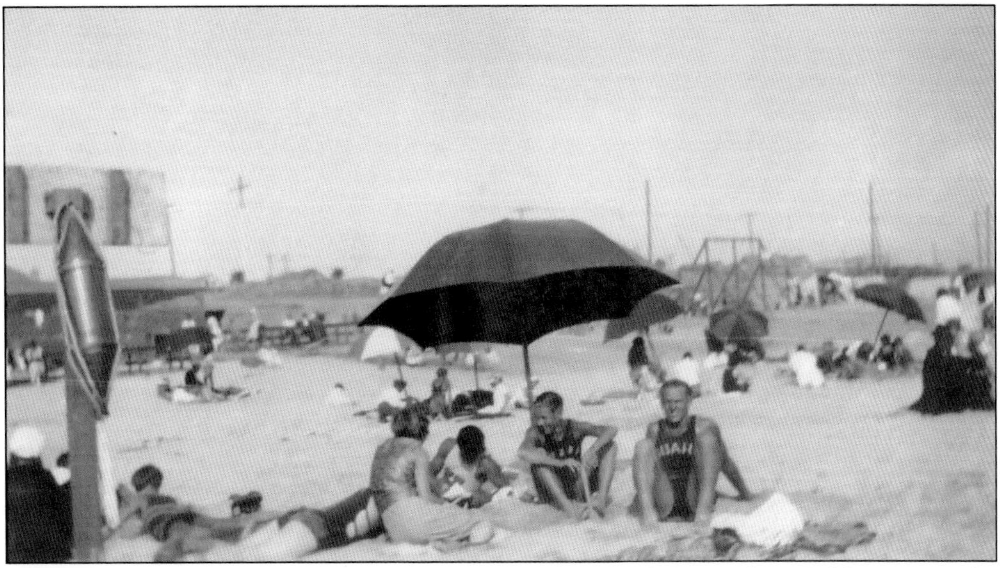

Bud and Clare "Van" Hoorbreke, seen in this 1925 photograph from Johnie Belshe, protect the east side of the pier. Also working but not shown are Cecil Jenks and Angelo Molica. In 1924, East Ocean Boulevard made the connection with Newport Beach. The same year saw the police department purchase its first lifesaving equipment, a Lung Motor, although it was too cumbersome and far from the beach to be effective for the lifeguards.

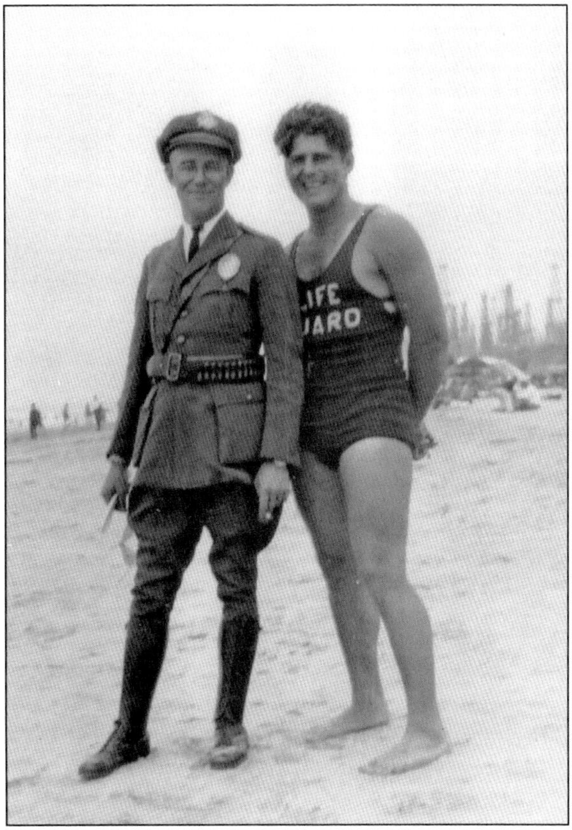

From *The First 80 Years: History of the Huntington Beach Police Department* by Michael Biggs, this 1927 photograph shows police officer La Verne Keller with Harry Lee on the west side of the pier. Keller was also the commander of the HB American Legion post and became the chief of police in 1932 during the early Depression years.

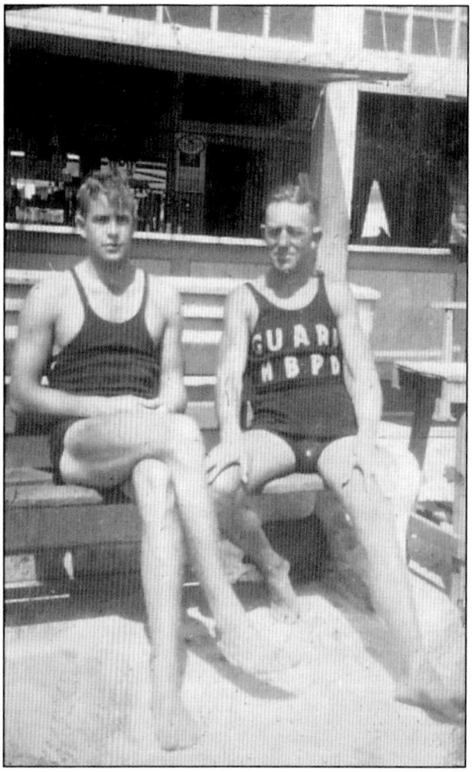

Police chief Jack Tinsley selected Fred Ott for head lifeguard in 1927, and in this photograph from the same year, Ott (right) and lifeguard Bob King, a popular star high jumper from Stanford, sit in front of the concessions between the Plunge and the Dance Hall. Higgins recalled that Ott was a weak swimmer and determined it must have been a political appointment. In the early oil boom years, the city was not very interested in the beach and consequently hired mostly football players, track stars, and personal favorites.

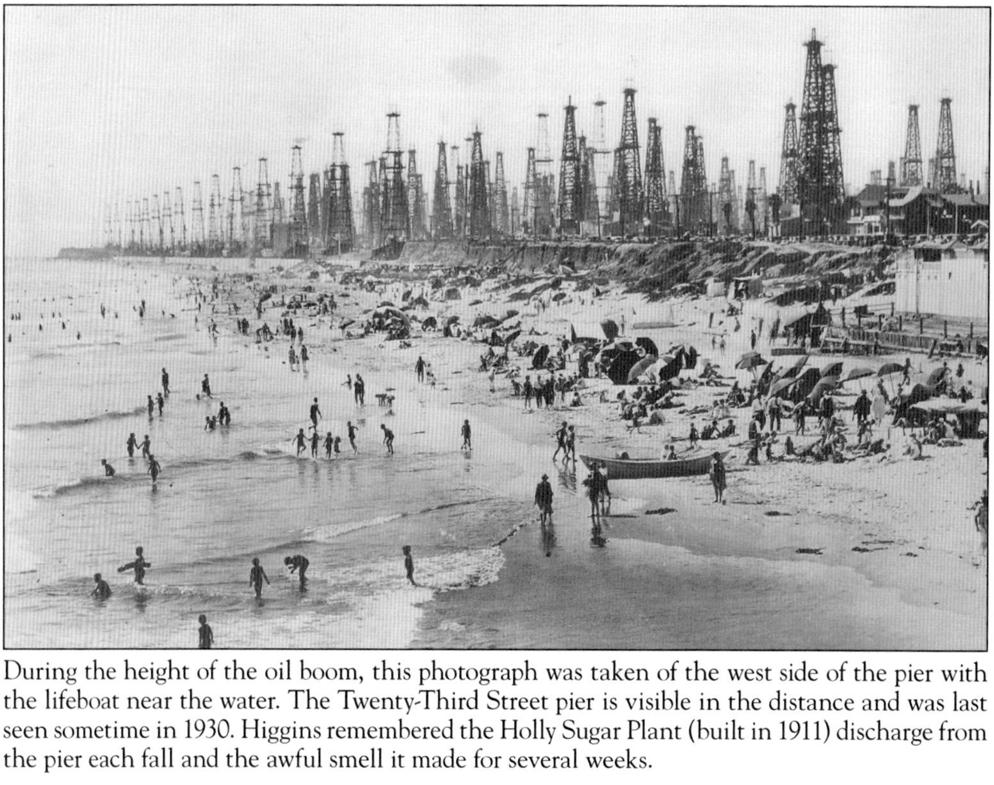

During the height of the oil boom, this photograph was taken of the west side of the pier with the lifeboat near the water. The Twenty-Third Street pier is visible in the distance and was last seen sometime in 1930. Higgins remembered the Holly Sugar Plant (built in 1911) discharge from the pier each fall and the awful smell it made for several weeks.

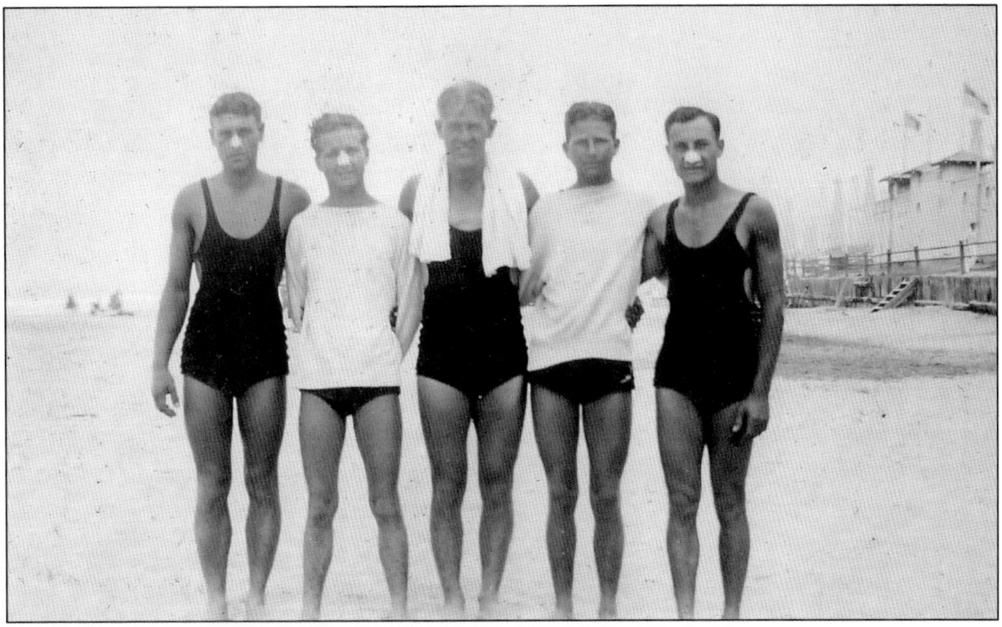

In this 1926 or 1927 photograph, the "Beach Gang," as they liked to be called, stands together with the Plunge and wood bulkhead in view. From left to right are Pete DiFabio, Glenn ?, teenaged Bud Higgins, Bub ?, and Angelo Molica.

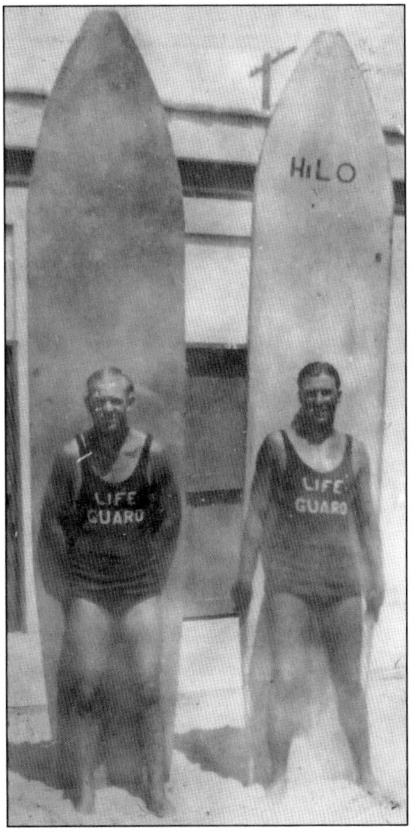

In August 1927 (possibly 1928), Higgins (left) and Belshe made these two surfboards from a single 20-foot plank of kiln-dried redwood. They were inspired by Duke Kahanamoku, whom they met and later invited to surf the Huntington Beach Pier. The Duke was an Olympic champion swimmer and was recognized as "the Father of Surfing." In 1925, the Duke lived in Newport Beach and surfed the Corona Del Mar breakwater near the Bath House

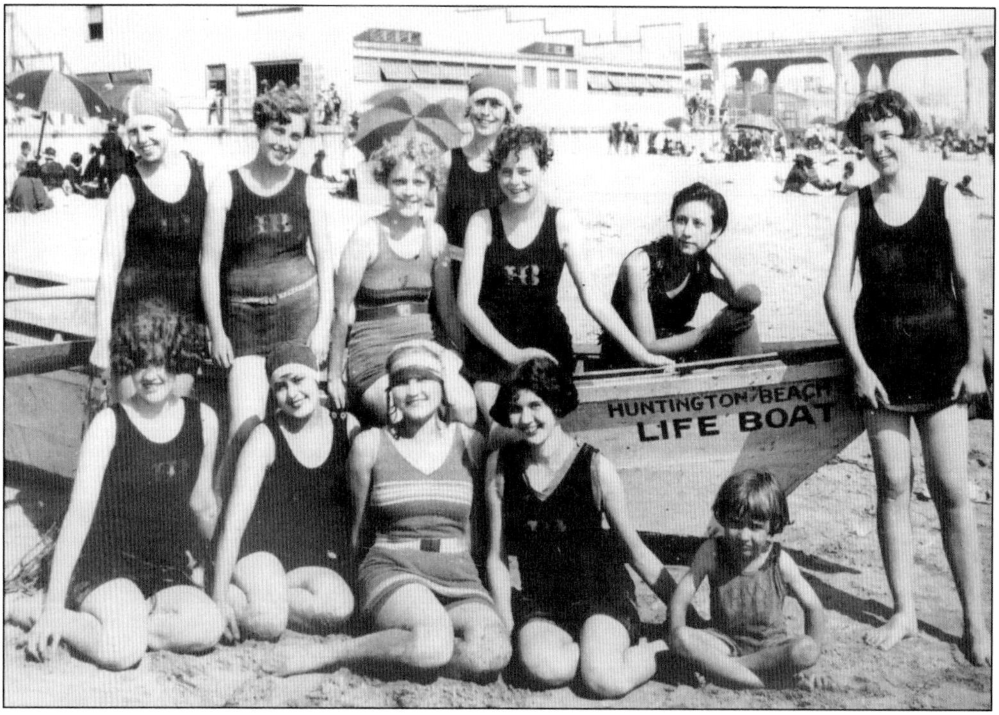

The "Beach Girls" took over the HB Life Boat in this 1930 photograph; behind them is the Dance Hall next to the concrete pier. The first lifeboat, or dory, was likely built in 1902 along with the new wooden pier. The last wooden dory, according to Higgins, broke up and disappeared sometime in the early 1940s.

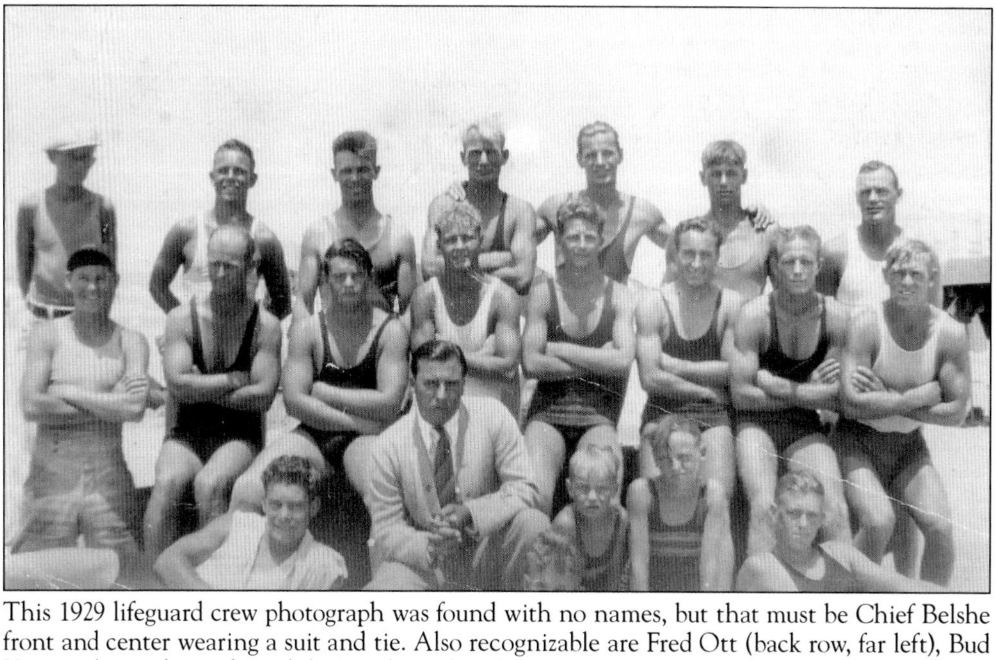

This 1929 lifeguard crew photograph was found with no names, but that must be Chief Belshe front and center wearing a suit and tie. Also recognizable are Fred Ott (back row, far left), Bud Higgins (second row, far right), Angelo Molica (second row, third from right), and Clare "Van" Horbeck (first row, far right).

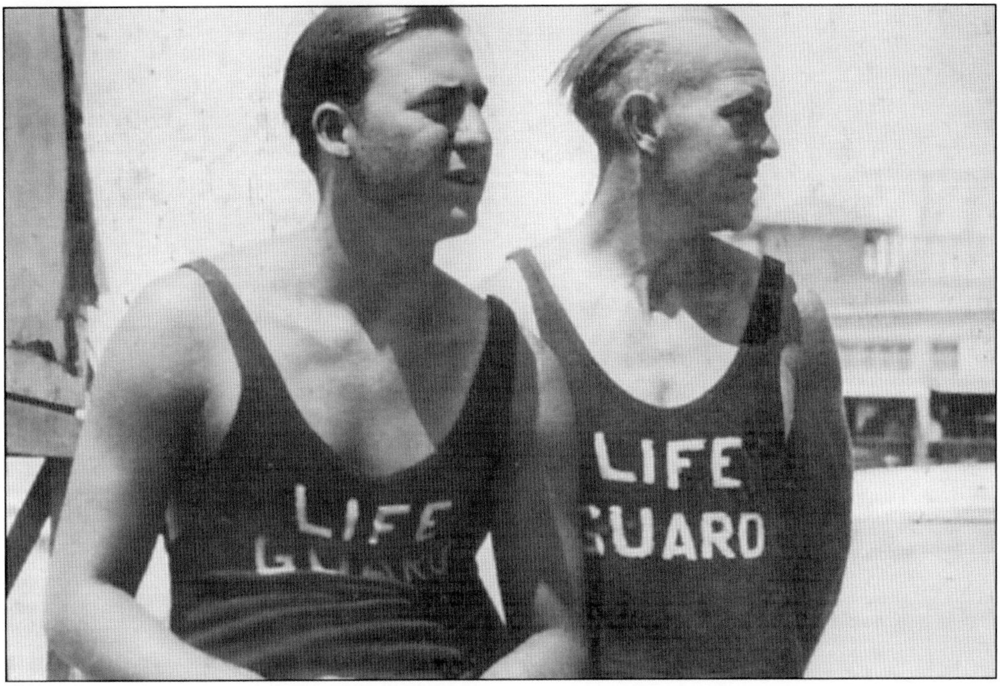

Taken in 1930, this may be the best lifeguard photograph of both lifeguard chief Gene Belshe (left) and later chief Bud Higgins together. They are recognized as lifesaving pioneers. During their long public safety careers, Huntington Beach assigned Belshe as the assistant police chief in 1941 and Higgins as fire chief in 1950.

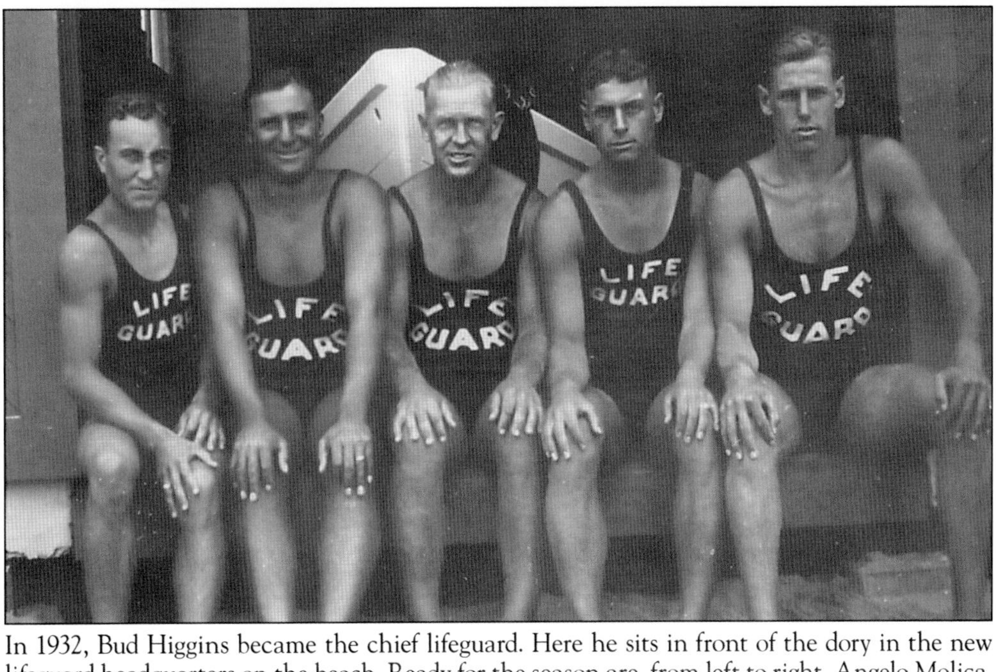

In 1932, Bud Higgins became the chief lifeguard. Here he sits in front of the dory in the new lifeguard headquarters on the beach. Ready for the season are, from left to right, Angelo Molica, Gene Belshe, Chief Higgins, Pete Di Fabio, and Clare "Van" Horbeck. In the same year, the first pedestal concrete towers were placed at Huntington Avenue and Third and Sixth Streets.

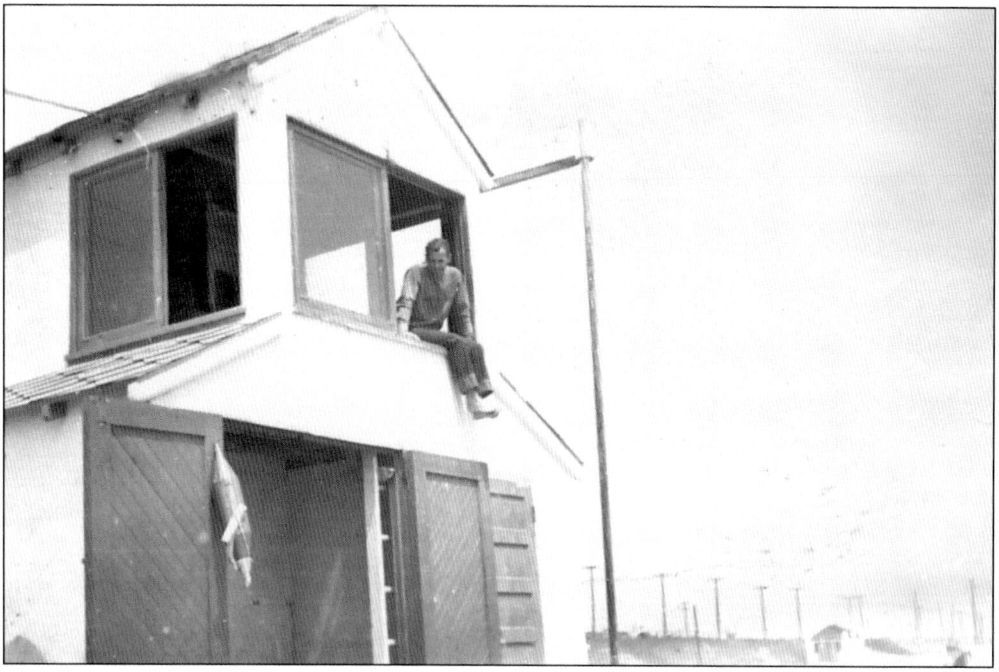

The new lifeguard headquarters provided safe storage for equipment and dry storage for the dory, in addition to an elevated viewing platform with a quick exit down the pole. The first Dwight's Beach Concession shared the back part of this building until 1939.

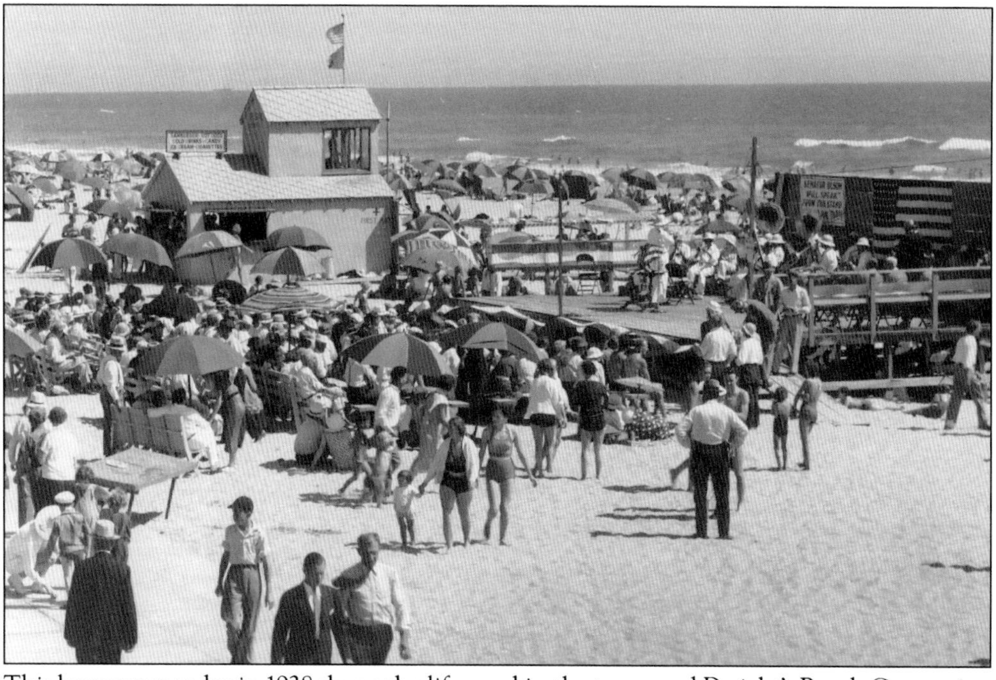

This busy summer day in 1938 shows the lifeguard in the tower and Dwight's Beach Concession open for business. The stage on the beach was the home of the Huntington Beach Band and, on this day, displayed a banner announcing that "Senator Olson will speak today." The next year, Dwight's moved to a second location: its own building farther back on the beach.

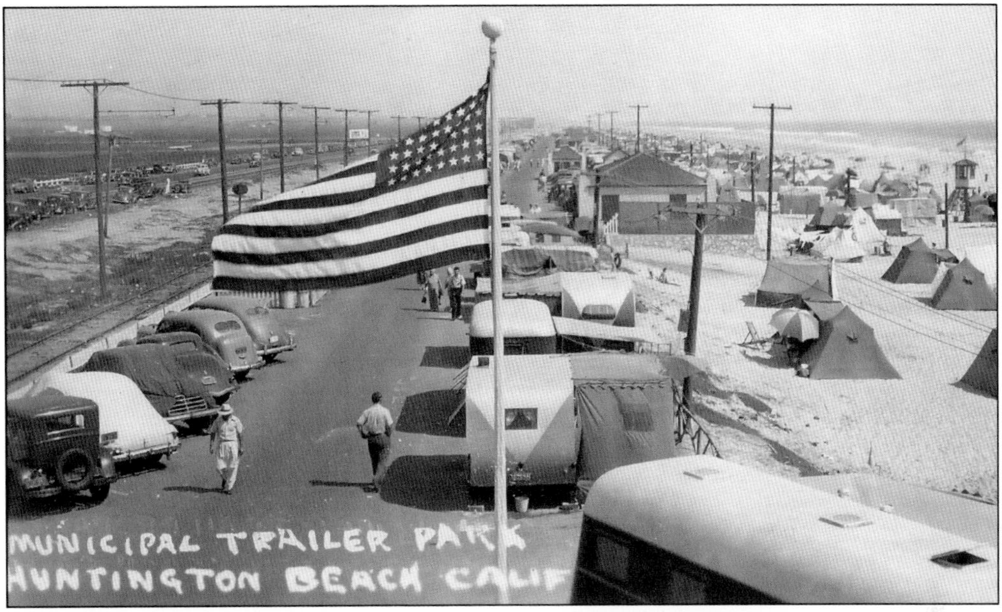

In 1927, the city leased the PCH campground from the Huntington Beach Company and named it the Municipal Trailer Park, the first of its kind in Southern California. An airplane is visible on the inland side of PCH, and on the right, notice the pedestal concrete lifeguard tower built in 1932.

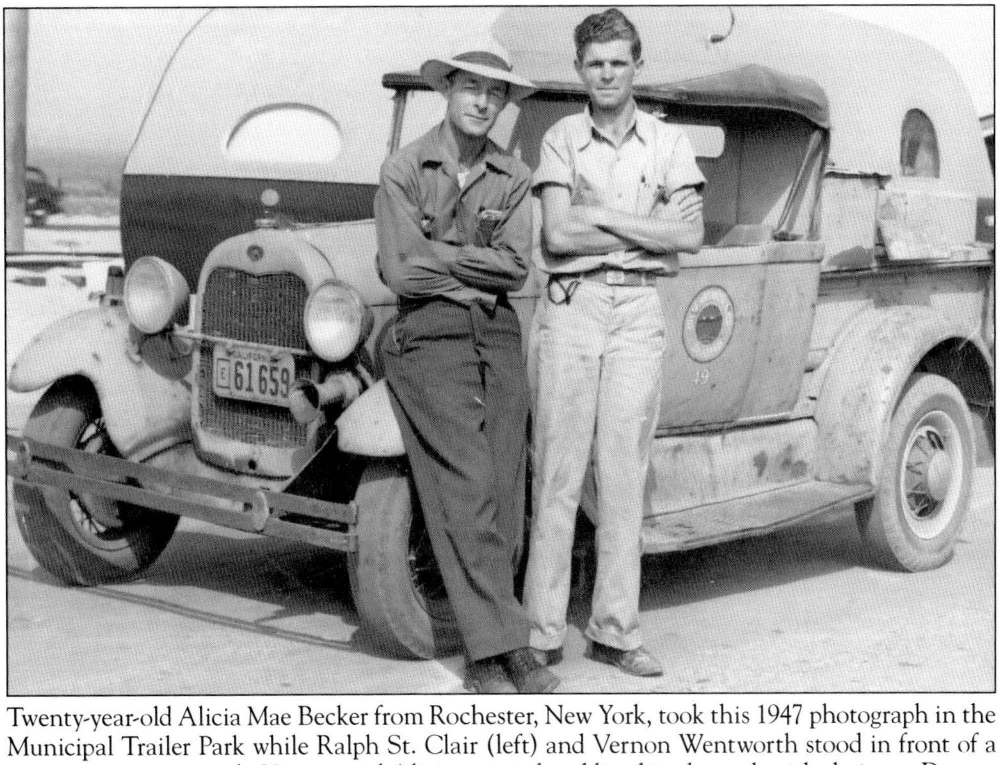

Twenty-year-old Alicia Mae Becker from Rochester, New York, took this 1947 photograph in the Municipal Trailer Park while Ralph St. Clair (left) and Vernon Wentworth stood in front of a city maintenance truck. Vernon and Alicia married and lived in the park with their son Duane. Alicia Wentworth later became the city clerk (1973–1988) and city historian (1989–2006).

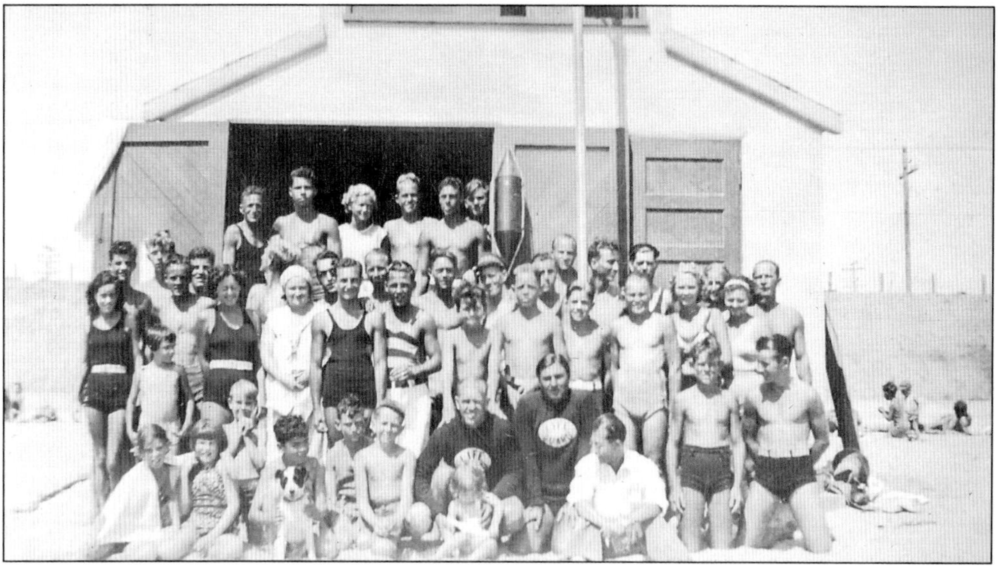

In the middle of the first row wearing dark shirts are Bud Higgins (with young daughter Darlene) and Gene Belshe (part-time lifeguard and full-time police officer). The rest are lifeguards, junior lifeguards, and friends. This building was torn down in 1939 and replaced by the similar but smaller tower No. 1. Lifeguard headquarters was moved onto the pier in 1935.

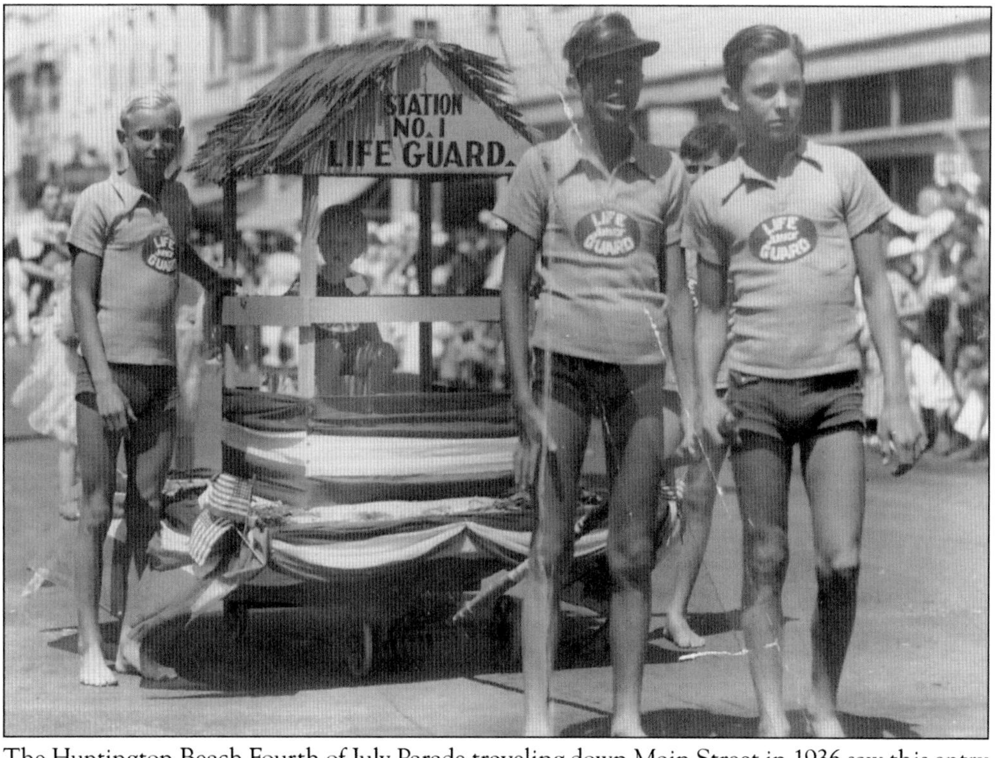

The Huntington Beach Fourth of July Parade traveling down Main Street in 1936 saw this entry of junior lifeguards and their "Station No. 1 Lifeguard" tower. This parade entry was the first-place winner of the $7 prize. In the photograph are, from left to right, Bud Redline, infant Darlene Higgins, Ike Thomas, Earl Conrad (partially hidden), and Galen Hasson.

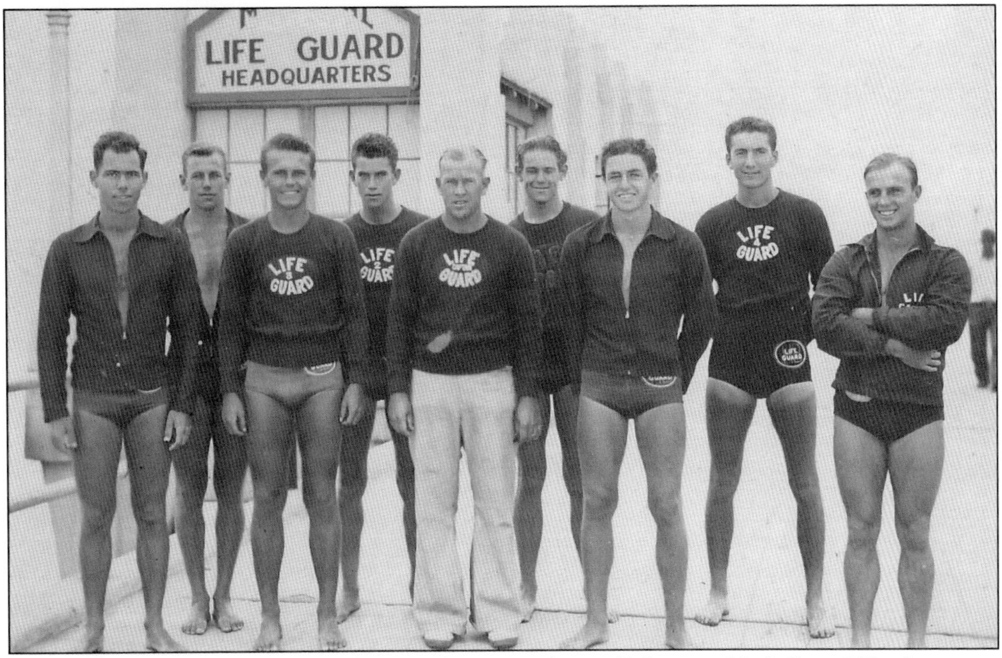

This 1937 crew photograph was taken on the pier in front of Municipal Life Guard Headquarters. Standing with strong legs and summer tan lines are, from left to right, Ed Ewing, Clare "Van" Horbeck, Bob Hilton, Nolan Hasson, Chief Bud Higgins (in long pants), Bill Farquar, Don Winters, Gale Bergey, and Lawrence "Porry" Patrick.

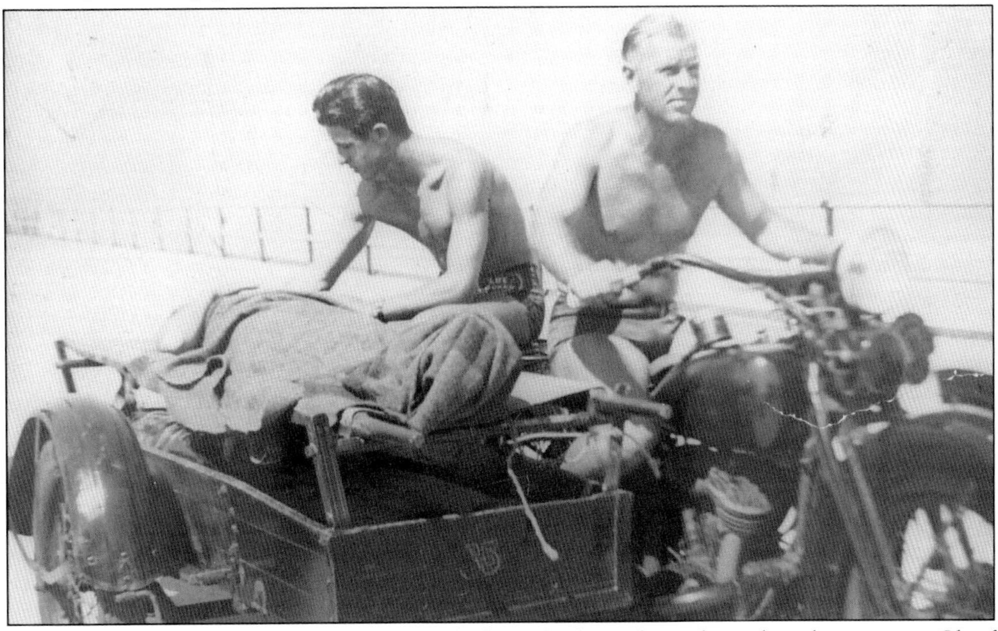

In 1935, the lifeguards received this motorcycle and sidecar from the police department. Chief Higgins (right) and Lt. Don Winters race off the pier with a patient in what appears to be a simulated response. Winters became a navy pilot and was downed in the Pacific during World War II. His name can be found today on the list of Huntington Beach heroes on the World War II Memorial Monument outside of city hall.

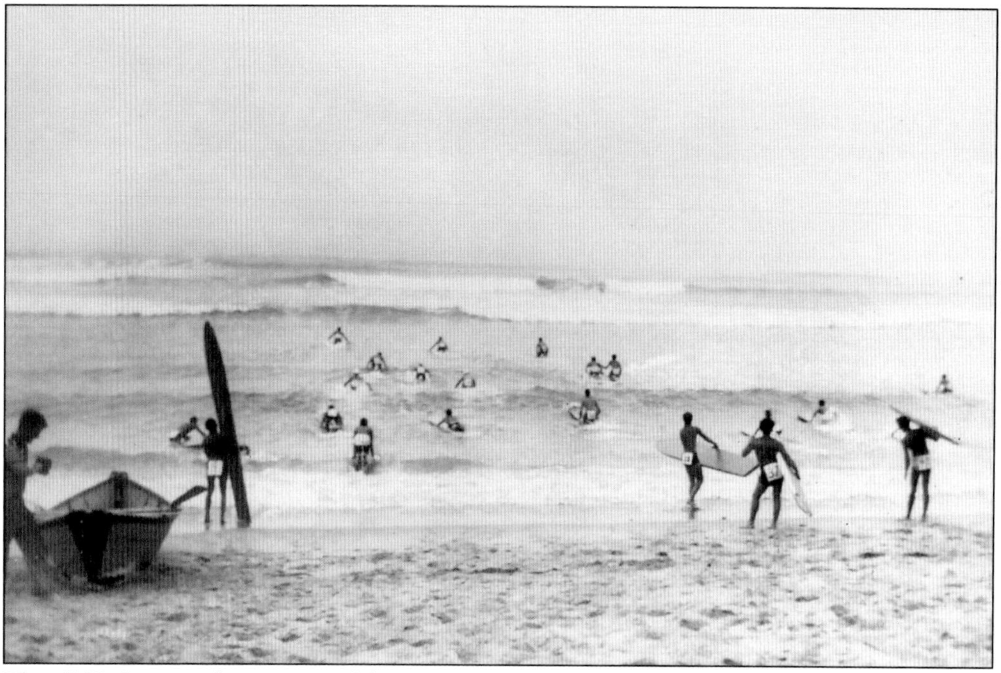

This 1938 photograph, courtesy of the Huntington Beach Long Board Crew and Marylin Noth, is of an early Huntington Beach Pier surf contest. The contestants and lifeguard dory were on the west side of the pier. According to Higgins, the first surf contest in Huntington in 1933 had big surf, was sponsored by the lifeguards, and was won by contestant Dave Beall of Santa Ana.

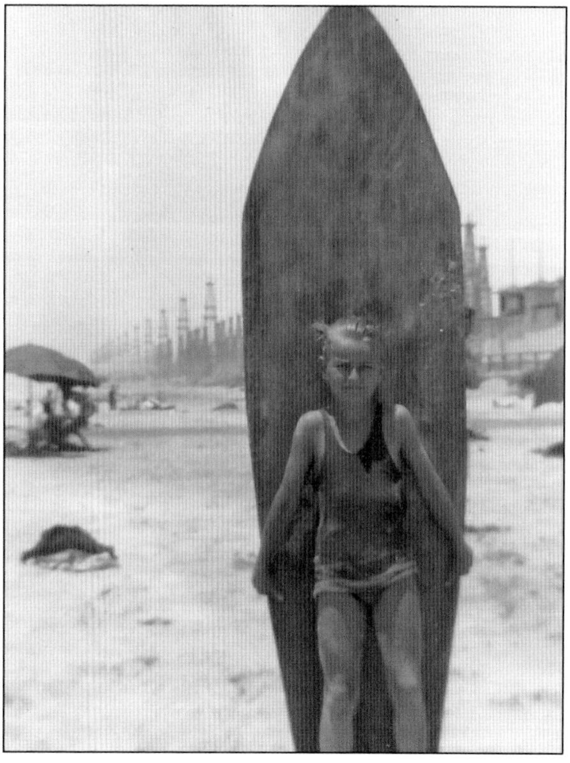

This photograph was possibly taken in 1928 on the west side of the pier and shows a confident young boy with an intimidating piece of lumber. He was likely a junior lifeguard and belonged to the "lifeguard gangs."

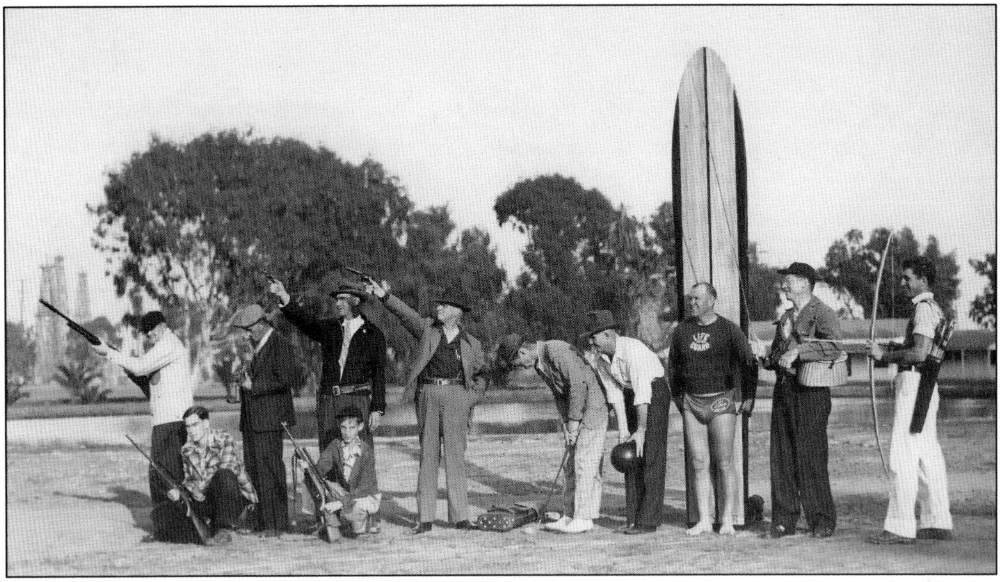

Pictured is a 1939 gathering to honor various Huntington Beach sports at Lake Park near the casting pond. From left to right are Roy Rafferty (skeet shooting), two unidentified boys from Dodges Rifle Club (kneeling), Perry Huddle (camera), Jim Clarke (handgun), Rev. Luther Arthur (handgun), Clayton Alridge (golf), Mickey Rafferty (bowling), Bud Higgins (surfing), Beryl Harper (fly casting), and Bill Wardwell (archery).

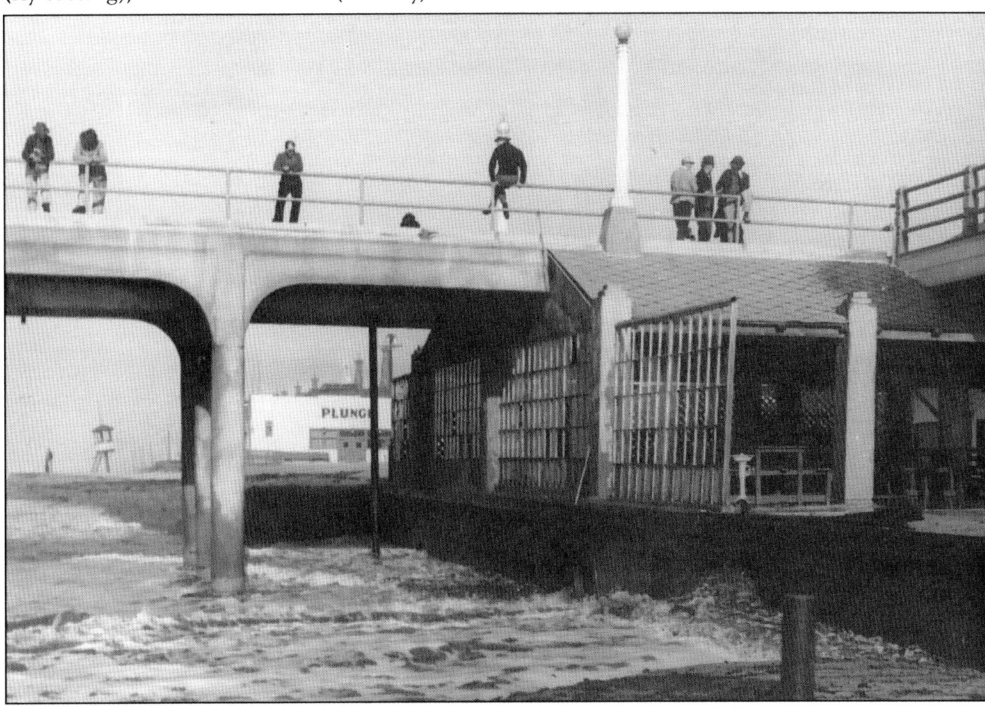

On September 12, 1939, the California coast was hit by a tropical hurricane, or a Mexican chubasco, and Huntington Beach recorded waves as high as 23 feet. Buildings on the pier were demolished, and 294 feet of pier deck and pilings went missing. This photograph shows the water up to the base of the pier with the Plunge and the lifeguard tower in view.

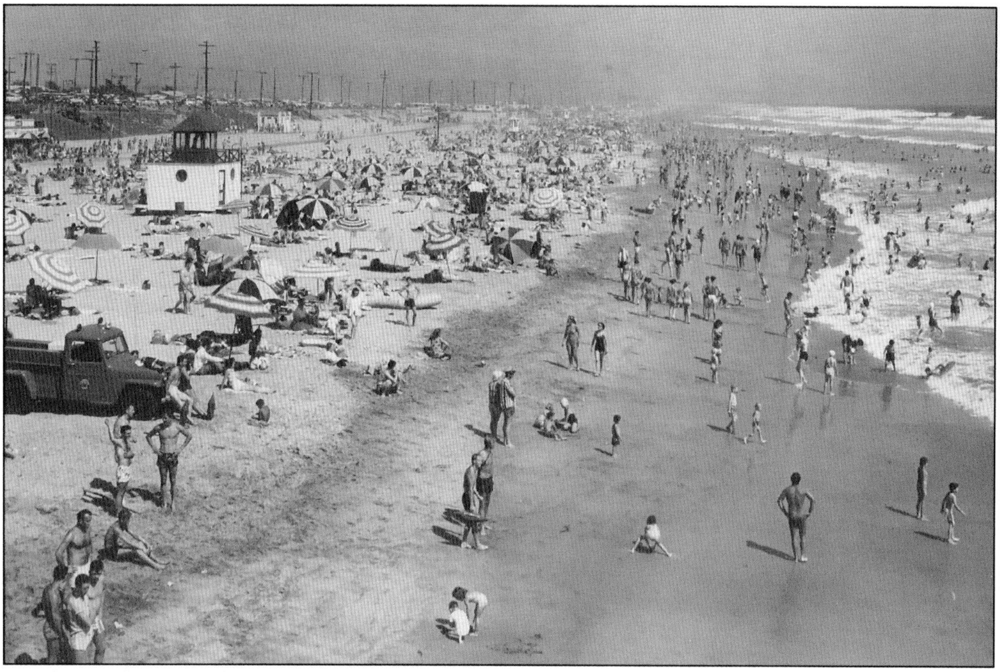

"Wide Beaches and plenty of sunshine," was written on the back of this July 4, 1940, photograph. The box-like building with deck is the new Tower No. 1, the truck and lifeguards with buoys are busy next to the pier, and the new Dwight's concession is partly visible on the left, as are the cement lifeguard towers down the beach.

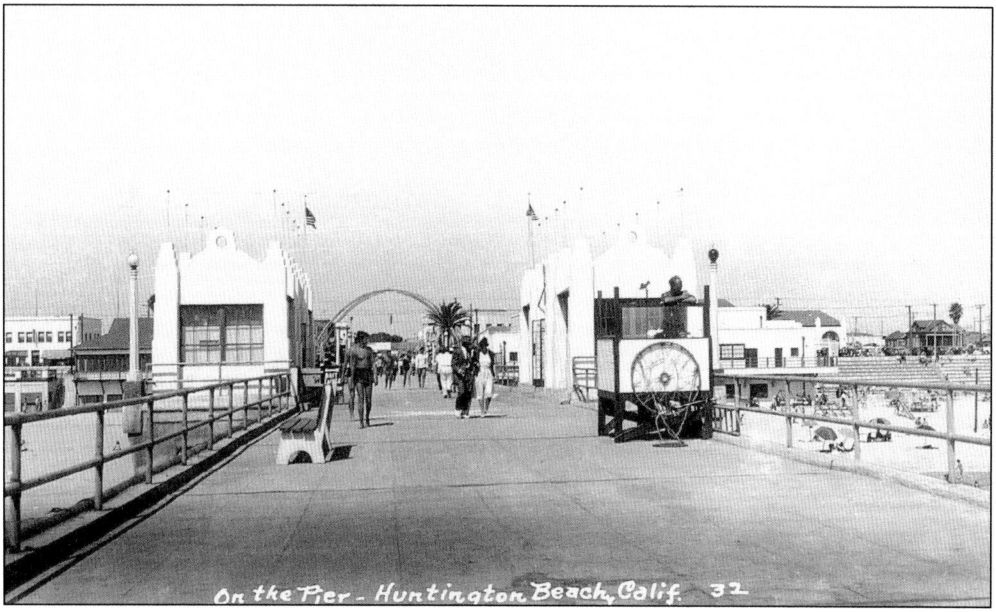

In 1932, this lifeguard station was in use with a telescope and pier rescue net. In 1935, lifeguard headquarters moved to one of the so-called "sun buildings" on the pier and quickly had a lookout built on top. For years, the city council denied the lifeguards the right to build a new tower farther out on the pier, which would have cut down the glare, and is where present-day Tower Zero is located. The landmark Huntington Beach steel archway, built in 1929, was taken down in 1941.

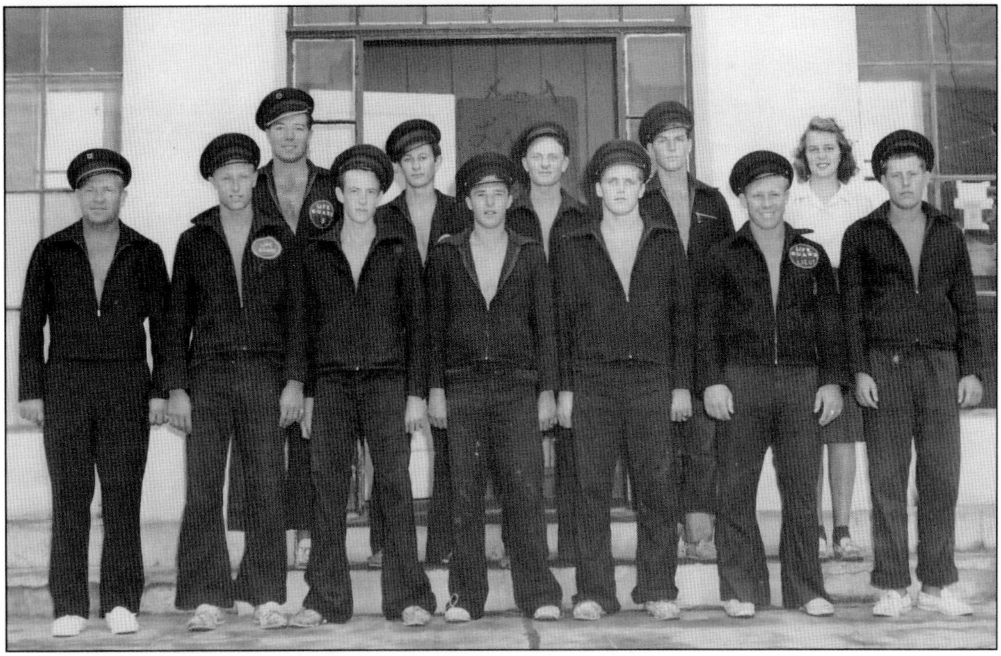

During World War II and after Pearl Harbor was attacked on December 7, 1941, the availability of qualified lifeguards was limited. Here, in the summer of 1942, the lifeguard crew was so young that the lieutenant was reportedly only 16 years old. Incredibly, the mostly Huntington Beach High School students who worked as lifeguards persevered. They recorded zero drownings for the next four years.

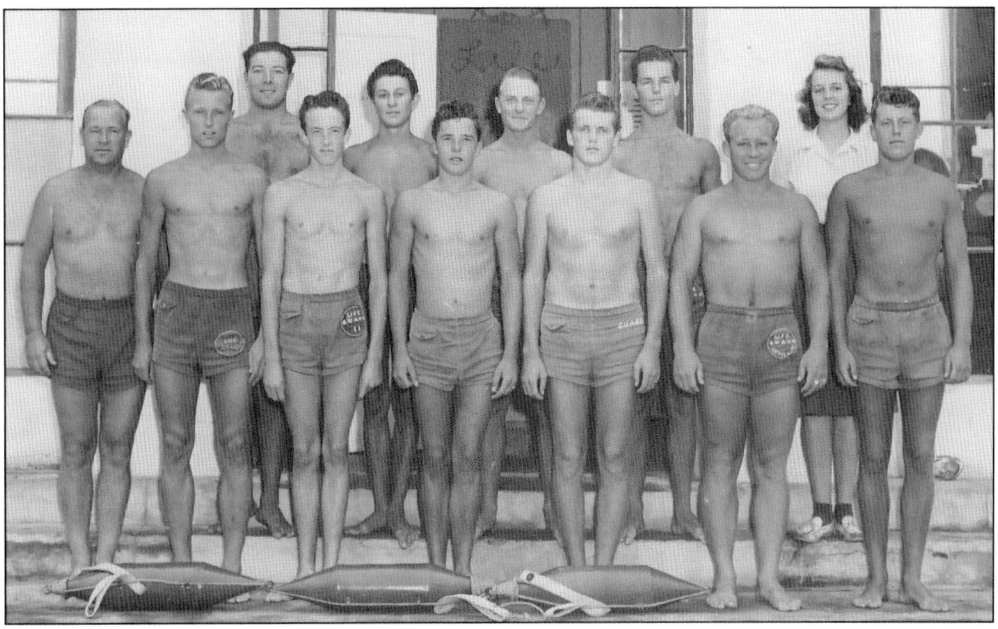

Here the same 1942 crew poses in front of Municipal Life Guard Headquarters on the pier, showing their physiques and torpedo rescue cans made of metal. From left to right are Chief Bud Higgins, Bob Hoyt, Bob Bermudez, Walt Dabney, Lewis Ross, Jack Cockrell, Chuck Lawson, Bob Murray, Bucky Wells, Lt. Bob Tucker, Barbara Jean Bristol, and John Overmyer.

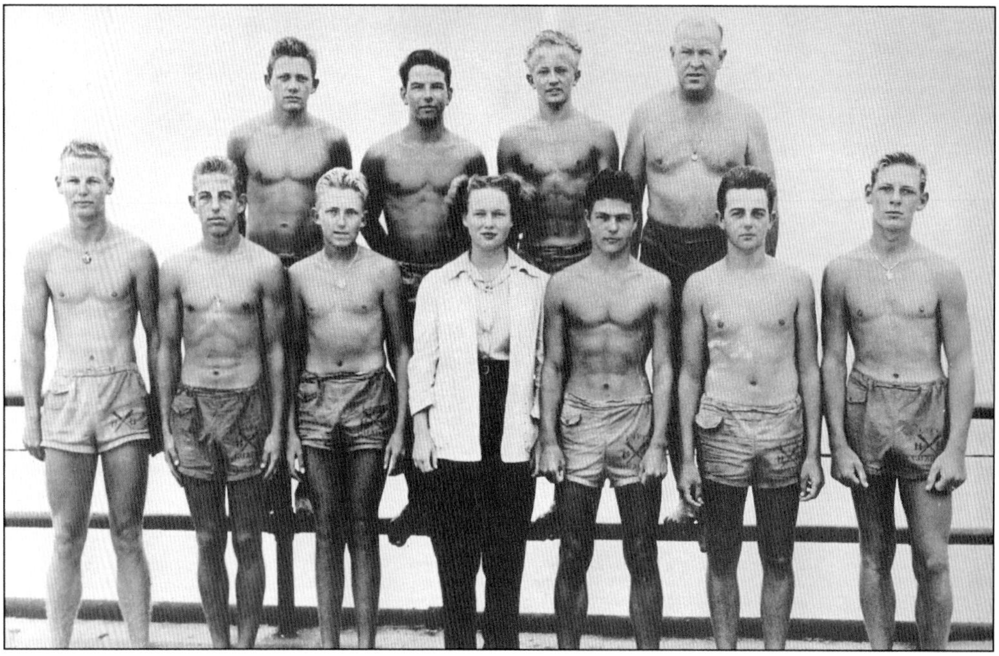

In July 1944, the lifeguards appear to be even younger but are also still in high school. Standing on the pier are, from left to right, Tom Hendrickson, Elmer Combs, Fred Swartz, Howard Ethington, Jack Dowty, Betty St. Clair, Eddie Brown, Vern Seltzer, Chief Bud Higgins, Harlo LeBard, and Loren Thornton.

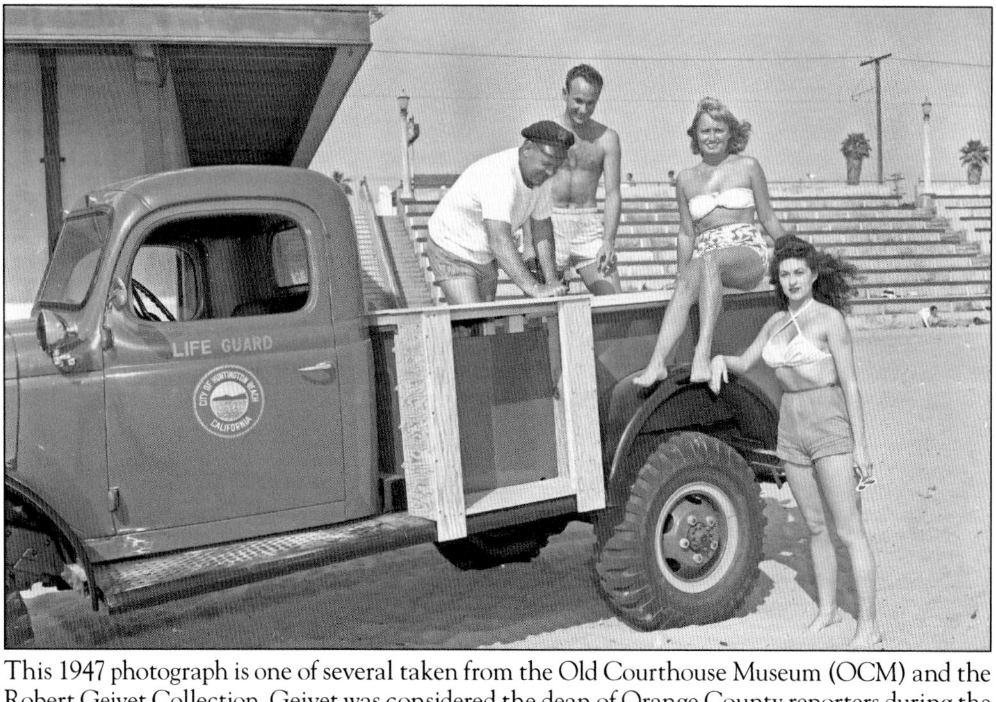

This 1947 photograph is one of several taken from the Old Courthouse Museum (OCM) and the Robert Geivet Collection. Geivet was considered the dean of Orange County reporters during the postwar era, 1946–1962. Chief Bud Higgins is shown here fabricating an addition to the lifeguard truck with a few supportive beach patrons.

“We lived in the Huntington Beach Municipal Trailer Park,” was written on the back of this photograph. The young lad pictured is George “Fred” Merch, the nephew of Alicia Wentworth, a past city clerk and Huntington Beach historian.

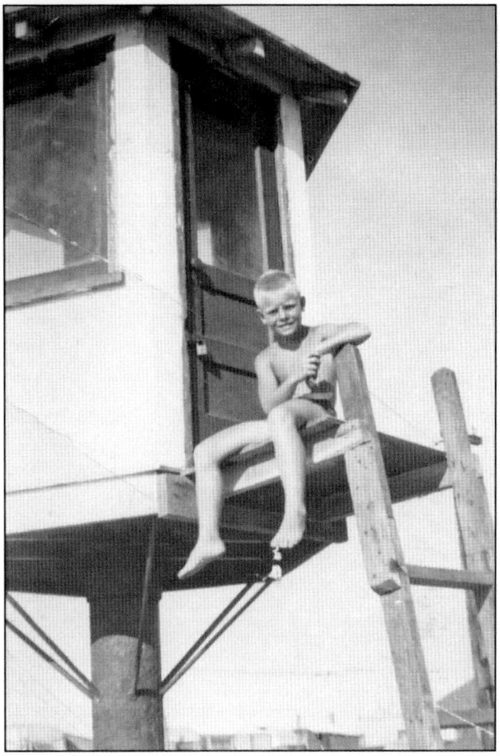

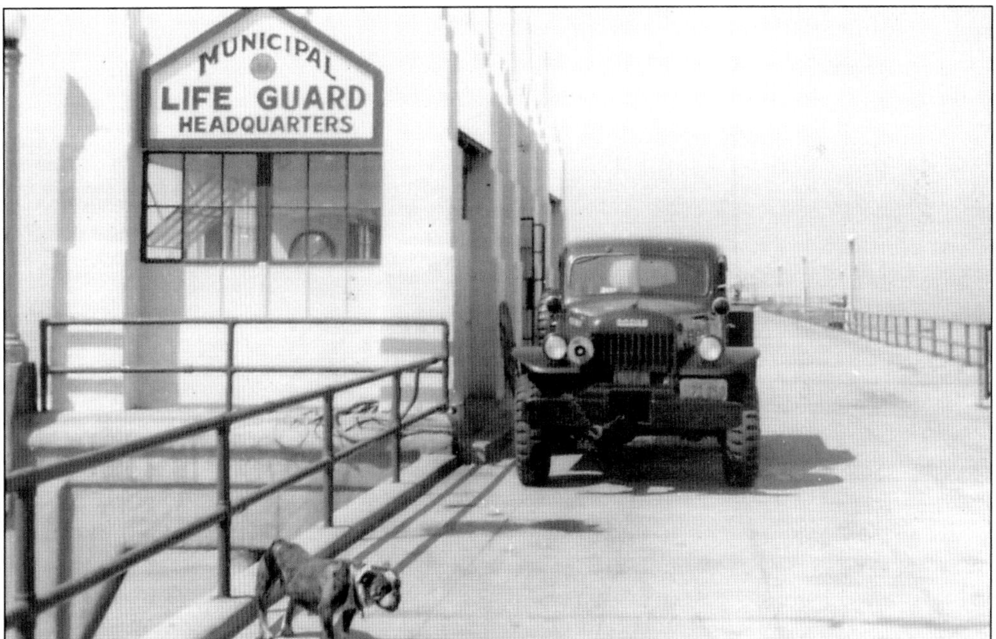

Bud Higgins on occasion during his career was known to have his pet dog at the beach and on the pier. Pictured in 1941, Lady is ready to follow Higgins and the other lifeguards just about everywhere. Lady was famous for jumping off the pier after the lifeguards, liking it, and swimming back to shore, sometimes without assistance.

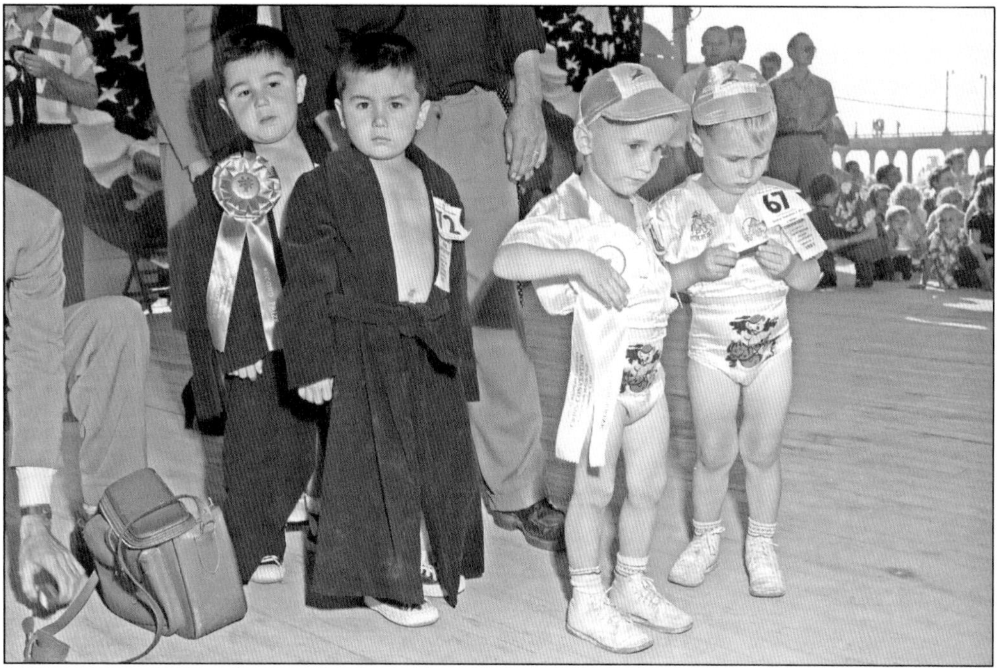

The annual Southern California Twins Convention, which was sponsored by the chamber of commerce, was held in Huntington Beach for many years. In September 1948, the 11th beach festival of the Huntington Beach Twins Convention had 600 sets of twins. This September 2, 1951, OCM photograph shows the 14th twins convention, which was the last one held in Huntington Beach.

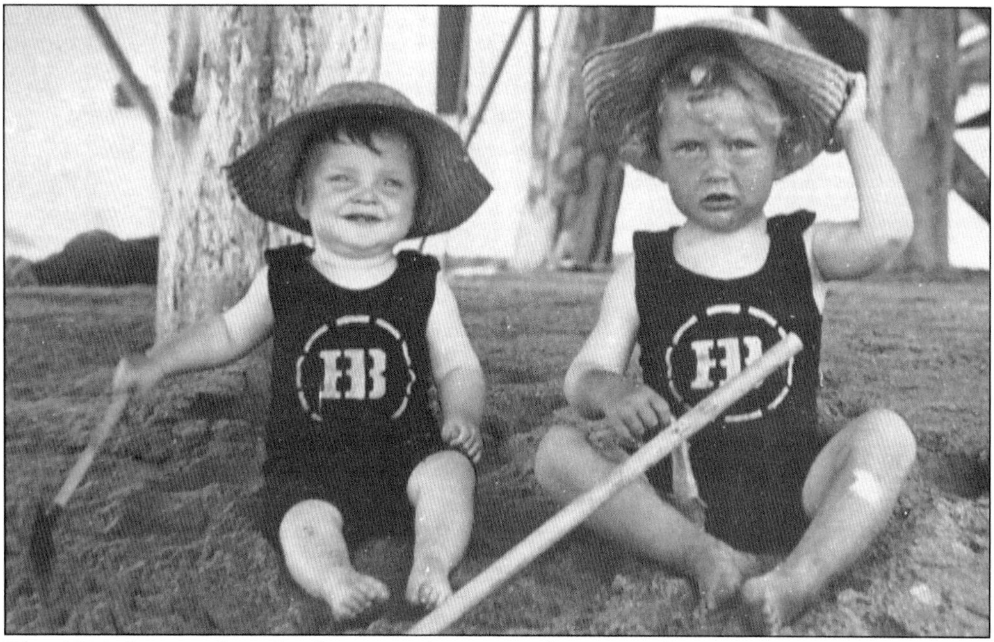

This 1906 photograph under the original 1902 wooden pier, called "Sunshine and Shadow," is a Huntington Beach classic and is from the office of the city clerk, as are many photographs in this book. These toddlers' names were not recorded and remain a mystery.

Two

CHANGING OF THE GUARD 1950–1966

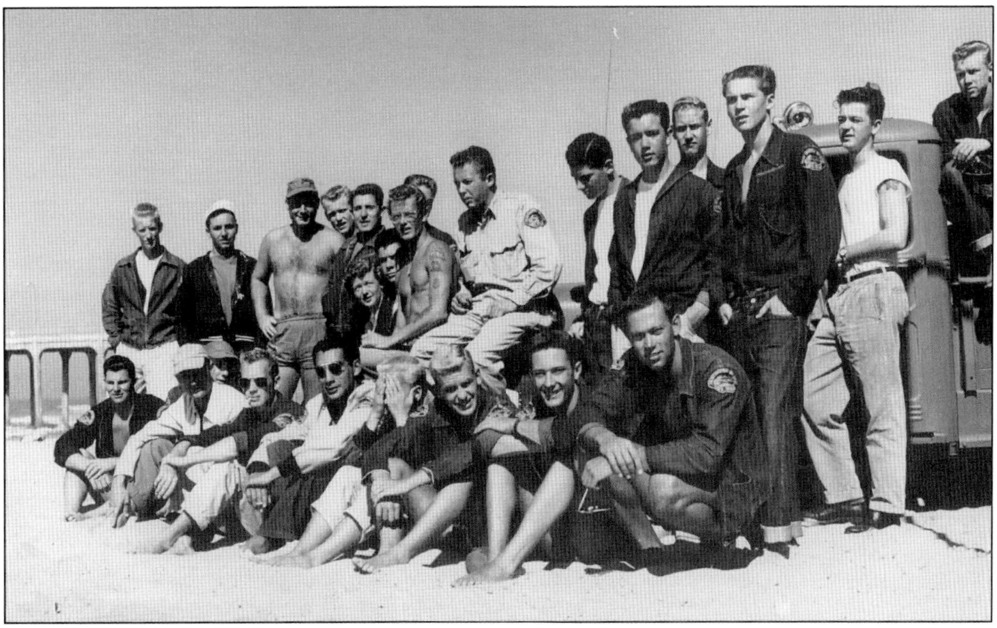

In 1950, chief lifeguard Bud Higgins was appointed the Huntington Beach fire chief, replacing Jack K. Sergeant. During the next few years, the lifeguards would see four new chiefs. This 1952 crew photograph is a classic sign of the times and has Chief Fred Swartz (second row, center with patch on shoulder), Capt. Rocky Freeman (left of Swartz with tattoo) and Frank Ciarelli (seated immediately below Swartz).

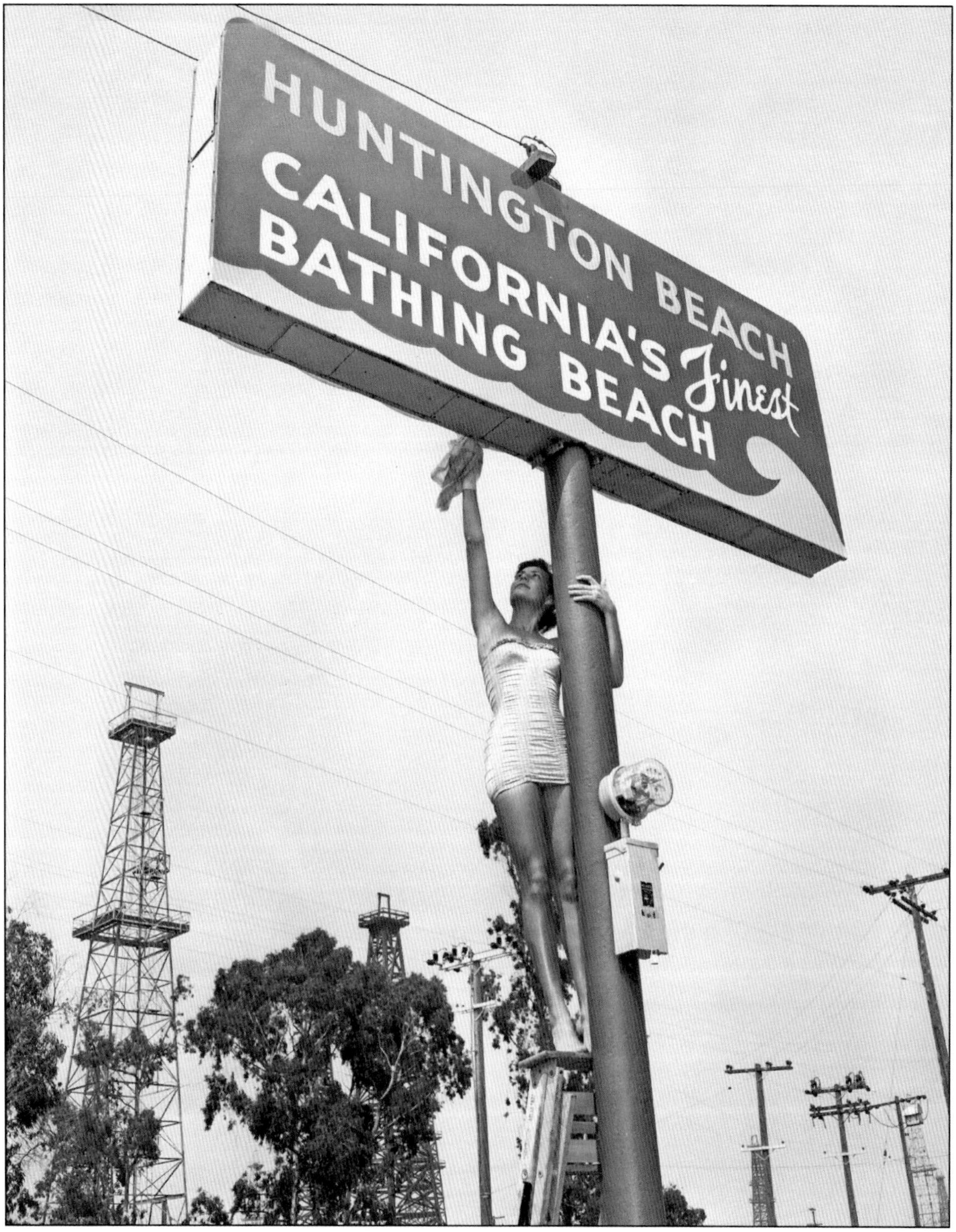

"Huntington Beach Sign, Carole Cuff, 17, HB May 23, 1952" was the attached label on this photograph. This unique photograph was also on display at the Old Courthouse Museum in the same building as Orange County clerk archivists Phil Brigandi and Chris Jepson, who helped uncover historical facts for this book.

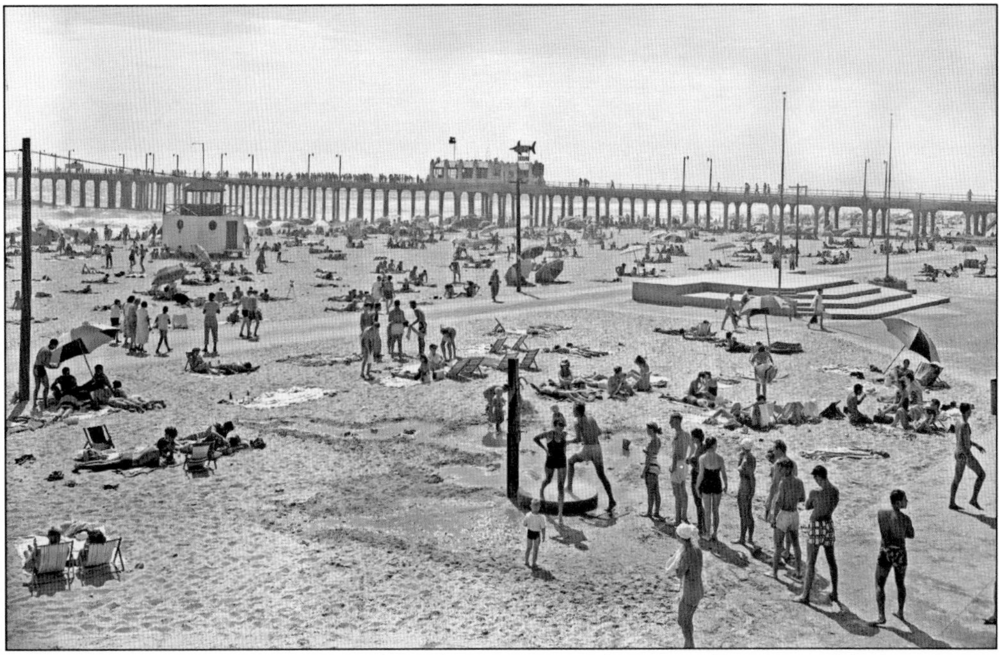

"Huntington Beach Strand 7-27-52," from the OCM, provides an excellent view of the large Tower No. 1, the newly built concrete stage, the large and very loud speakers (taken from a battleship) on top of lifeguard headquarters on the pier, and the prominent swordfish sign. Barely visible farther out on the pier is the first open-deck Tower Zero.

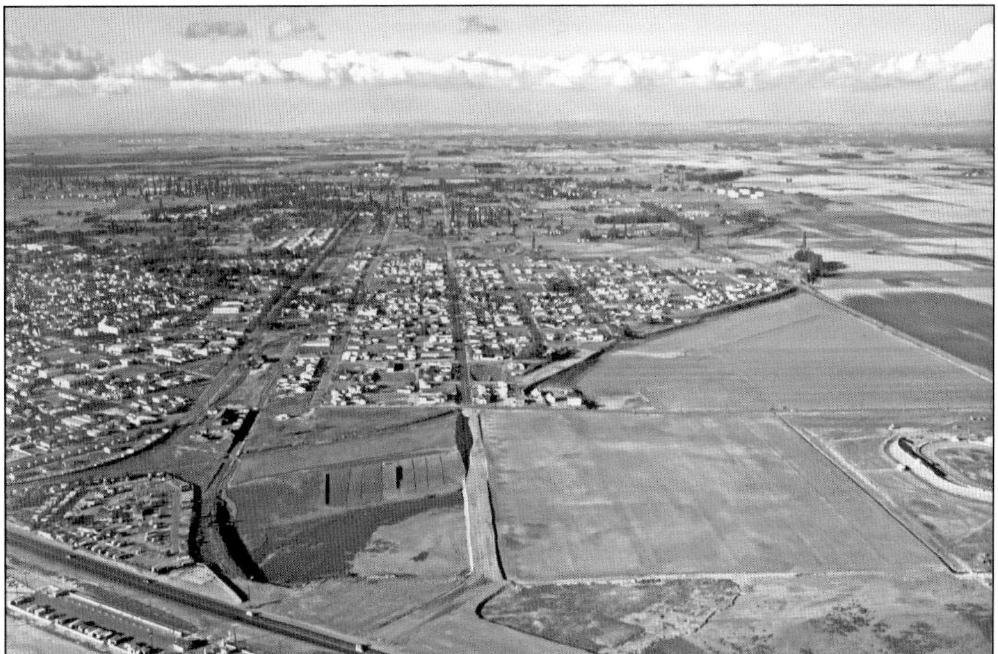

This February 22, 1951, OCM photograph shows a bird's-eye view of the city beach, the Municipal Trailer Park, and a fresh young town. A portion of the Talbert Race Track, also known as the Huntington Beach Speedway, can also be seen on the right.

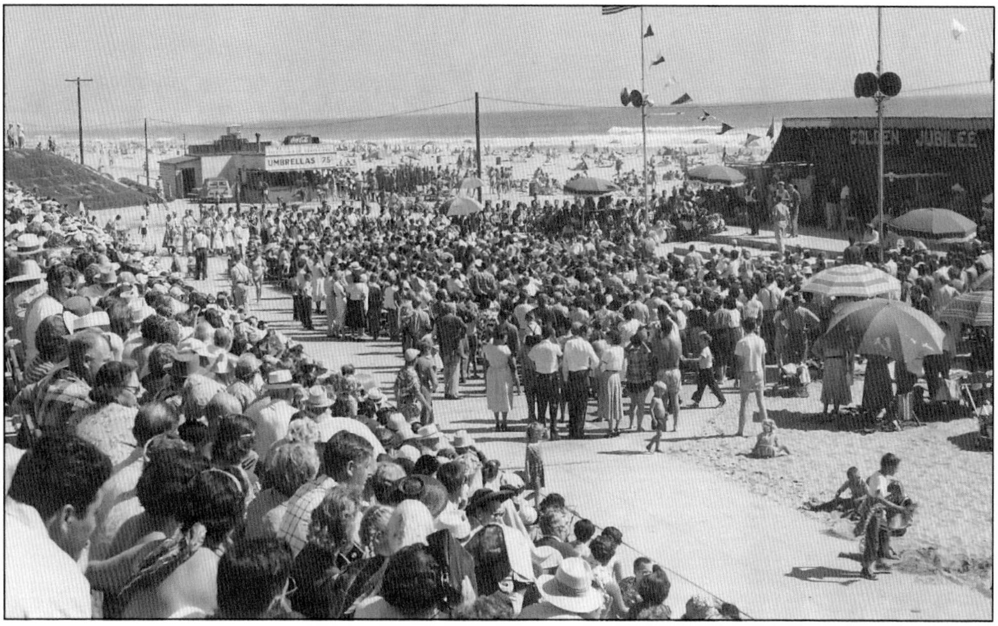

The City of Huntington Beach celebrated its 50th anniversary, the Golden Jubilee, on July 4, 1954. It was here that George A. Reynolds was recognized as the town's first constable, lifeguard, and organizer of the first city band, somewhat of an institution. At age 84, Reynolds recalled he allowed no drownings, "but I sure pulled some foolish people out of the ocean."

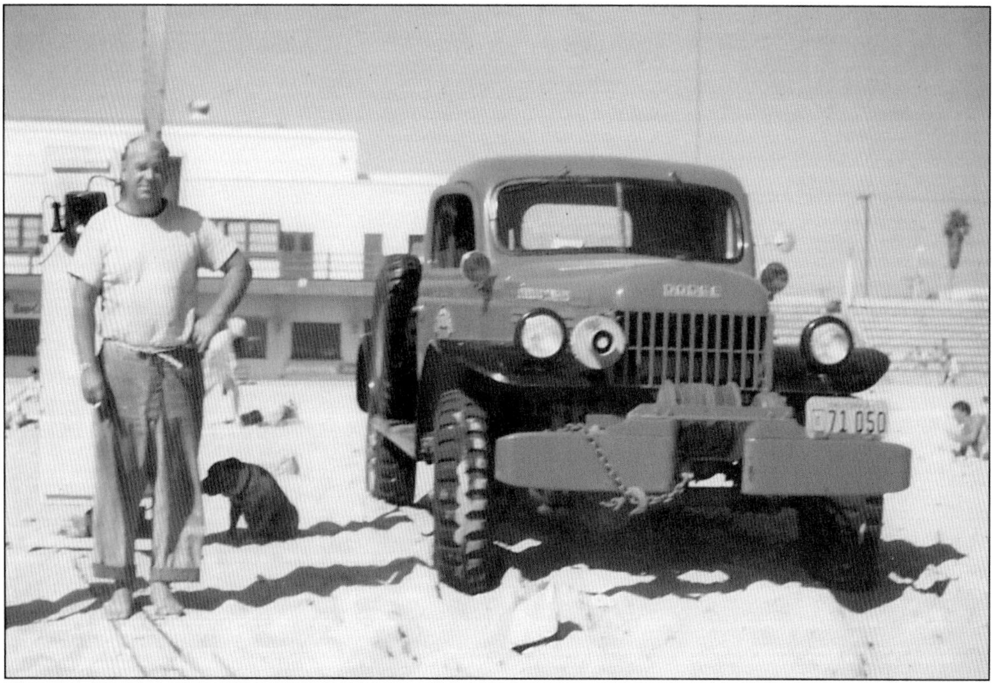

This photograph taken after 1950 has fire chief Bud Higgins working a lifeguard shift next to the pier in what is now the Tower No. 1 area. In 1950, Higgins quickly placed the lifeguards under the fire department. Bud appears to be in good company with his dog Squint, a cigarette in hand, and ready for a telephone call from HQ.

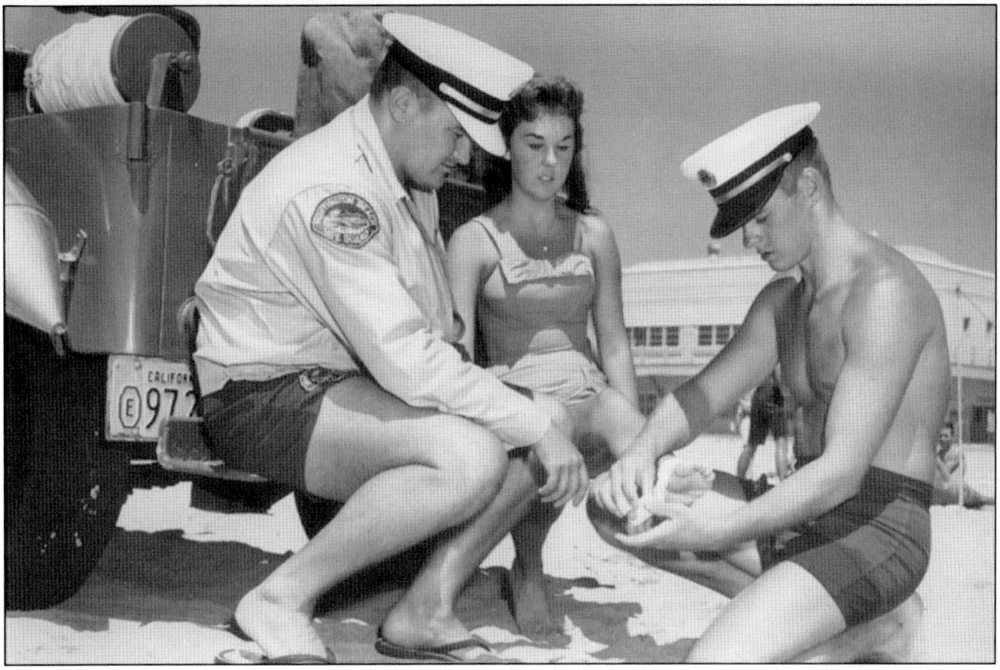

Capt. Vince Moorhouse (left) and Lt. Max Bowman take a moment to provide medical attention to this young girl's foot in 1956. Moorhouse began his lifeguard career in 1949 and soon after joined the navy as a member of the Underwater Demolition Team (UDT). He was an UDT instructor and combat veteran. Moorhouse returned to Huntington Beach in 1955 as a lifeguard lieutenant.

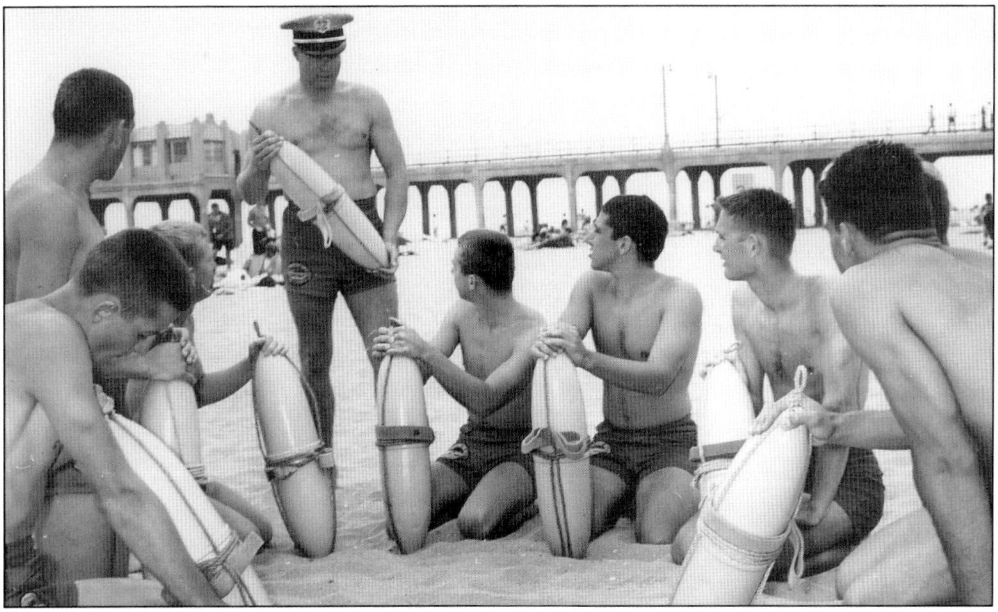

Lifeguard cadet training instructor Doug D'Arnall takes the lead of what is called the "School for Skilled" in 1959. Here is a fine example of finely wrapped torpedo rescue cans or buoys made of aluminum. Earlier technology produced the Peterson tube or belt and later the plastic Burnside buoys commonly used today. Both Pete Peterson and Bob Burnside were Los Angeles County lifeguards and legendary watermen.

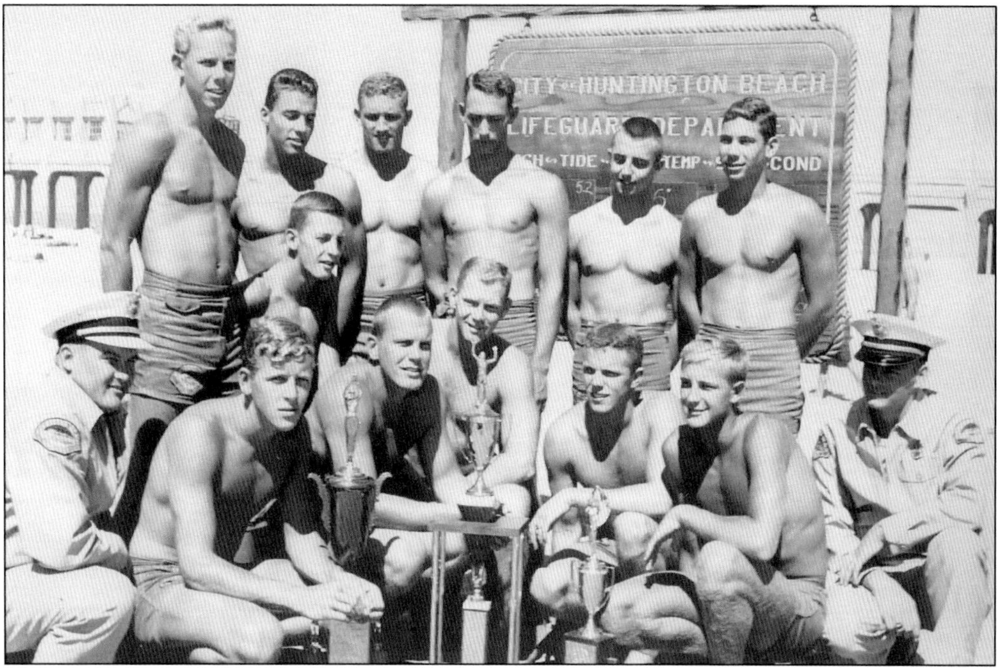

This photograph is titled "How sweet it is," and indeed it was sweet in 1958 to win first place at the Southern California Swim Championships at the Los Angeles Coliseum swim tank. The Huntington lifeguards were known for their swim and water polo skills and won their last title in 1950. In 1959, they took first place again with the slogan "two down, one to go for complete possession." They won again in 1960 and kept the perpetual trophy.

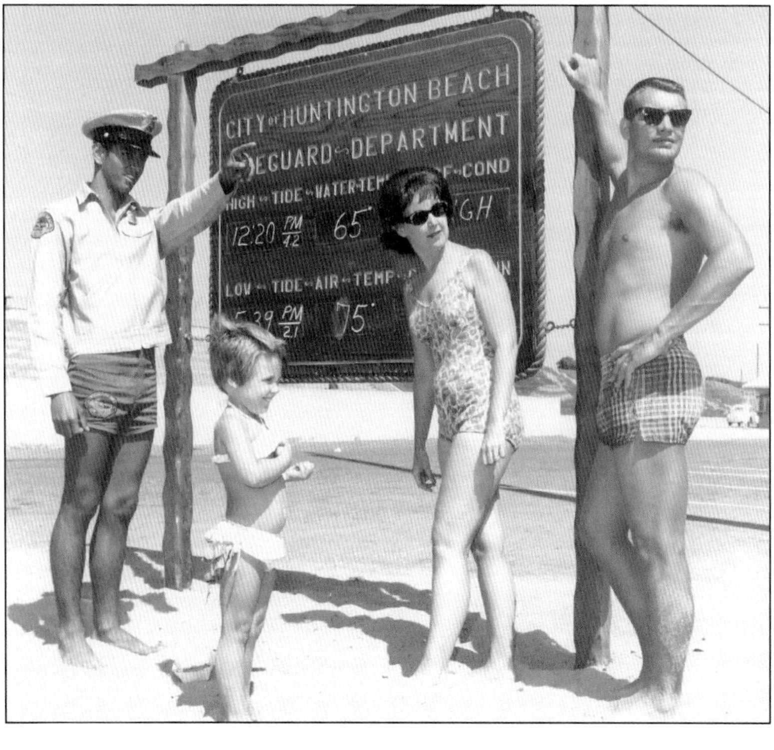

This weather board, shown in 1960, advised the public of the daily beach conditions and was located directly outside the lifeguard headquarters. Lifeguard Harold Lewis, stepson of Harlo LeBard, shows this young family the information of the day.

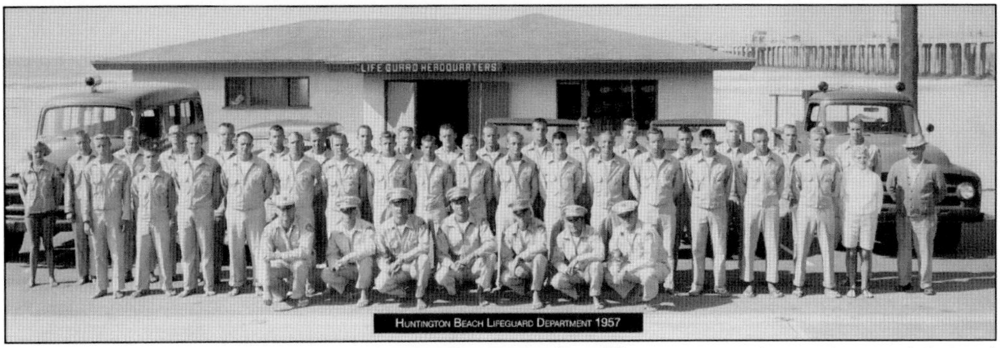

In 1957, the new chief lifeguard, Vince Moorhouse, gathered his crew together at the new lifeguard headquarters. The lifeguard department had just separated from the fire department, and the "changing of the guard" was complete. Moorhouse held the title of chief until 1984. Kneeling from left to right are Chuck Manley, Max Bowman, Kae Ewing, Ken Koster, Mike Henry, Buddy Belshe, and Chief Moorhouse.

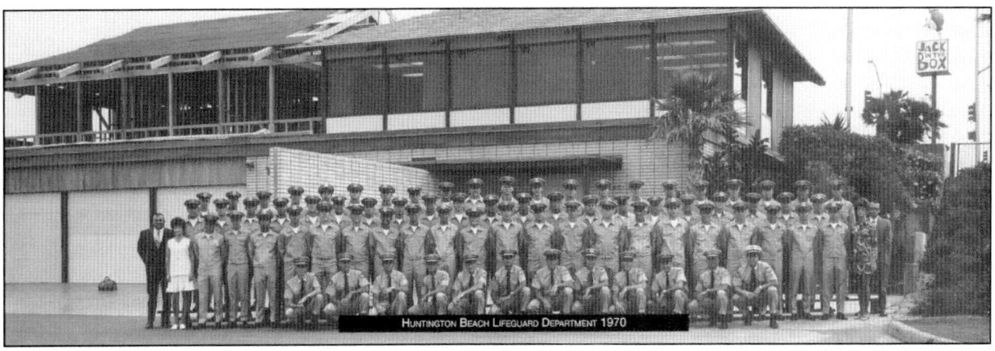

In 1970, in the again new lifeguard headquarters with addition in progress, the professional lifeguard crew stands at attention. Chief Moorhouse stands to the far left and Captain Bowman to the far right with an impressive group of lifeguards. Kneeling from left to right are lifeguard peace officers Mark Bodenbender, Brian Gerold, Lynn Lockyer, Ray Clever, Jim McKay, Bill Richardson, Winn Condict, unidentified, Tim Greaves, Mike Mills, Walt Sawyer, and Doug D'Arnall.

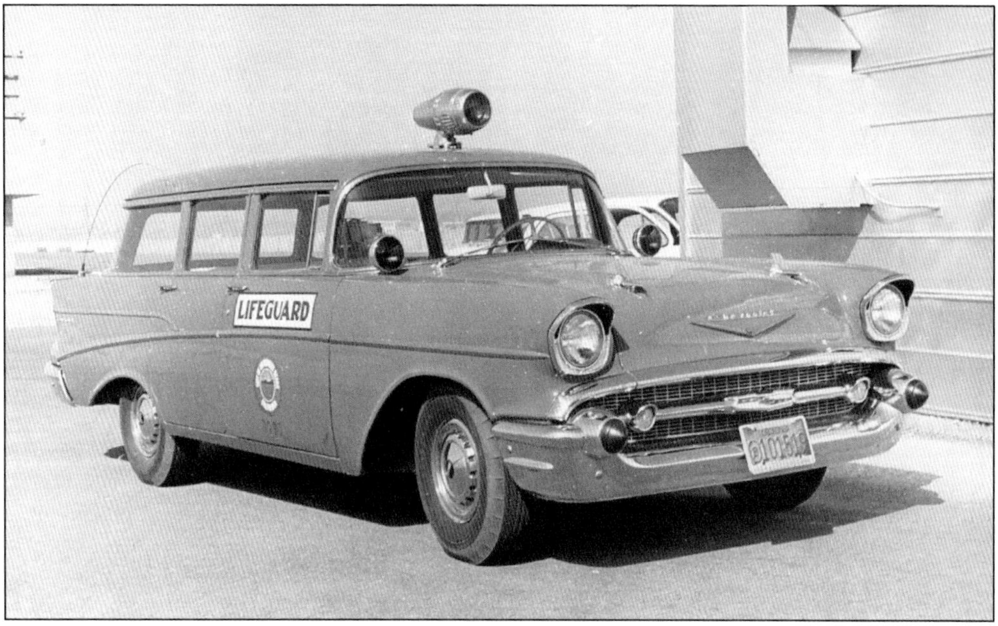

The fleet of lifeguard vehicles over the years would make a great addition to any car show, like the popular Saturday morning Huntington Donut Derelicts at the corner of Adams Avenue and Magnolia Street. This lifeguard's 1957 Chevy Bel Air Nomad would fit right in.

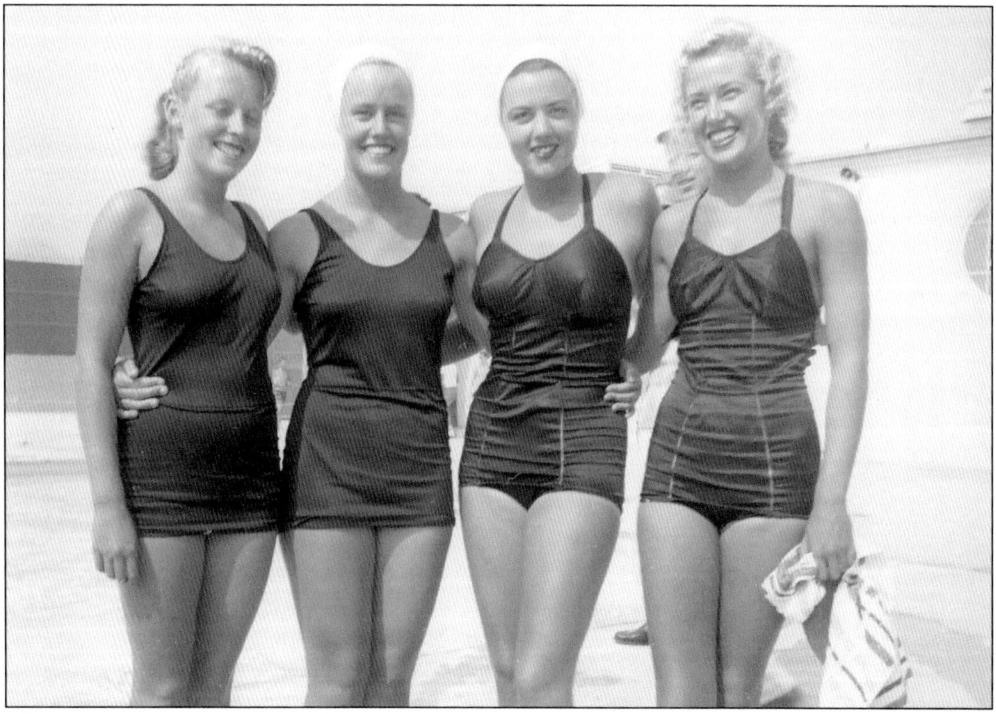

These four women are all excellent swimmers, and two have something very special in common: Darla Austin (far right) and Stephanie Belcher (second from right) were the first female Huntington Beach lifeguards in 1955. They guarded the bay side of Anderson Street, now Huntington Harbor, and gave swimming lessons.

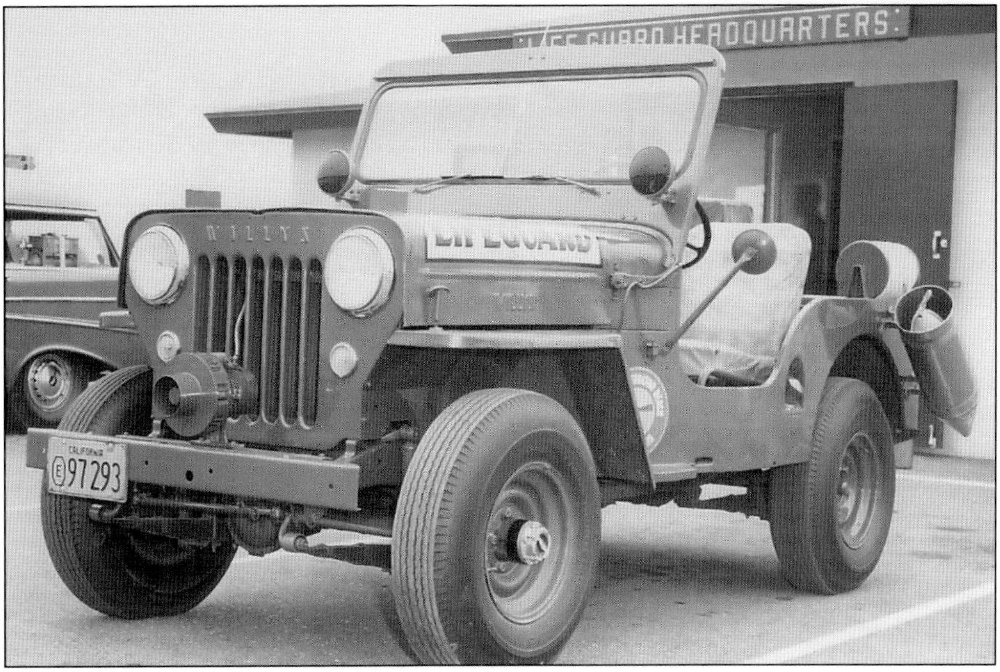

The old 5210 Willys four-wheel drive jeep is at the ready in front of lifeguard headquarters, later the junior lifeguard headquarters. The torpedo rescue can holder and rescue line are classic examples of the early equipment of the day. Farther in front of the vehicle would have been the concrete stage or bandstand and bleachers.

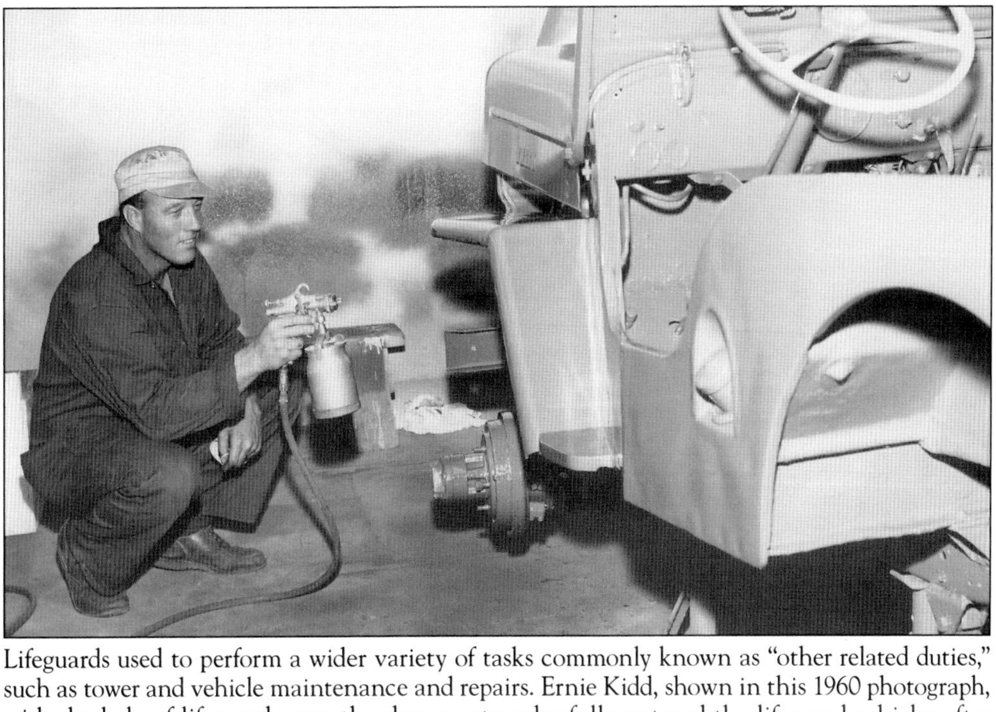
Lifeguards used to perform a wider variety of tasks commonly known as "other related duties," such as tower and vehicle maintenance and repairs. Ernie Kidd, shown in this 1960 photograph, with the help of lifeguards, was the shop master who fully restored the lifeguard vehicles after the saltwater damaged them.

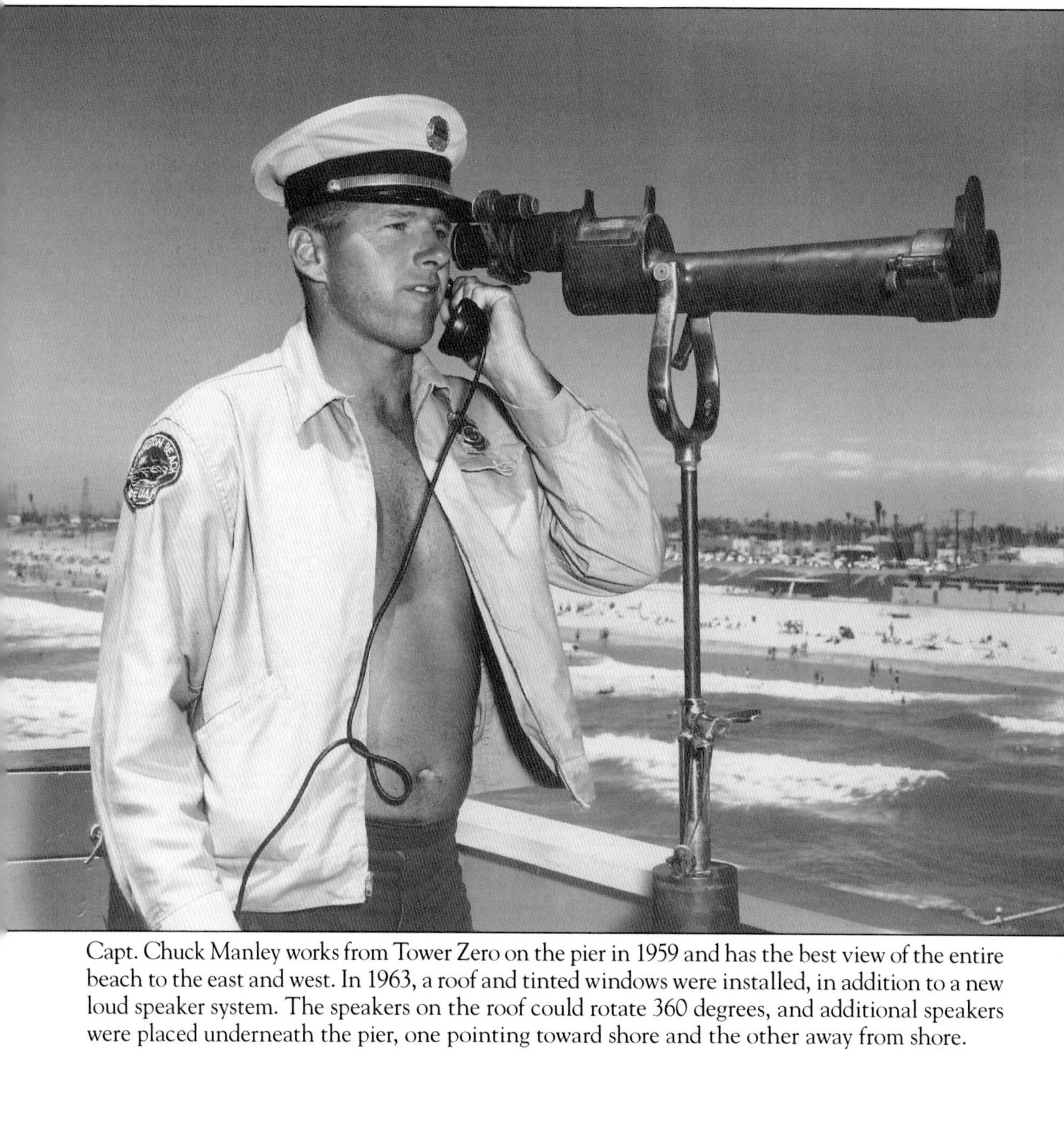

Capt. Chuck Manley works from Tower Zero on the pier in 1959 and has the best view of the entire beach to the east and west. In 1963, a roof and tinted windows were installed, in addition to a new loud speaker system. The speakers on the roof could rotate 360 degrees, and additional speakers were placed underneath the pier, one pointing toward shore and the other away from shore.

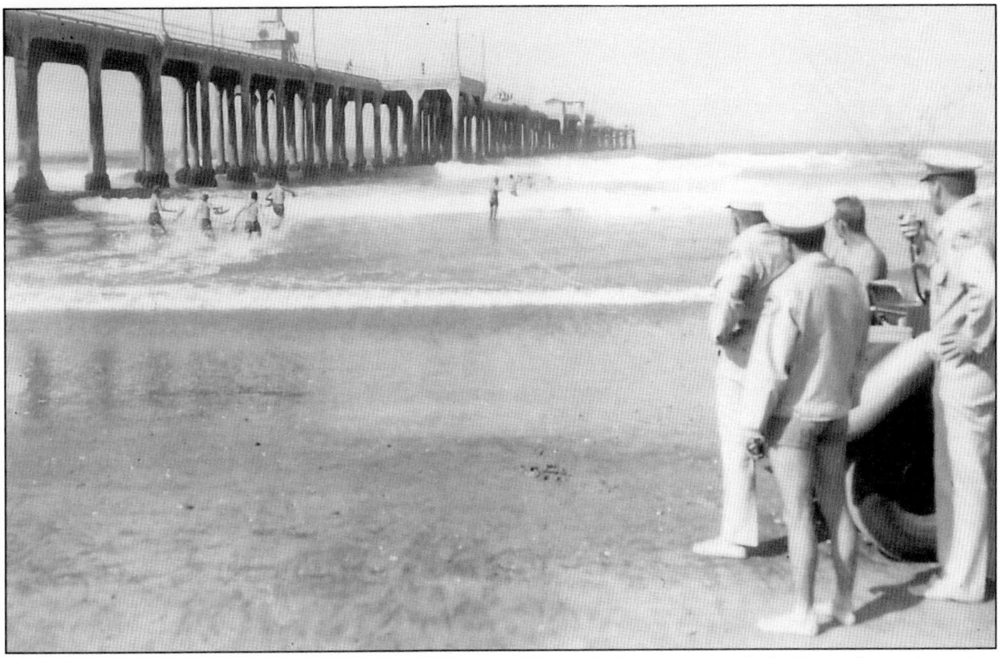

Soon after 1960, the rarely used method of rescue line deployment ended. Here the swimming lifeguard was attached with a belt to the line, collected the victim, and then was pulled back to shore by lifeguards on the beach.

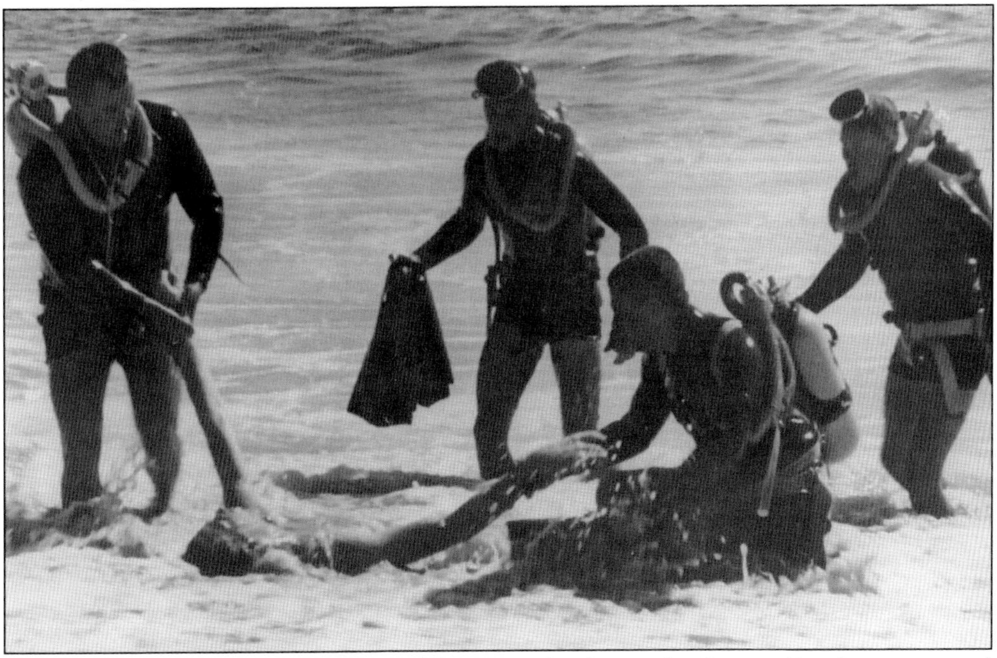

This 1960 body recovery of an 18-year-old marine who drowned at Laguna Beach was a mutual aid effort by the Laguna Beach Lifeguards and the Huntington Beach Dive Team. On occasion and even today, any Southern California lifeguard agency may request mutual aid for an event such as the search and recovery of a presumed drowning victim. In this photograph are, from left to right, Chief Moorhouse, Max Bowman, Doug D'Arnall, and Mike Hennessey.

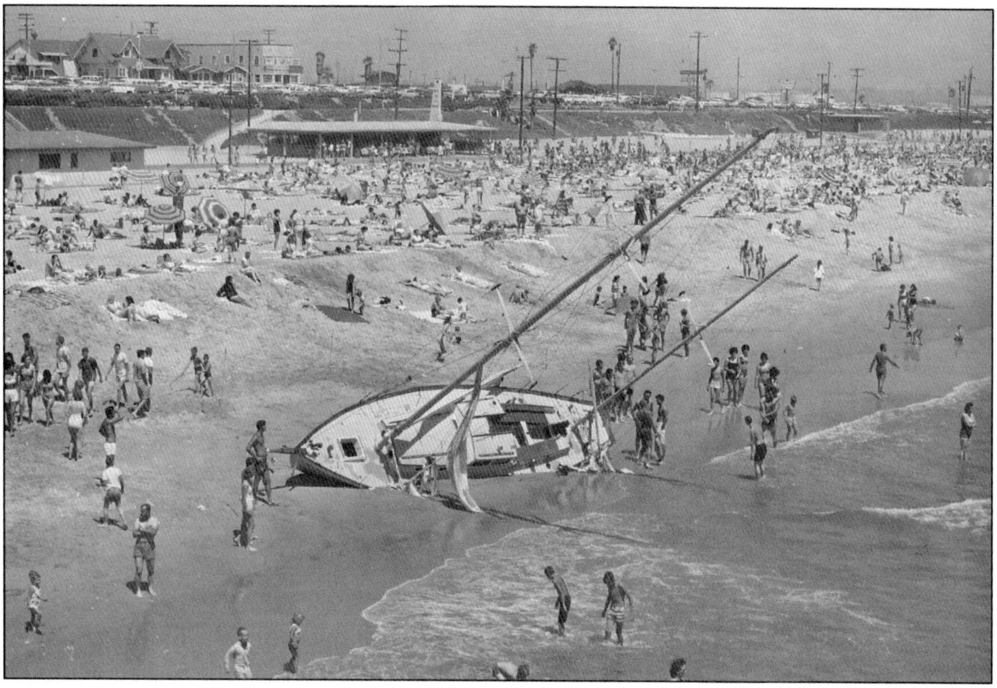

This once beautiful, two-masted sailboat, a ketch, was found on the beach close to the pier one morning. Boat rescues are common with a primary mission of preventing the often distressed vessel from entering the surf-line and hitting the beach.

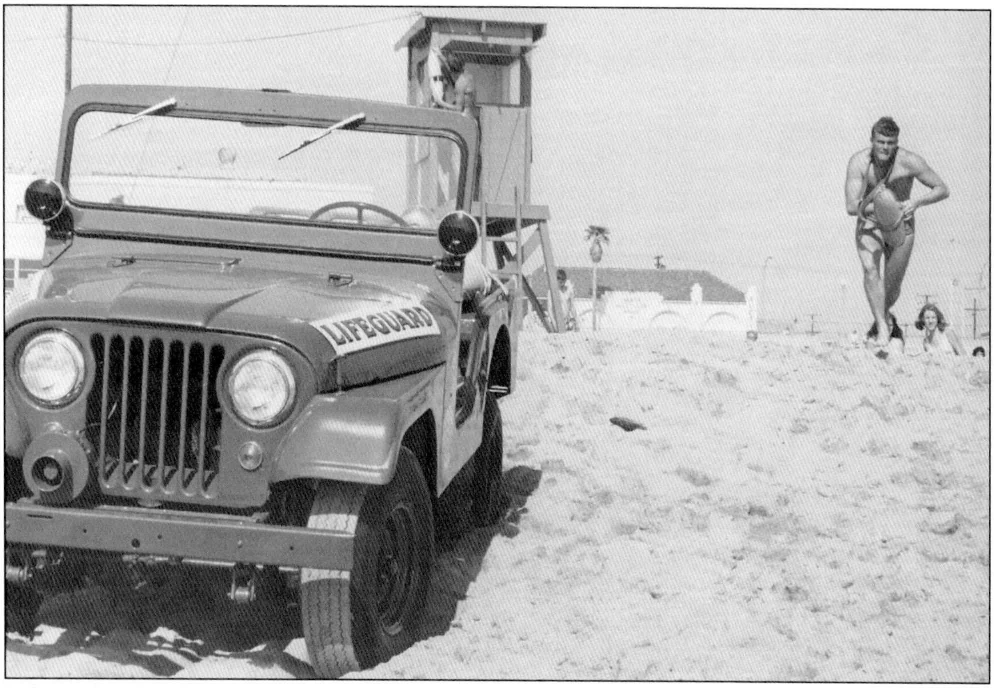

Lifeguard Mike Thurston responds to this 1966 rescue from Tower No. 1. Hopefully, the lifeguard unit operator has not already left and beat Thurston to the rescue. In 1967, the old wooden box towers began to disappear and were replaced by new models a few towers at a time.

Pier training is an integral part of the job at Huntington. On busy days with a strong side current moving toward the pier, Tower No. 1 (next to the pier) and Tower Zero are "doubled up." The extra lifeguards are needed in order to handle the activity. Pier jumps, climbing the rope ladder, and the old pier "Jennie" (a rare piece of lifeguarding equipment no longer in use) are part of training.

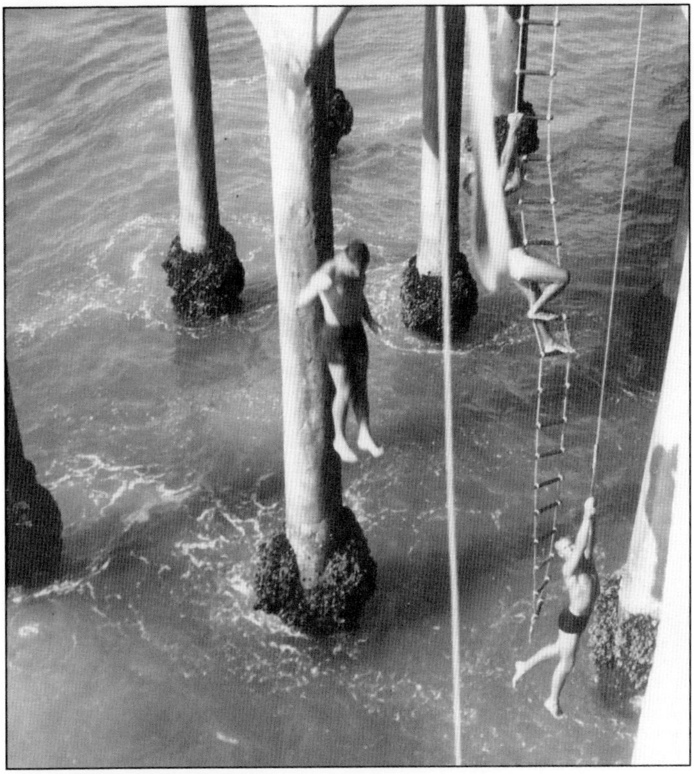

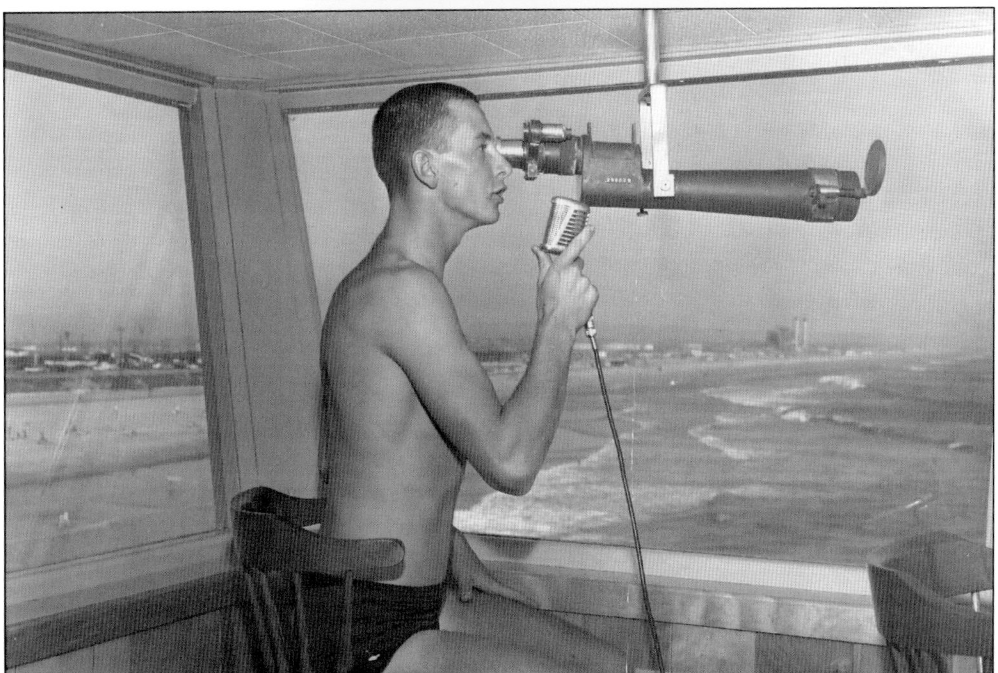

Here, in 1963, Bill Richardson sports a fresh haircut and department-issued Speedos while in Tower Zero. With binoculars originally from a Japanese war ship, he can see clearly to the Newport pier and Long Beach. Here he looks out to sea, possibly for a boat in distress.

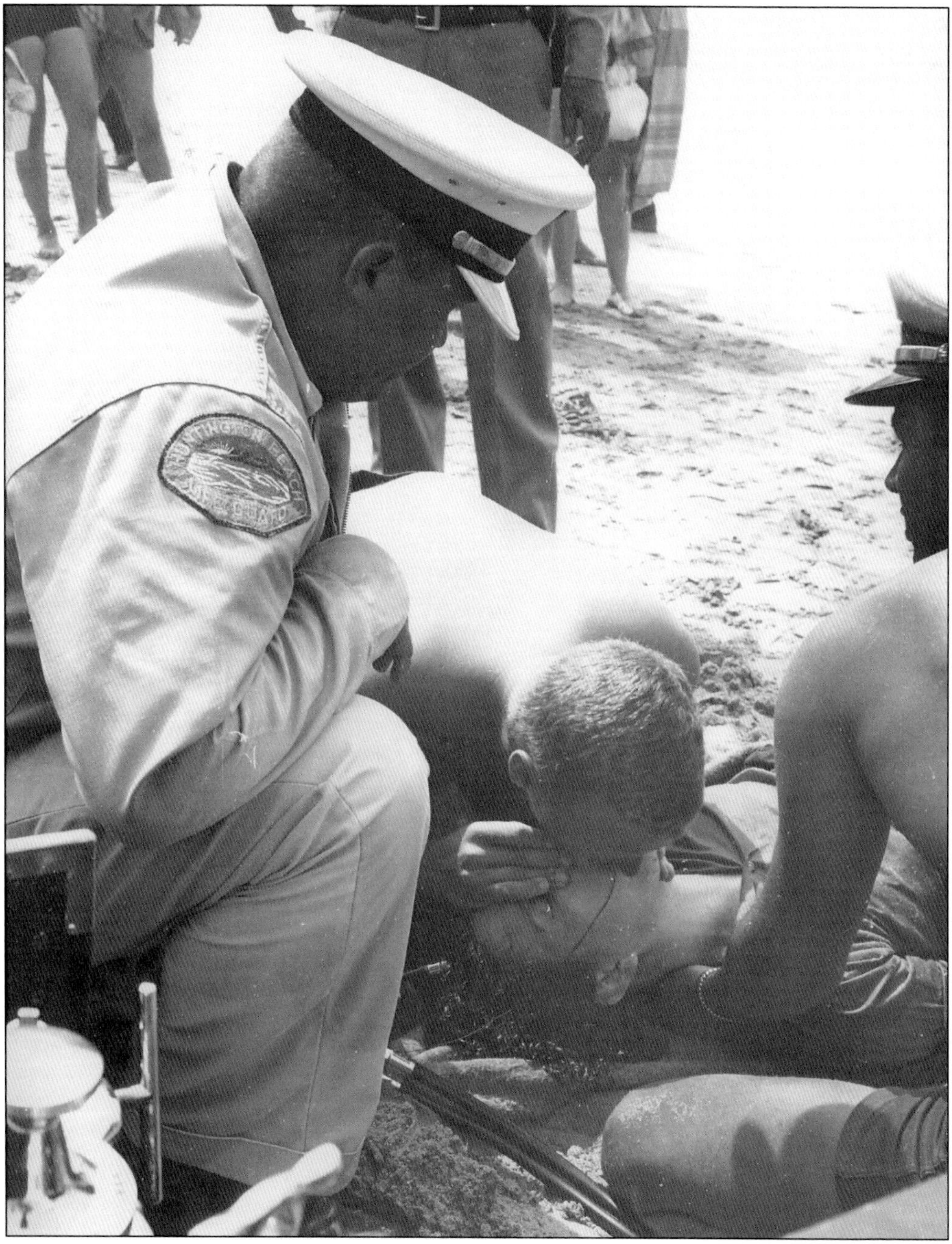

Chief Moorhouse watches his lifeguards perform CPR and try to save this person's life west of the city near the bluff area. This victim, one of three drownings, was on board a small boat that capsized in the surf-line during extremely foggy weather.

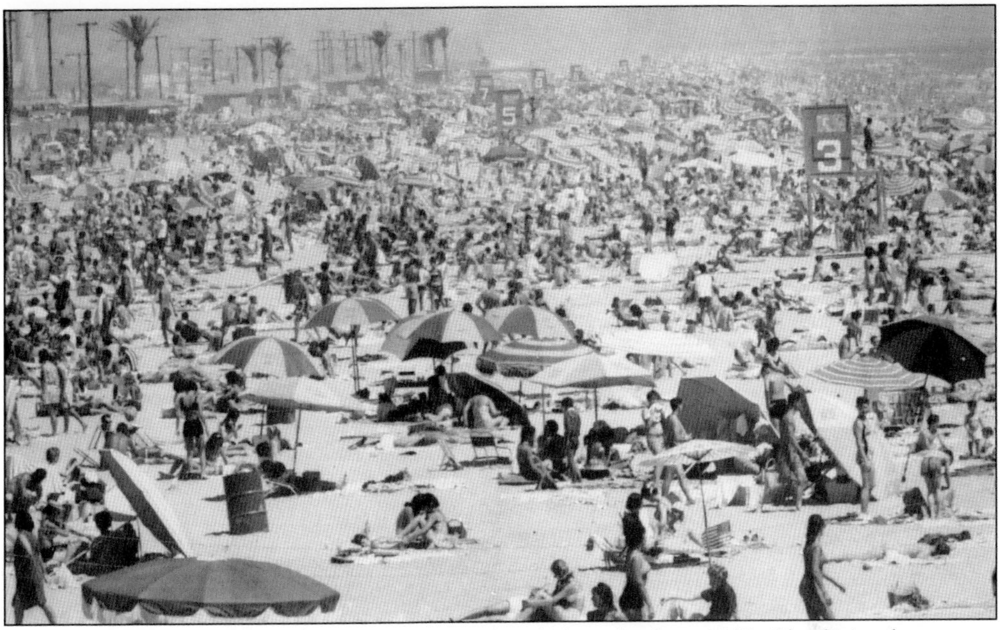

Area One, or the south side of the pier, was already busy back in 1960. Chief Moorhouse was instrumental in perfecting the perimeter defense system of lifeguarding the beach. The surveillance assigned each tower would extend to the next tower when the lifeguards left to make a rescue. The jeeps, Tower Zero, and eventually the rescue boats would do the same and ensure the proper resources for the smallest or biggest incident.

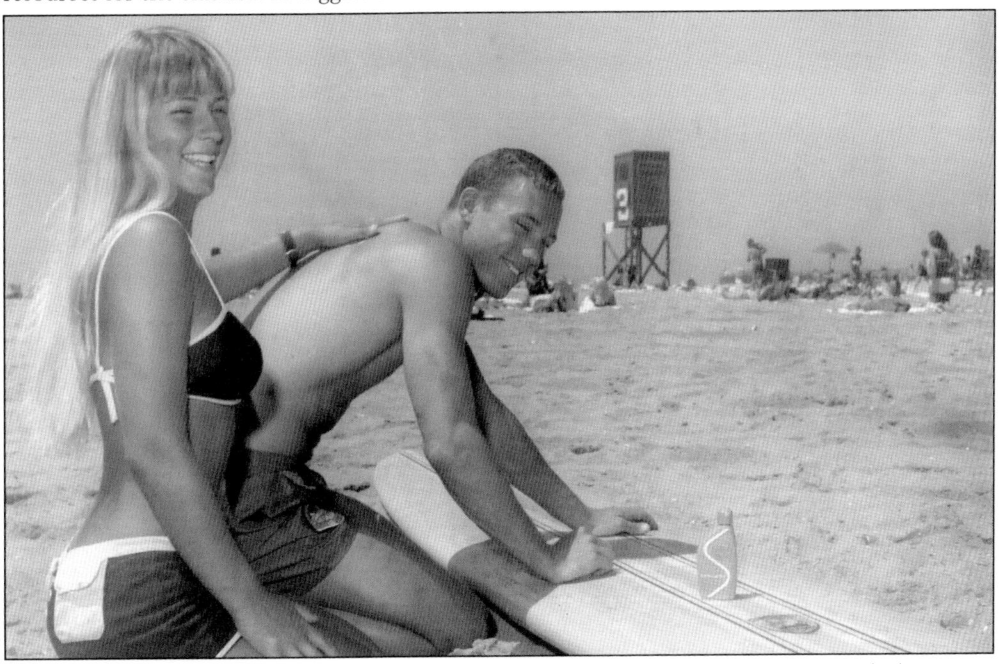

This 1960 south-side photograph shows Jan Gaffney ready with a bottle of Sea and Ski suntan lotion and lifeguard Russ Webb with his Gordie surfboard. Gaffney was crowned the 1965 Queen of the U.S. Surfboard Championships and now owns and operates Jan's Health Food Bar downtown on Main Street. Gordie's surf shop, the first in Huntington, opened in 1955.

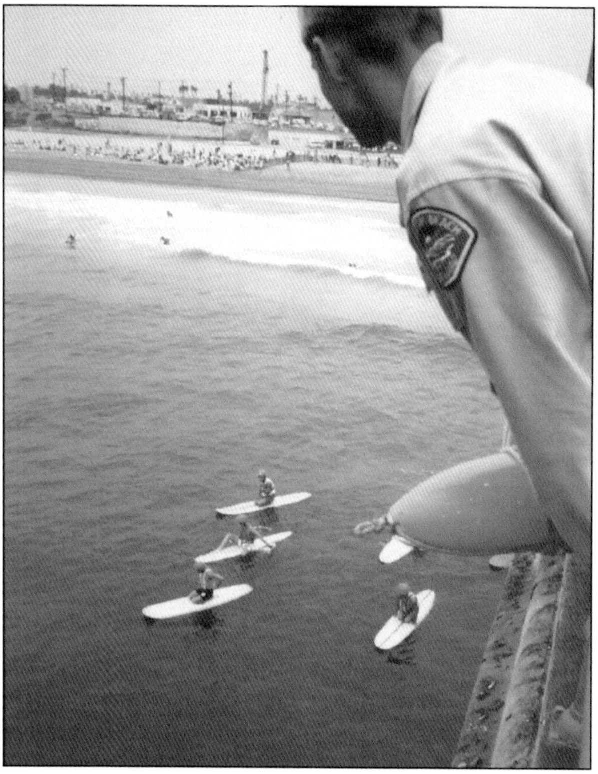

The lifeguard on the pier during the 1964 West Coast Surfing Championships checks on the surfers paddling out for the next heat. In 1959, the first West Coast Surfing Championships were held in Huntington Beach, organized by Long Beach State student Peter Bertran, Norm Worthy of the recreation department, and Vince Moorhouse. The first champion was Jack Haley of Seal Beach.

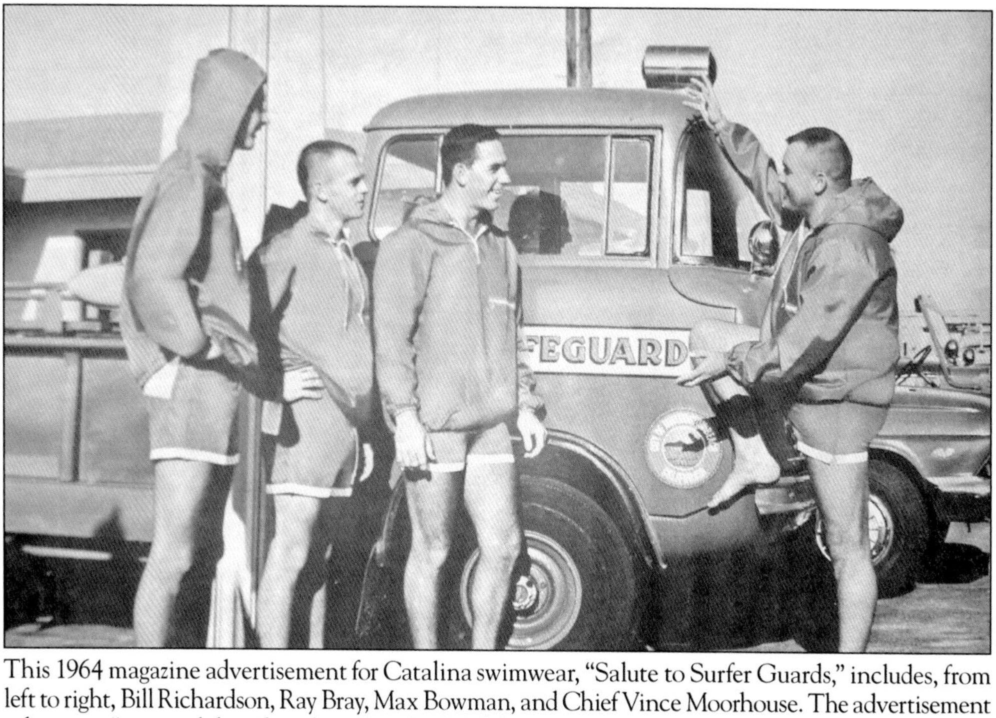

This 1964 magazine advertisement for Catalina swimwear, "Salute to Surfer Guards," includes, from left to right, Bill Richardson, Ray Bray, Max Bowman, and Chief Vince Moorhouse. The advertisement salute was "a special dip of our board to the HB lifeguards for their courageous efforts establishing high standards of safety, rules, regulations, and etiquette emulated internationally."

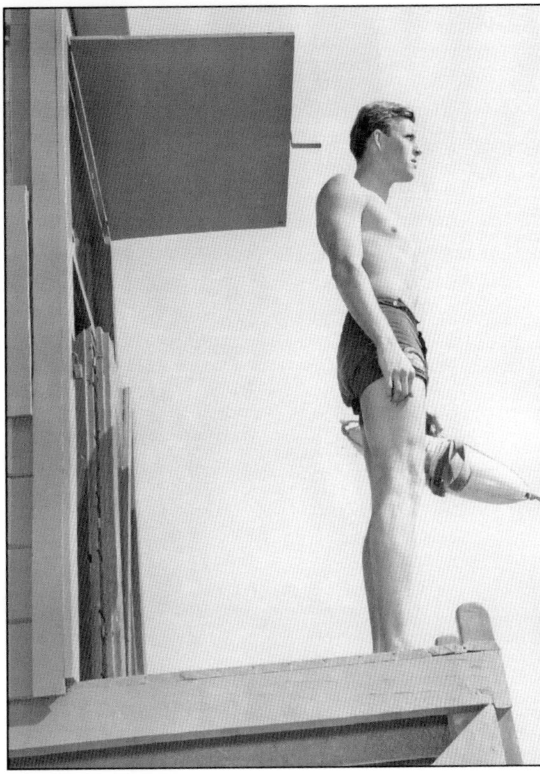

In this training sequence, lifeguard Winn Condict stands ready on the deck of Tower No. 1 and looks for a potential rescue in the water. Upon the command of Raymond Bray from the jeep, Winn leaps off the deck with torpedo buoy in hand. Today large sand mounds are maintained in front of the towers by the invaluable beach maintenance crew to prevent unnecessary knee or back injury while responding to rescues.

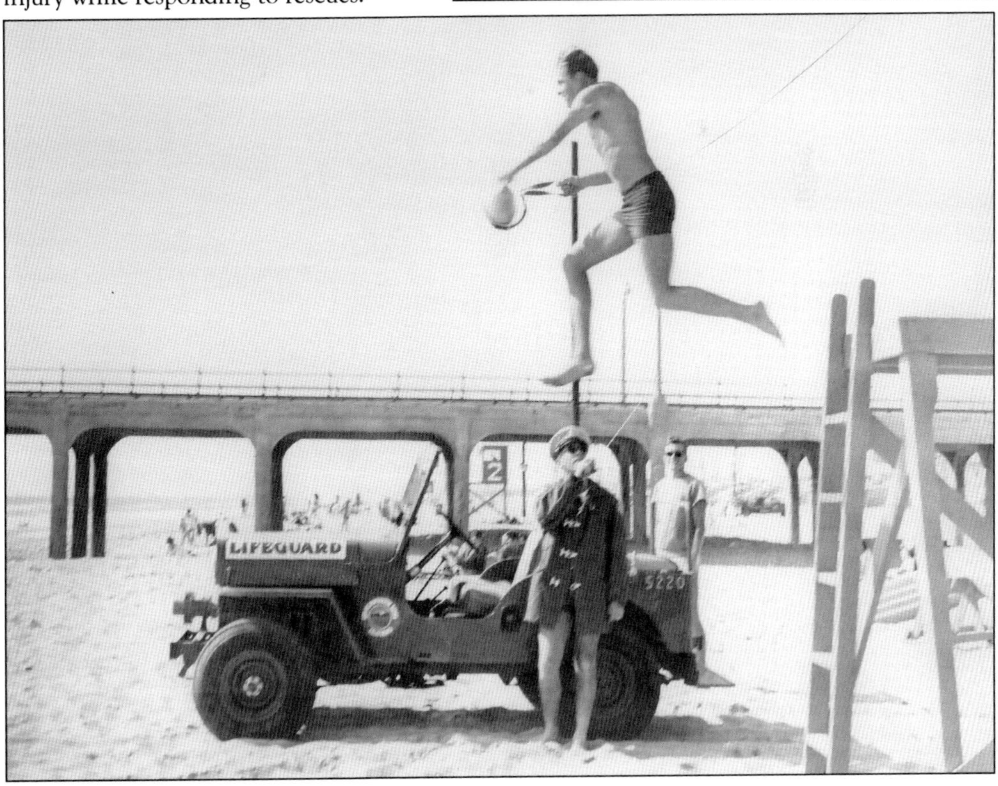

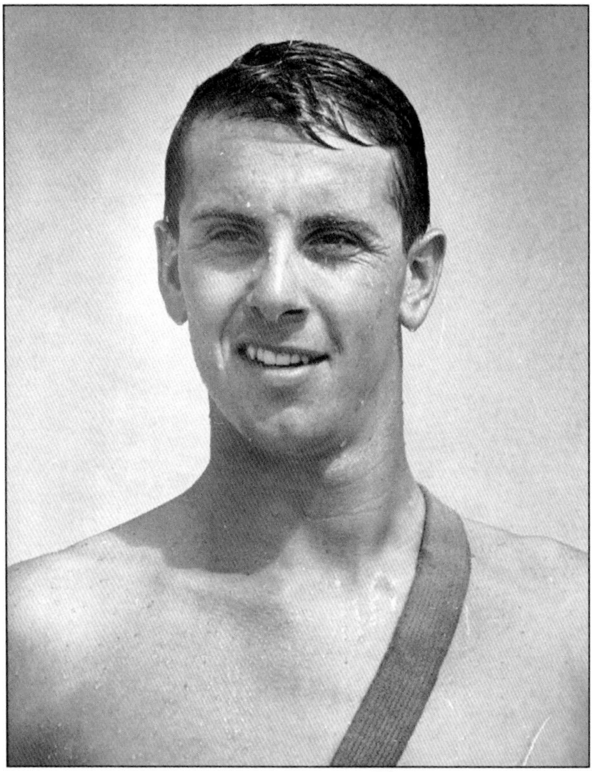

On March 14, 1964, lifeguard John Freenor responded from the pier with a paddleboard to an emergency call several hours into working the night shift (24-hour patrol). Freenor rescued four men from a downed navy helicopter a half mile off the end of the Huntington Beach pier. "Glad to be alive" was the common phrase among the navy helicopter personnel who nearly lost their lives that early morning off the coast of Huntington Beach. Freenor received several awards from the city and the local American Legion post. Below, the U.S. Navy awarded Freenor the highest peacetime award offered by the navy—the Navy Silver Life Saving Award.

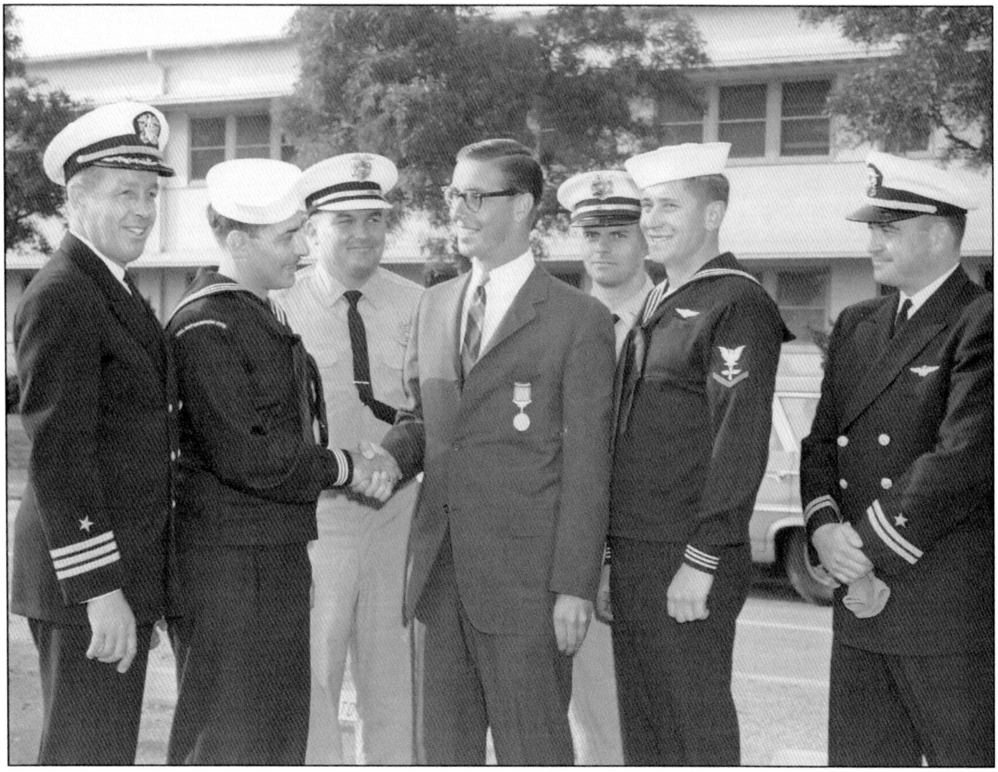

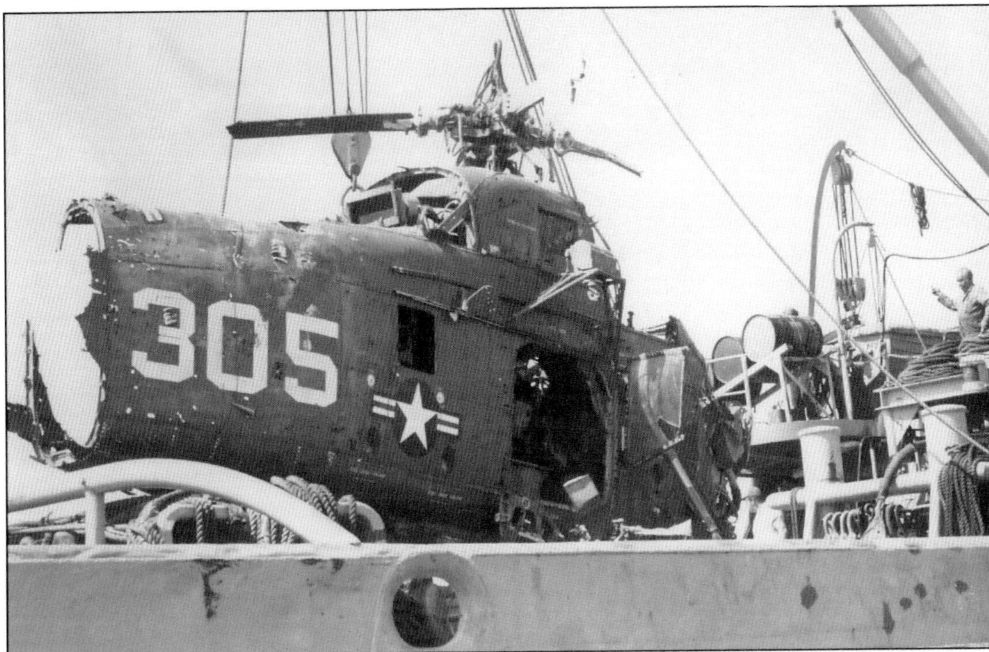

The day after the valiant Freenor rescue, the navy helicopter salvage operation was visible from the end of the pier. The twisted metal and fuselage were pulled up from the ocean depth of 40 to 50 feet and taken away.

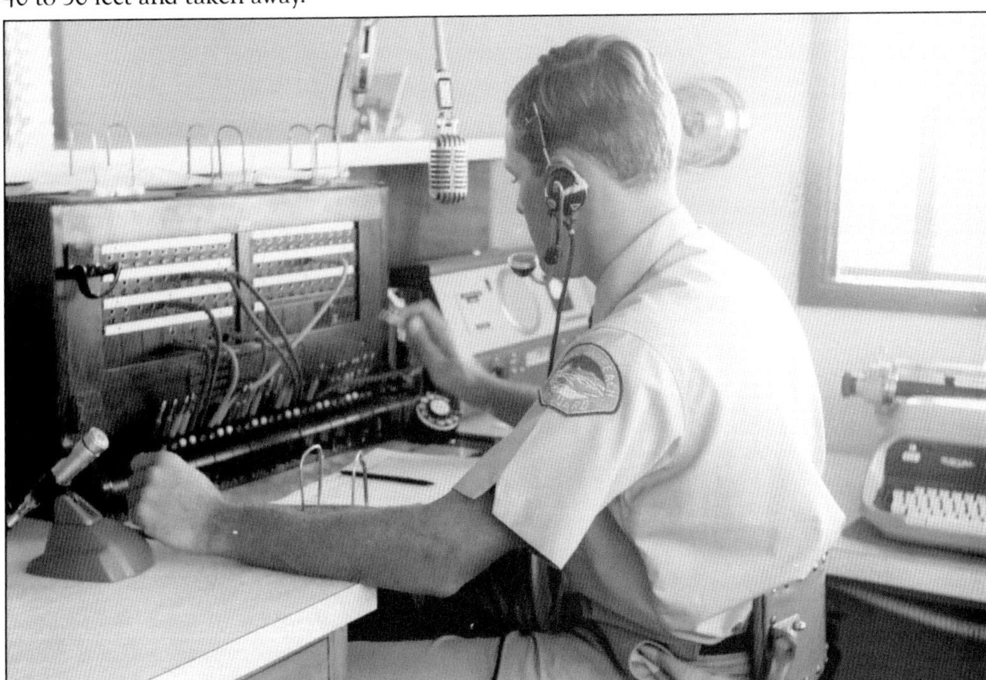

In this 1964 photograph, dispatcher Winn Condict was assigned to the vintage PBX telephone switchboard at the new lifeguard headquarters at Lake Street and PCH. The PBX was first used in the lifeguard headquarters on the pier in the 1930s, moved in 1957 to lifeguard headquarters on the beach, and finally retired in 1990.

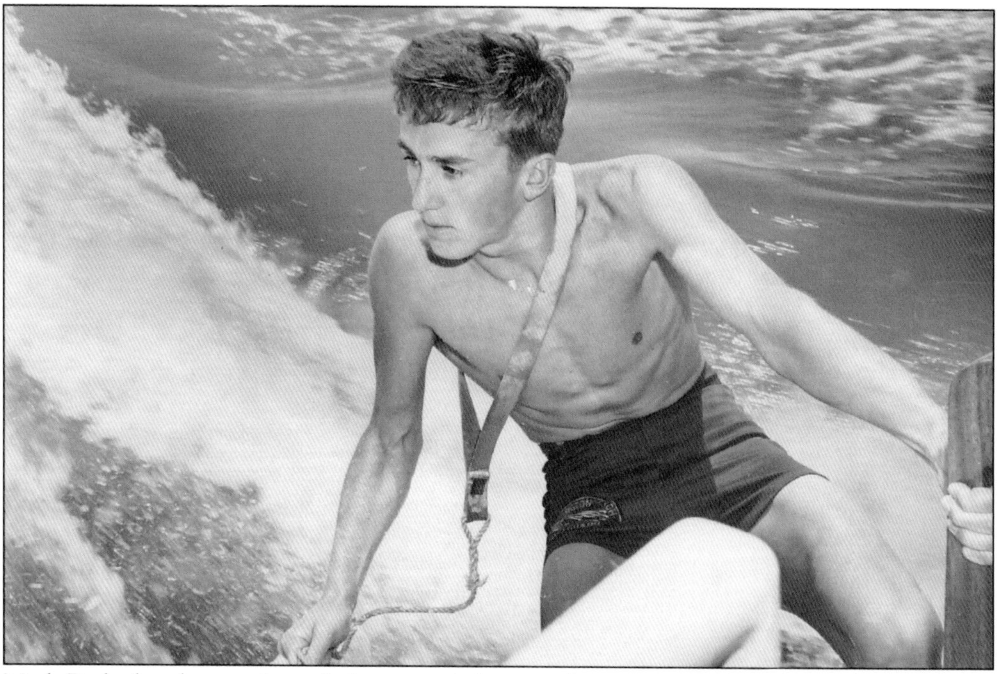

Mark Bodenbender stands ready for a speed drop on the new rescue boat *Sentinel* 5240 in this 1964 photograph. After the lengthy design, production, and now maiden voyage, the *Sentinel* and later *Guardian* proved to be valuable assets.

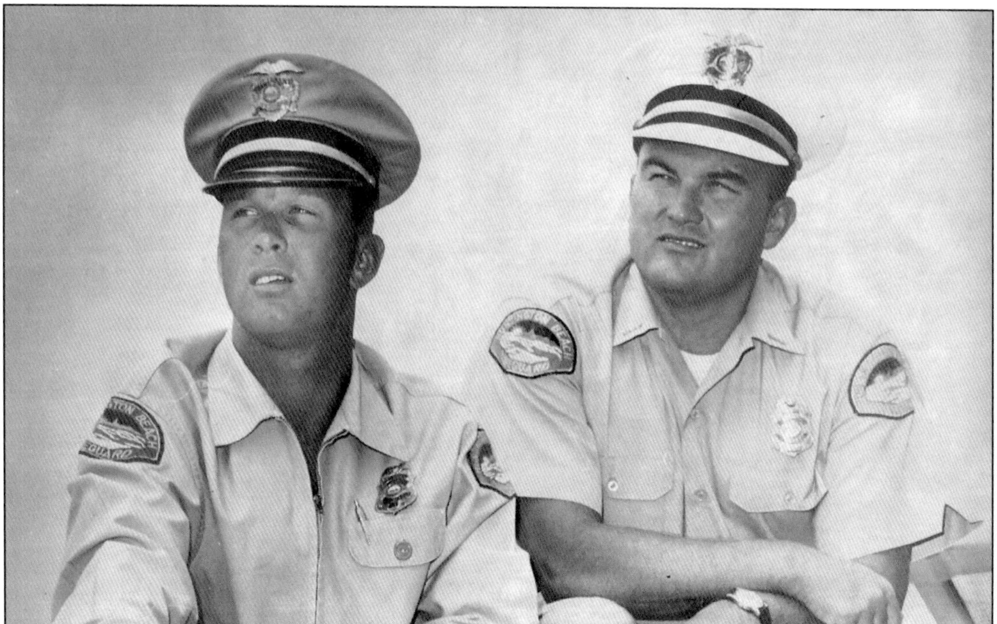

On May 13, 1964, Lt. Walt Sawyer (left) and Chief Moorhouse responded to a downed helicopter two miles off shore near the oil platform "Emmy" using the new *Sentinel* 5240. All three people survived the crash, were rescued by lifeguards, and were grateful to be alive. This was the second helicopter crash in two months off the shores of Huntington. Sawyer and Moorhouse each received a medal of valor.

Soon after Huntington Harbor opened, the Huntington Beach lifeguards provided the harbor patrol with three rescue boats. Here is the bow and crew of the *Sentinel* in 1965 with, from left to right, Walt Sawyer, Don Stewart, and John Setmire. In 1974, the Orange County Sheriff's Department began its harbor patrol program, ending the lifeguard program.

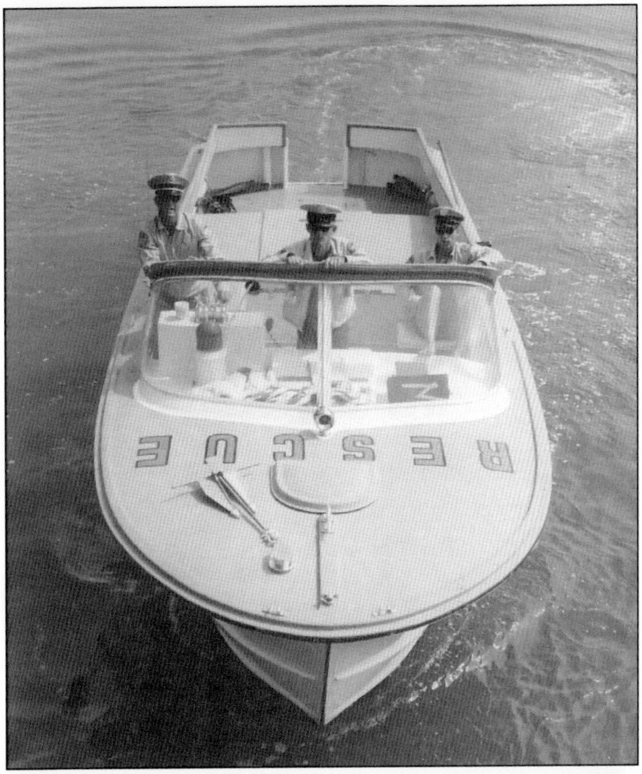

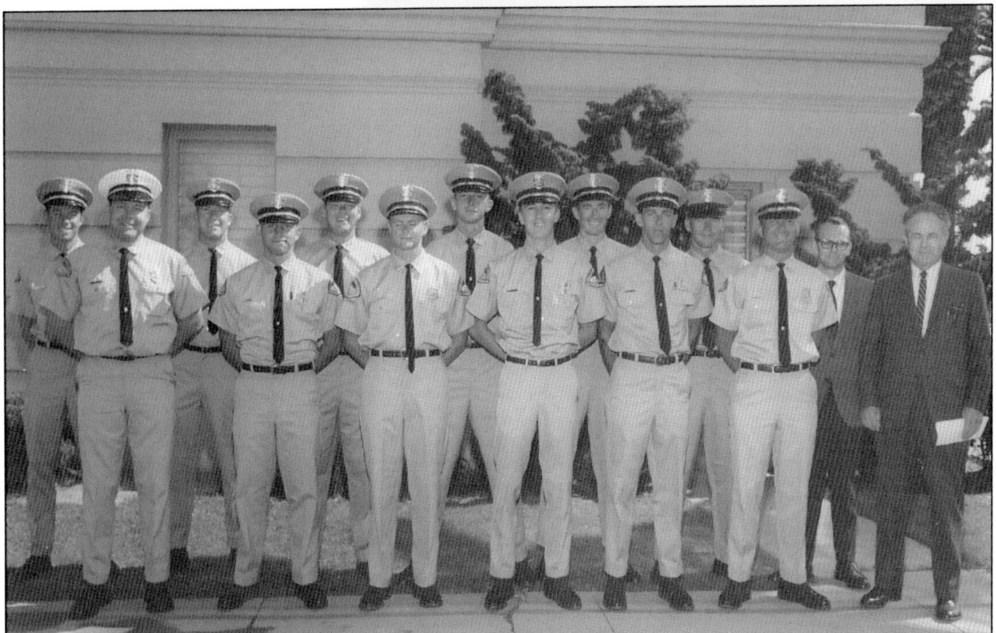

In 1969, the permanent lifeguard staff was deputized by police chief John H. Seltzer and recognized as "special officers." From left to right are Lynn Lockyer, Doug D'Arnall, Tim Greaves, Brian Gerold, Don Shuckman, Mike Thurston, Bill Richardson, Mark Bodenbender, Jim McKay, Jim Rayl, Randy Condict, Walt Sawyer, Max Bowman, and Chief Seltzer.

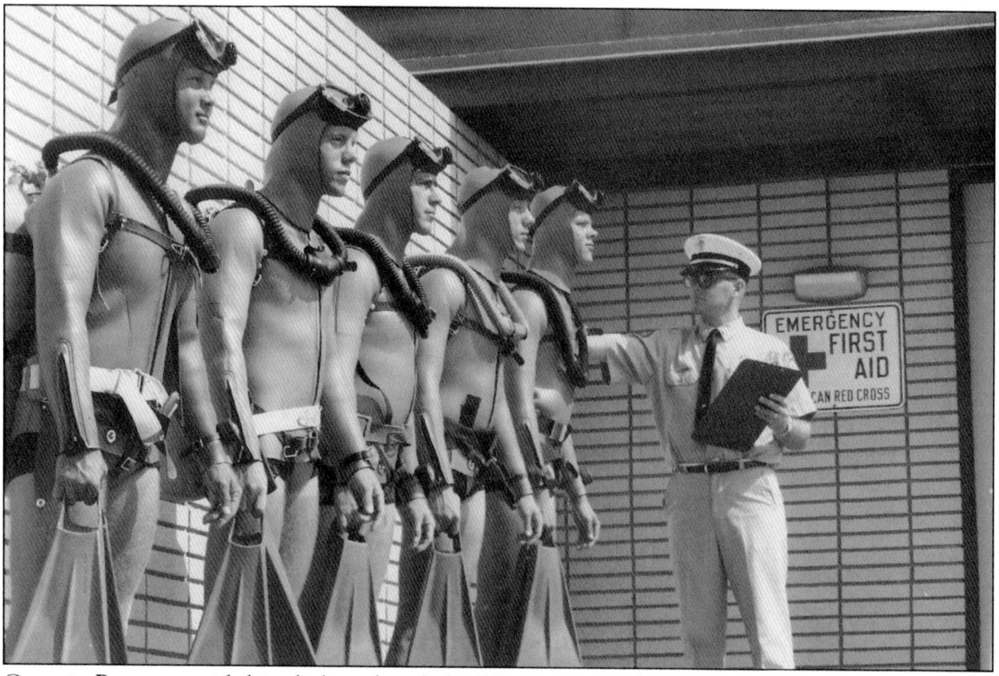

Captain Bowman with his clipboard and checklist inspects the SCUBA Dive Team in front of lifeguard headquarters. The dive team may be called to respond at the beach, inland, within the city limits, and outside the city for another agency's mutual aid request. From left to right are Walt Sawyer, Torrey Webb, Ray Bray, Russell Webb, and Hal DeJong.

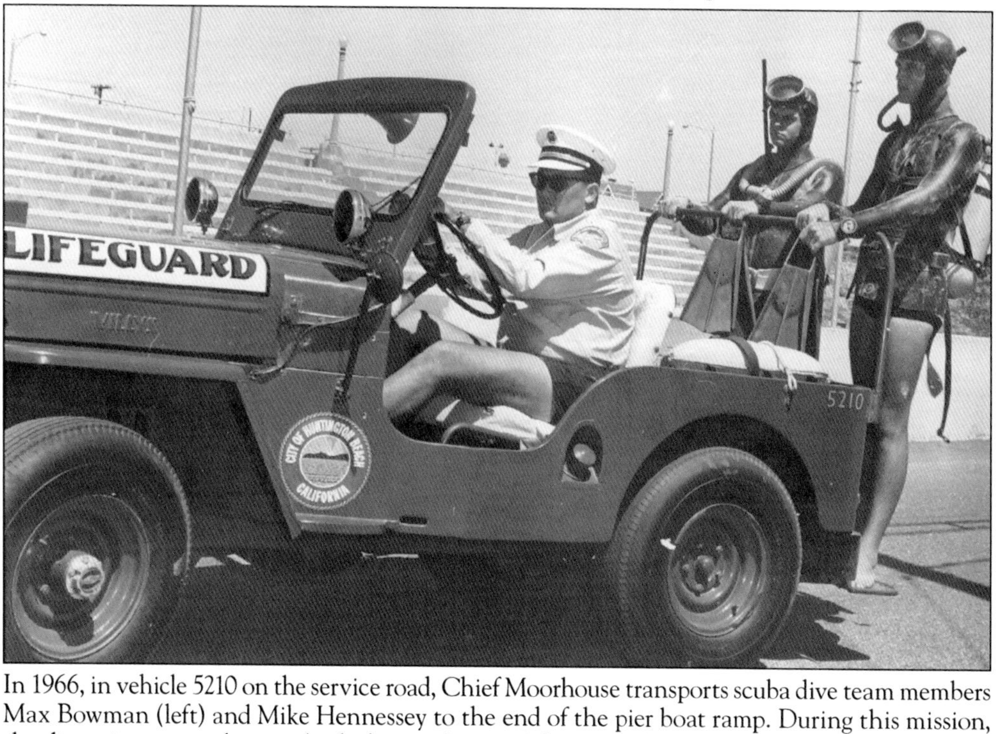

In 1966, in vehicle 5210 on the service road, Chief Moorhouse transports scuba dive team members Max Bowman (left) and Mike Hennessey to the end of the pier boat ramp. During this mission, the divers inspect and report back the condition of the pier pilings below.

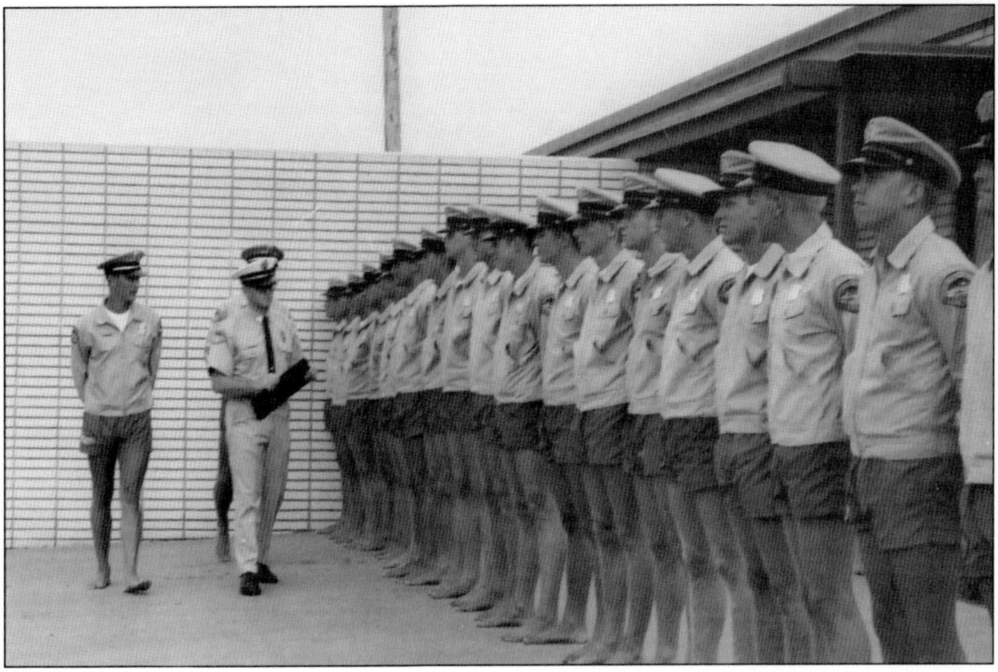

The lifeguard morning lineup and inspection was at the top of the hour with reporting time 15 minutes before. This 1966 lineup was led by Captain Bowman; Stan Reed is to the left of Bowman, and Bill Richardson is behind. Inspected men were clean and had a proper hair length (facial hair was not allowed), uniforms, badges, and the infamous "bag checks."

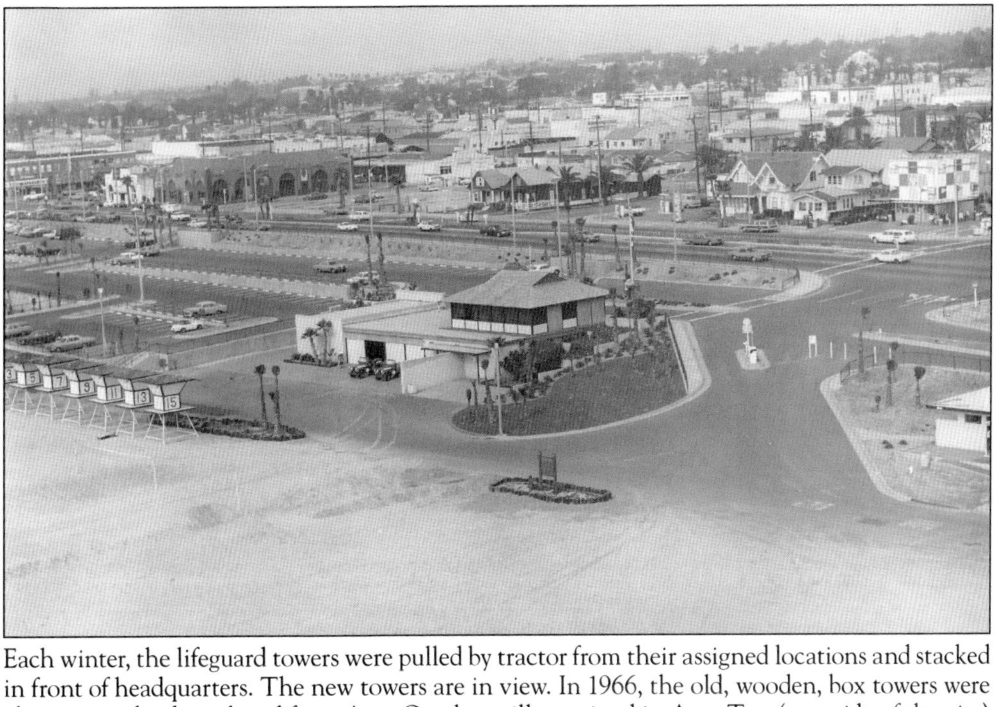

Each winter, the lifeguard towers were pulled by tractor from their assigned locations and stacked in front of headquarters. The new towers are in view. In 1966, the old, wooden, box towers were almost completely replaced from Area One but still remained in Area Two (west side of the pier) and Area Three (Orange County, Sunset Beach).

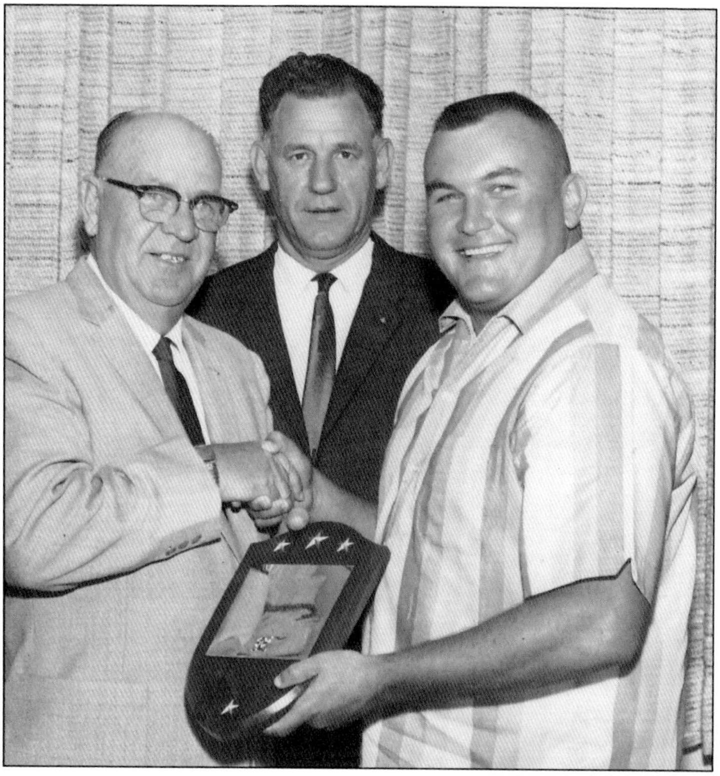

In 1965, Chief Moorhouse (right) presented this lifetime achievement award to Bud Higgins, retired Huntington Beach lifeguard chief and fire chief, during the Huntington Beach Surf Life Saving end of summer dinner. Official dinner guest, standing in the center, is Jake Stewart, Huntington Beach mayor (1960–1968).

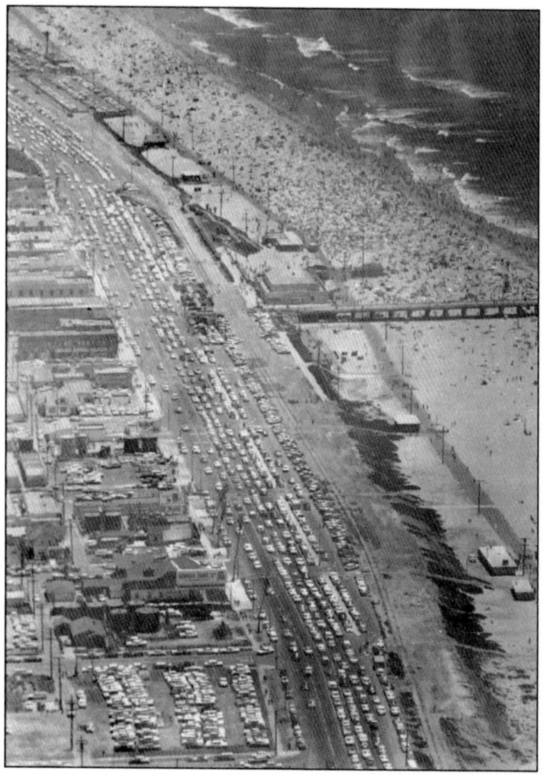

This photograph was taken from the police helicopter on July 4, 1964. The beach and the city are busy and ready for more changes to come. The Salt Water Plunge had just been dismantled, soon the first and only apartment building would be built on the beach, and the McDonnell Douglas Aircraft and Space Systems Center would open the following year.

Three

THE COASTAL PLAYGROUND 1967–1999

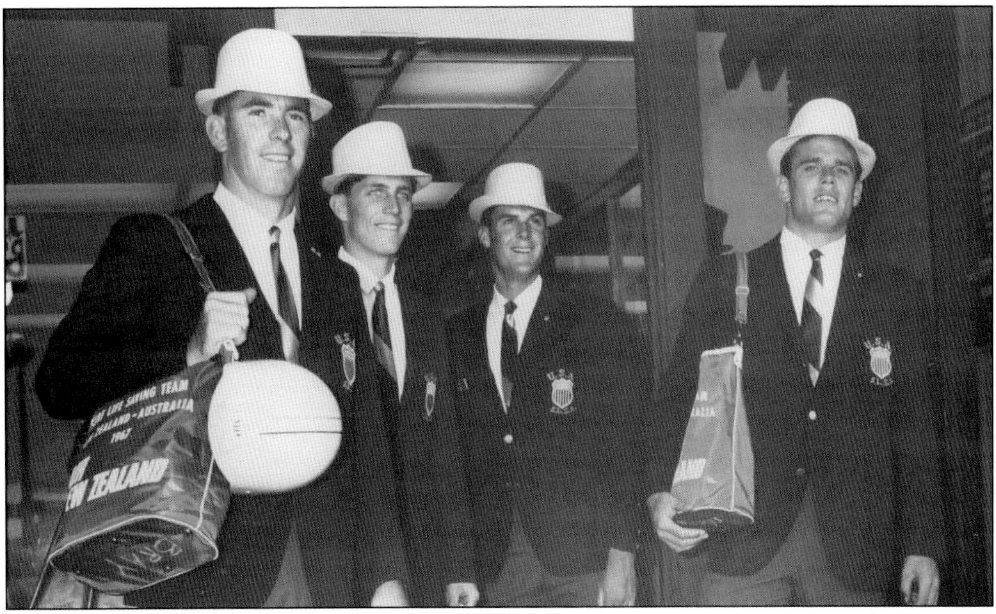

In 1967, the National SLSA sent a competition team to the Australian National Lifesaving Championships. Departing from Huntington Beach are, from left to right, Ray Bray, Spike Beck, Jerry McGraw, and Joe Metzger. Other team members included Bob Burnside, Rudy Kroon, Jon Helland, Doug Jensen, Howard Hendriskson, Eric Arneson, Jerry Bennet, Paul Cohee, Brian Gerold, Larry Hanes, George Loweree, Michael Bryant, Alex Nordhols, Chief Bud Stevenson, Chief Myron Cox, and Capt. Jim Richards.

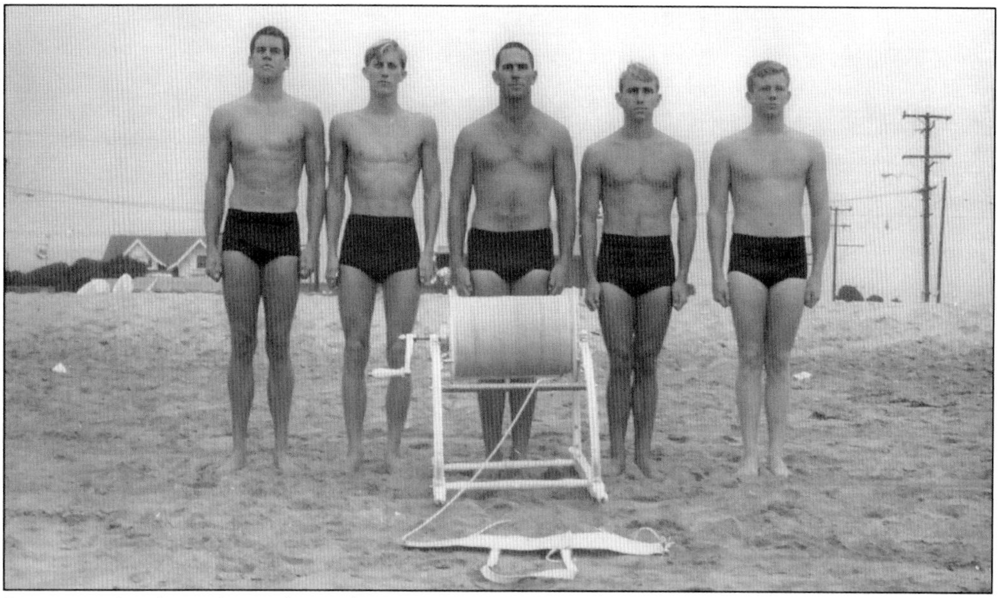

Preparing for Australia and standing at attention are, from left to right, Ken Hammer, Spike Beck, Ray Bray, Brian Gerold, and Paul Cohee with the Australian lifesaving reel. Spike Beck stunned the Aussies with his upset win in the junior belt race, the only non-Australian ever to win an Australian title to date. At Kiama Beach, New South Wales, the Americans accepted the invitation to enter the finals of the surf boat race, also making a surprise victory.

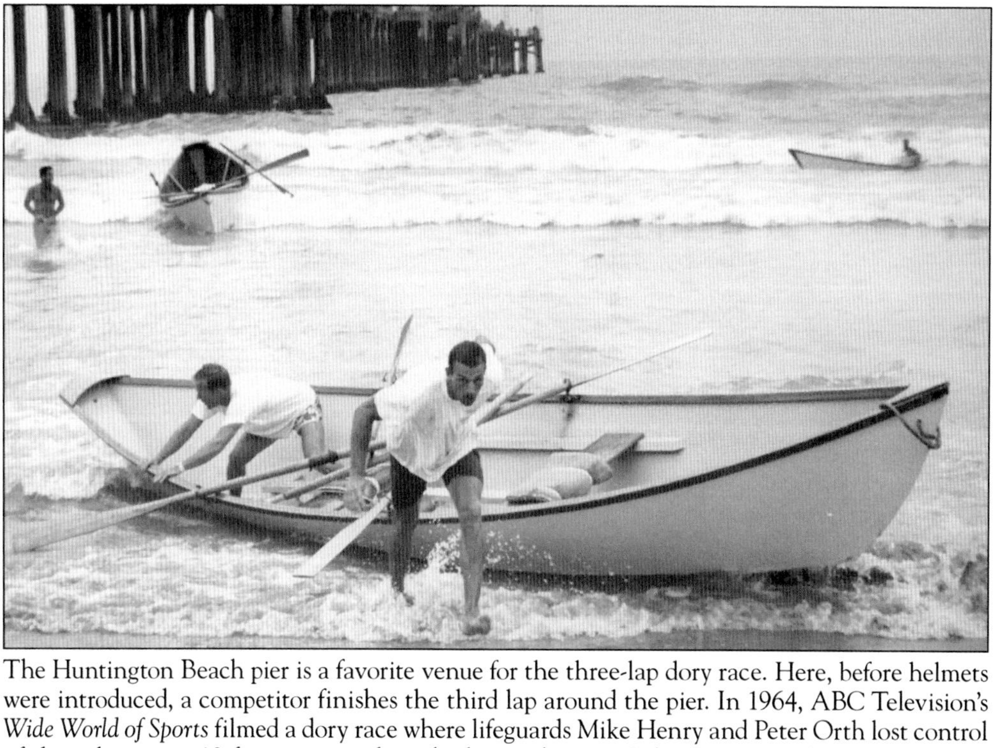

The Huntington Beach pier is a favorite venue for the three-lap dory race. Here, before helmets were introduced, a competitor finishes the third lap around the pier. In 1964, ABC Television's *Wide World of Sports* filmed a dory race where lifeguards Mike Henry and Peter Orth lost control of their dory on a 10-foot wave and crashed into the pier. It became one of the ABC Great Moments of 1964.

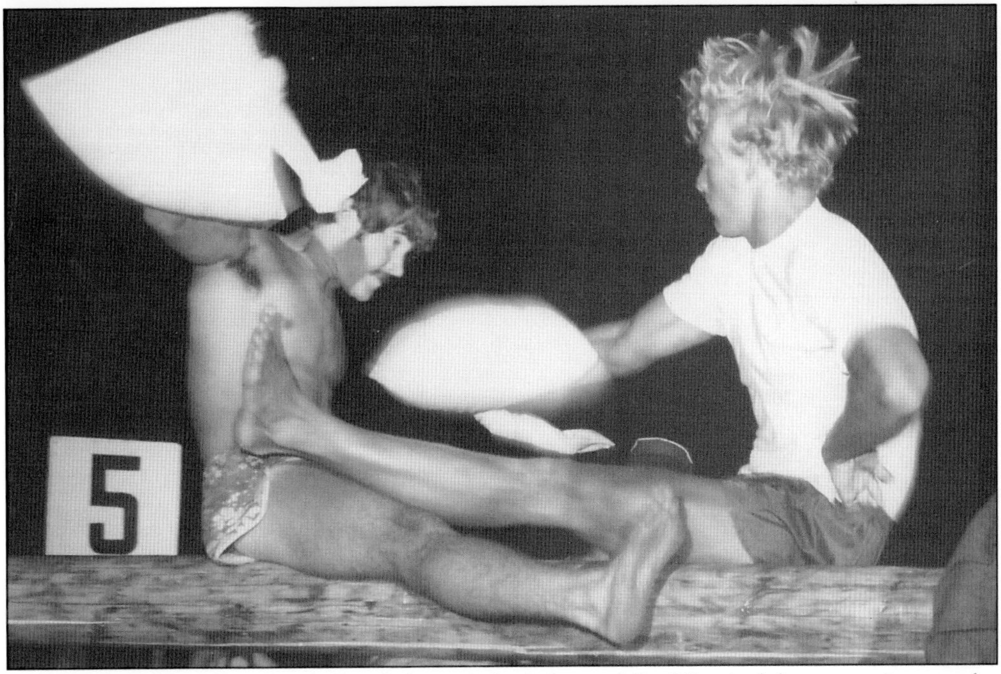

In the late 1960s, Huntington Beach hosted the Lifeguard Surf Festival for competitors under search lights placed on the pier and beach. Teams from up and down the coast would enter the host event, the five-man Roman chariot races sometimes called "shades of *Ben-Hur*." Shown here is the pillow fight event, a crowd favorite, until someone collected the errant knuckle sandwich.

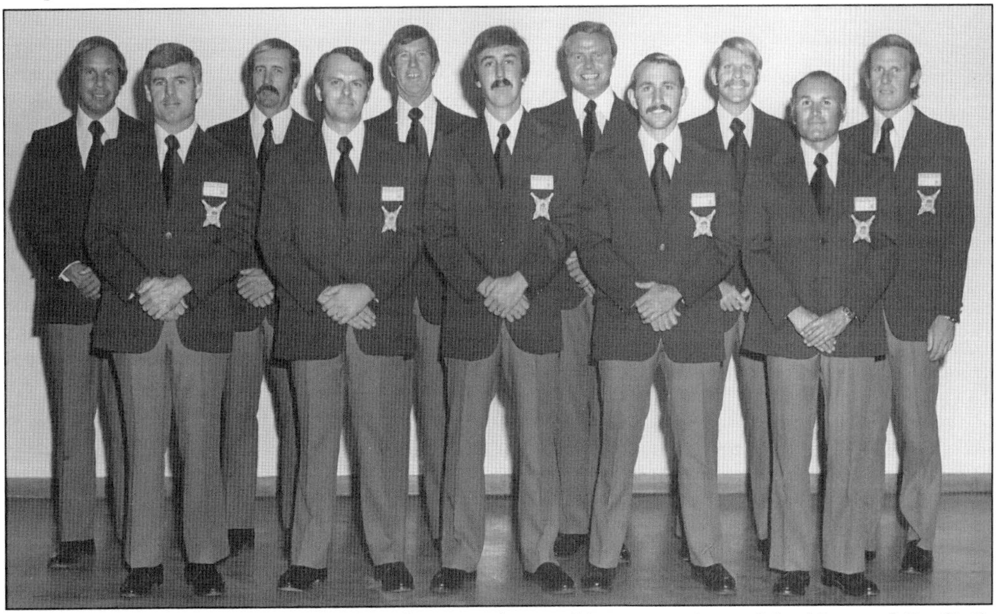

In 1964, Vince Moorhouse was a founding member and later president of the National Surf Life Saving Association, later named the United State Lifesaving Association. In 1971, this national lifeguard delegation went to South Africa; shown from left to right are Bill Owen, Tim Dorsey, Sheriden Byerly, Max Bowman, Paul Mathies, Mark Bodenbender, John Patty, Brian Gerold, Richard Mark, Buddy Belshe, and "Topper" Horack.

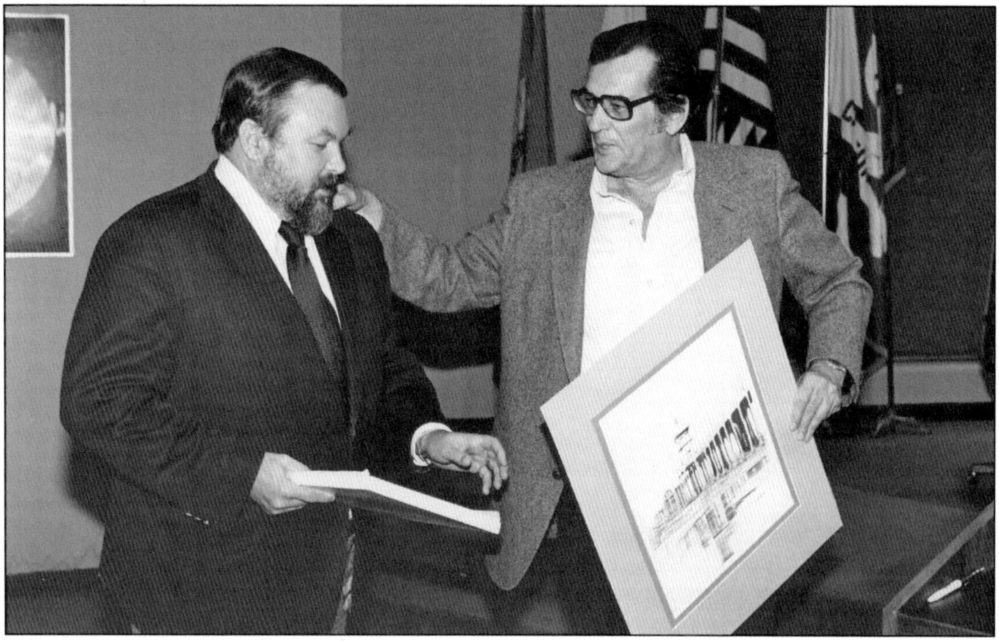

Vince Moorhouse (left) was appointed the director of the HB Harbors and Beaches Department in 1966 and was responsible for the capital improvements at the beach, which in turn provided substantial revenue for the city. Here in 1970, Moorhouse presents two-time mayor Jack Kelly a token of appreciation. Kelly was best known for his role as Bart Maverick in the popular 1957–1962 television series *Maverick*.

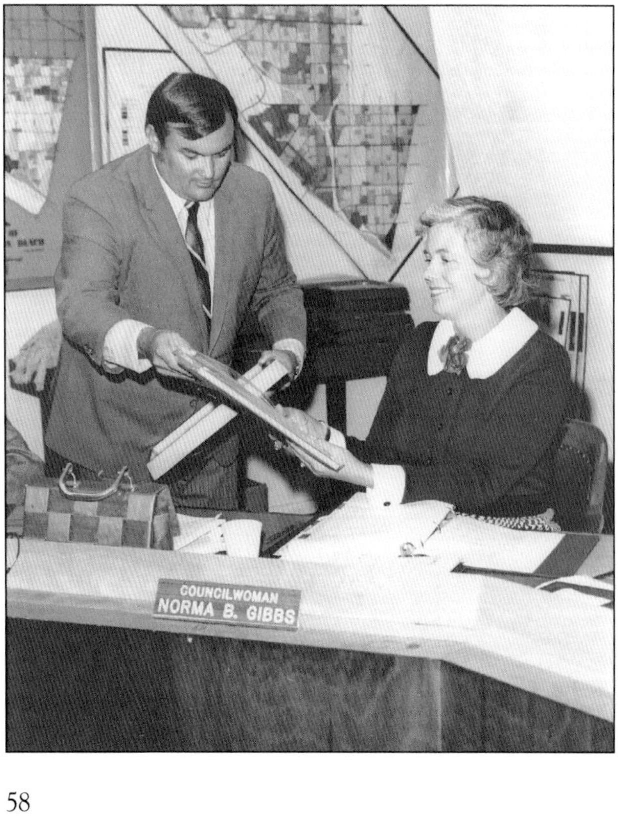

Vince Moorhouse in 1976 was elected president of World Life Saving. Here in 1972, Moorhouse is pictured with Norma Gibbs, the first Huntington Beach female council member and mayor (1975–1976). Her legacy includes the development of Huntington Central Park, many bicycle paths, beach and wetlands preservation, and the Sister City program.

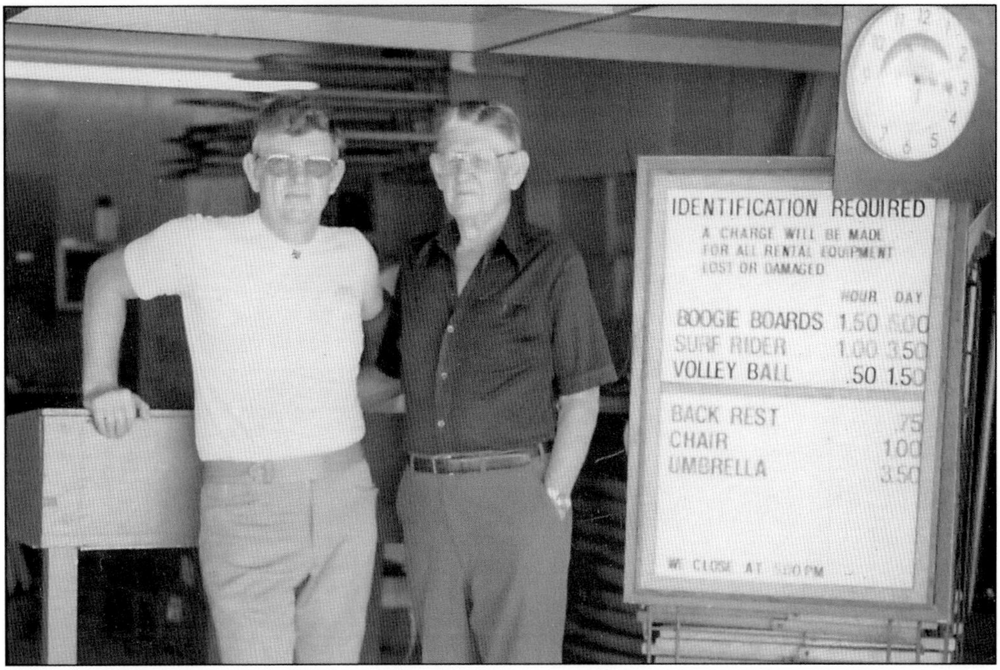

Taken in the early 1970s in Dwight's Beach Concession, from left to right, are Jack and Dwight Clapp. Dwight and his wife, Fae, started the business in 1932, made lots of hamburgers, and invented his famous "cheese strips" with sauce. Dwight's Drive-In opened at Beach Boulevard and PCH in 1949, and Jack took over Dwight's. Then in 1958, Jack founded Jack's Beach Concession, and later in 1975, his son Dave took it over—truly a family beach business.

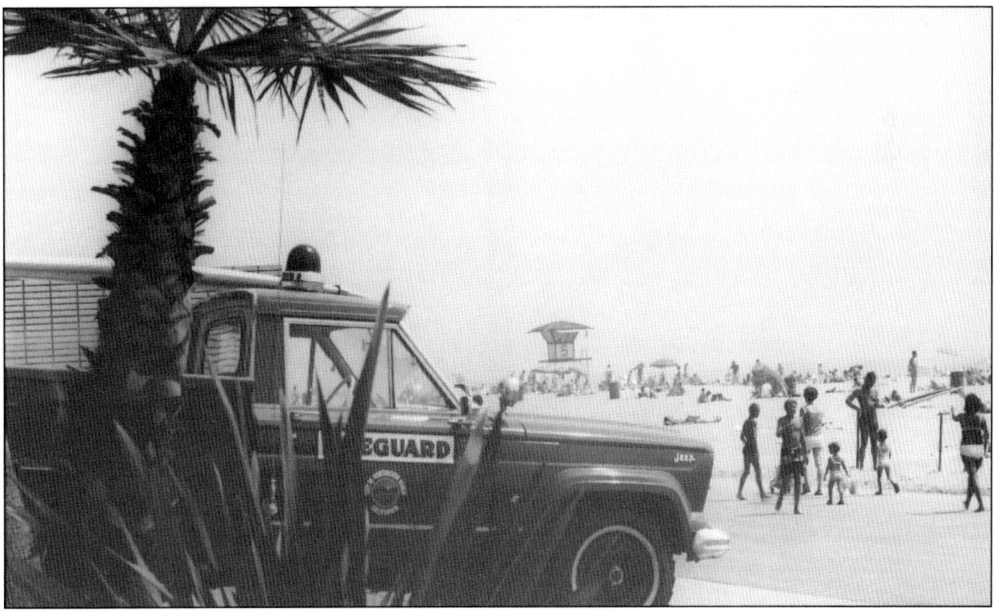

In 1970, the lifeguard truck with rescue paddleboard parks on the "Apron" in front of HQ. Stationed to the left in the building was the first-aid room guard ready to accept walk-in medical aids or assist the transport of patients to an ambulance or paramedics. During large or mass rescues in the water, the first-aid room guard would leave the building to assist.

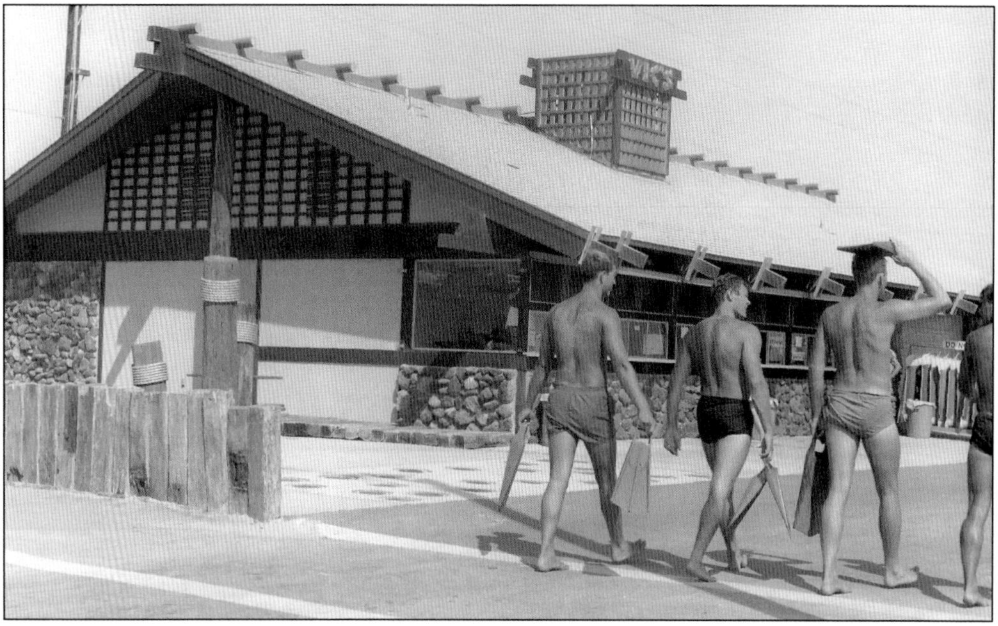

After a long day in the tower or jeep, the lifeguards would have some fun and go bodysurfing. During the big south swells, they would run to Beach Boulevard (one mile) and bodysurf back to the pier. Along the way was Vic's, a popular place to eat breakfast that was owned and operated by past lifeguard and USA Olympic water polo coach Monte Nitzkowski.

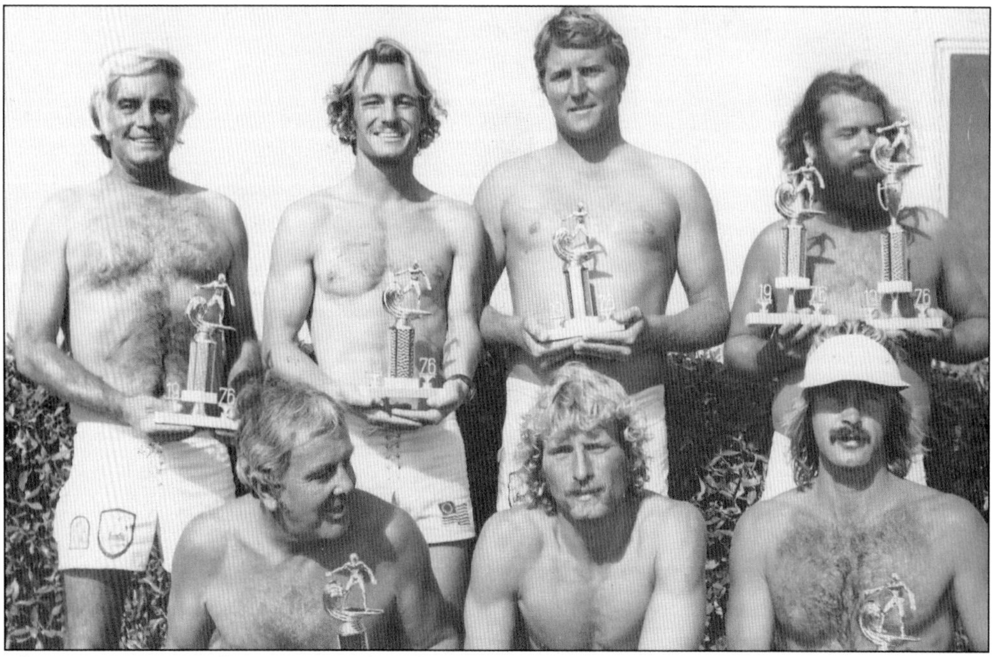

The Huntington Beach International Surfing Museum displays this photograph: Clean Sweep- "The Hole in the Wall Gang." This group made a clean sweep during the 1976 Western Surfing Association contest at the pier. Huntington Beach locals are, from left to right, (kneeling) Bob Carbonell, Bob Milford, and Chris Cattel; (standing) Bill Rainforth, Guy Grundy, John "Frog" Van Oeffelen, and John Boozer. The team was sponsored by Gordie surfboards and Nancy Katin surf trunks.

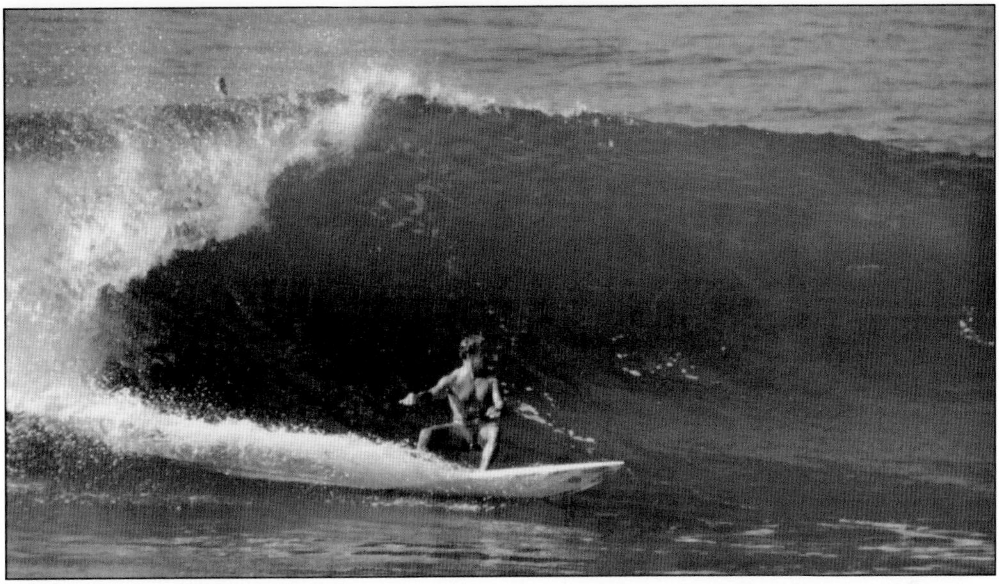

Chuck Linnen, in the mid-1960s, rips on this wave wearing an unauthorized pair of lifeguard trunks with patch. In 2003, Linnen was inducted a Local Hero in the Surfing Walk of Fame and in 2007 the Honor Roll with the HB Pier Surf Club "The Boys of 1955." Other Honor Roll HB lifeguards on the list are Bud Higgins, Rocky Freeman, Harlo LeBard, Dean Ashbrook, Frank Ciarelli, and Don Stewart.

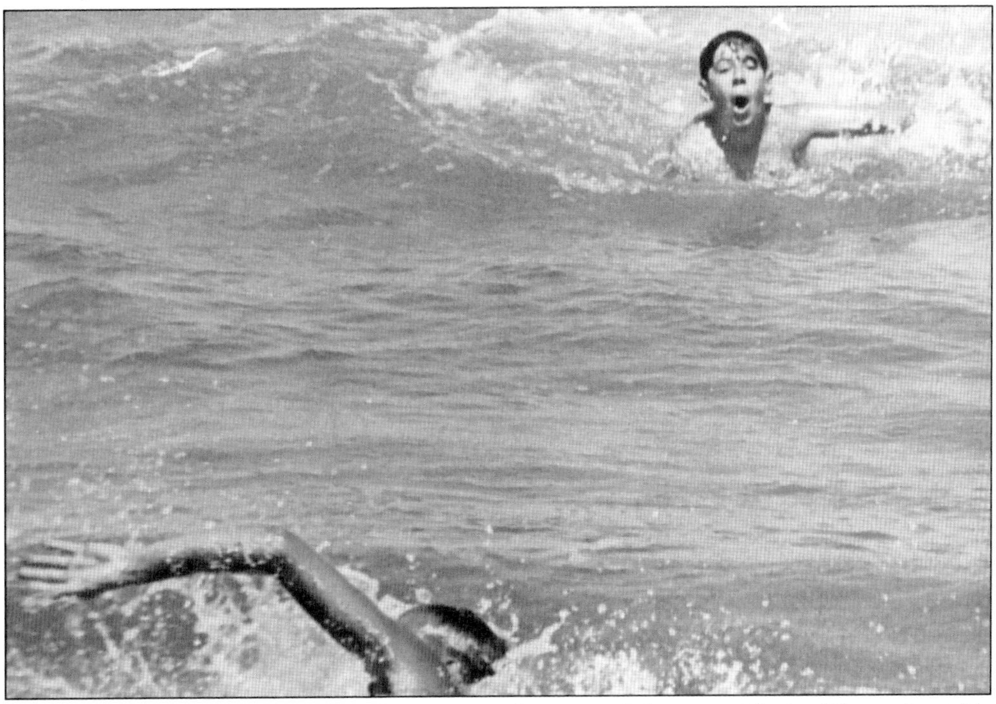

Here a young swimmer shows the classic signs of panic and distress with the lifeguard quickly approaching. Both are loaded with adrenalin and anticipation. From the files of the California Surf Lifesaving Association, with the motto "Lifeguards for Life," this photograph is a great representation of a rescue, or "906," in progress.

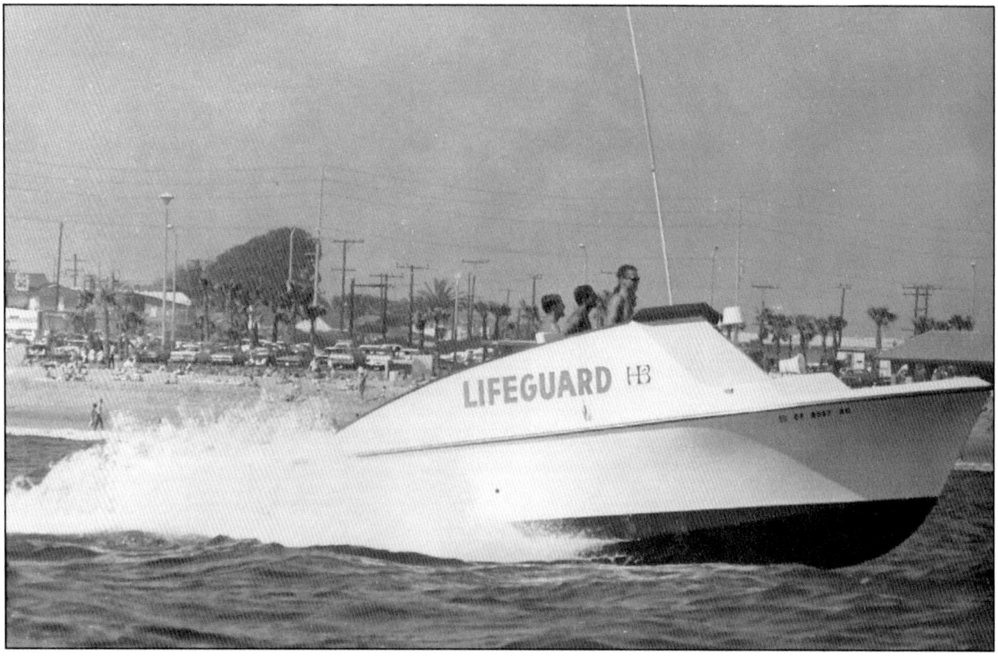

The rescue boat *Guardian* responds to a call, heading south in Area One in the early 1970s. Mindful of any offshore long distance swimmers, the *Guardian* responds to assist rescues made by lifeguards on the beach. The rescue boats provide critical backup for rescues and preventative actions.

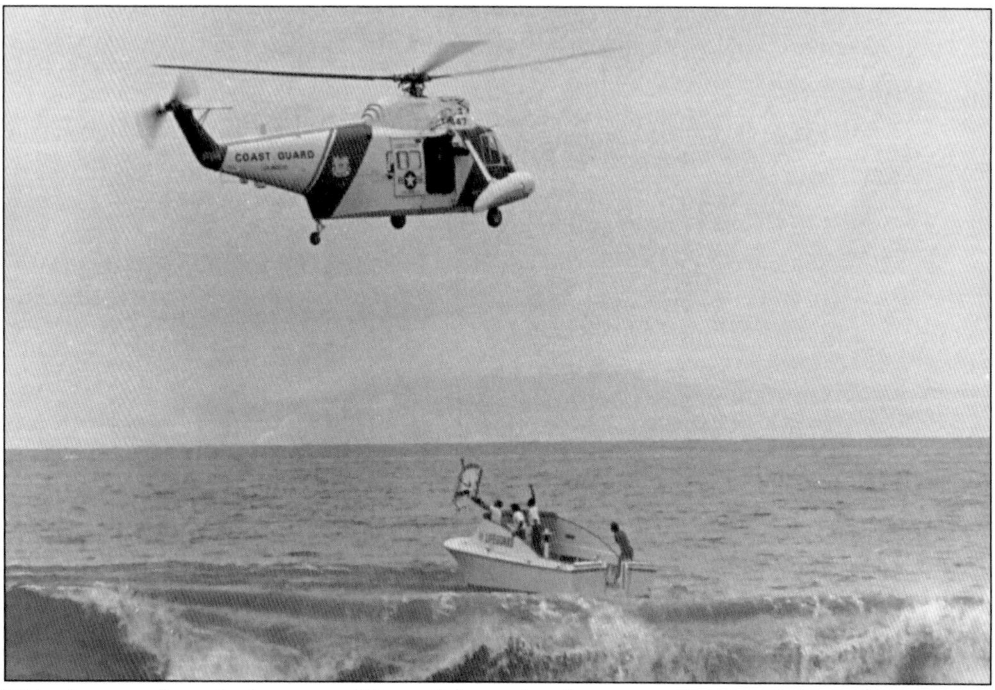

This photograph made the cover of *Ocean Lifeguard* in the spring of 1973 and shows the *Guardian* receiving a litter basket, or stokes, from the Los Angeles–based U.S. Coast Guard helicopter. This training exercise was held during the Second World Life Saving meeting, which was held in Huntington Beach.

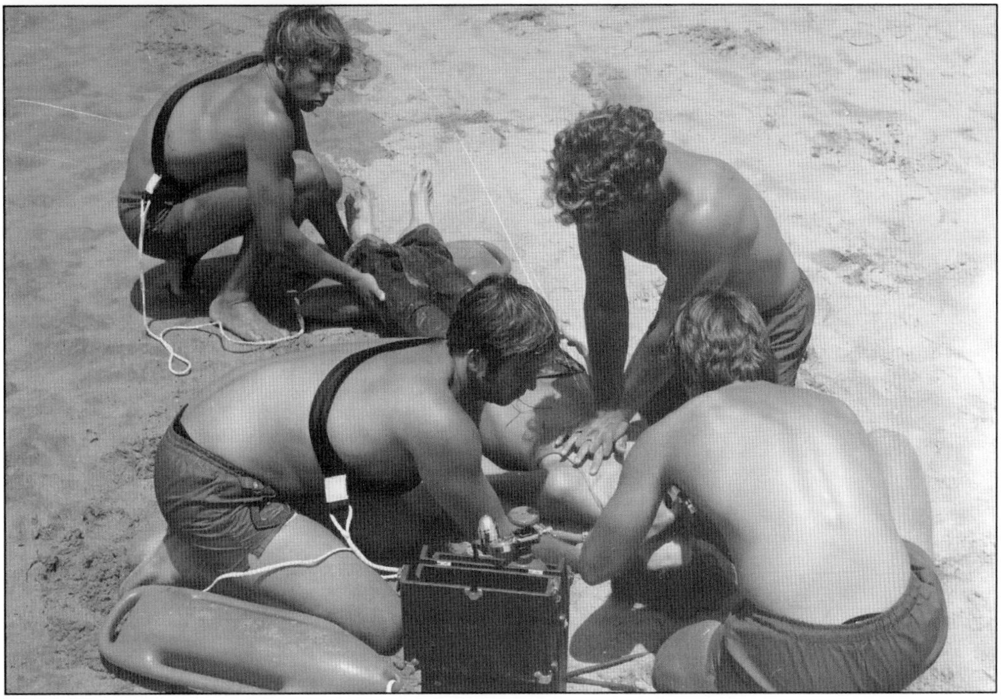

In 1975, lifeguards performed CPR on this victim and used the positive pressure resuscitator near the water's edge. Emergency Medical Technician (EMT) lifeguard supervisors and marine safety officers provide high-quality Basic Life Support (BLS) in preparation for the paramedics, who provide Advanced Life Support (ALS). On average, the paramedics can be on the scene in a few short minutes.

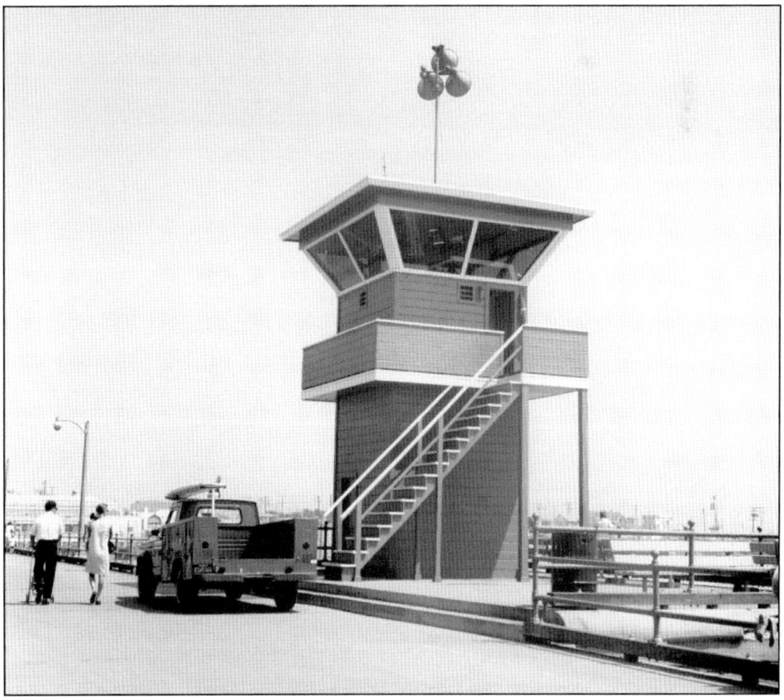

Freshly painted in 1975, Tower Zero commands a critical view of the beach and is sometimes called the "Eye in the Sky." The tower is operational 365 days during daylight hours and has the capability to telephone and radio dispatch as equal to that of the communications center in lifeguard headquarters on the beach.

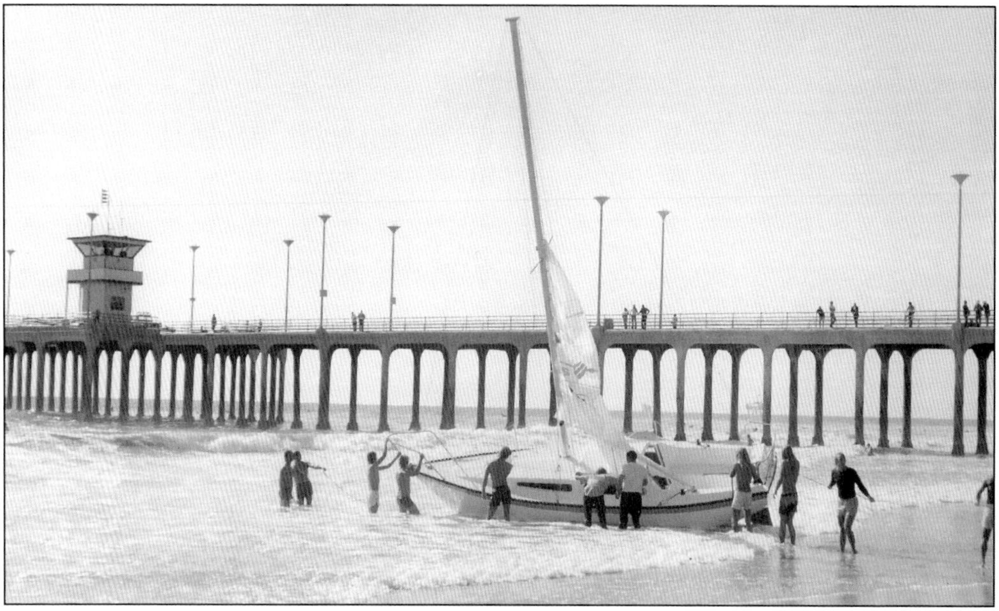

Boat rescues are common, although groundings such as this small sailboat are not. A boat of this size can easily be towed by lifeguards and kept outside the surf-line to wait for the lifeguard rescue boat or harbor patrol. This sailboat was later salvaged by being pulled off the beach by a tractor and removed by trailer.

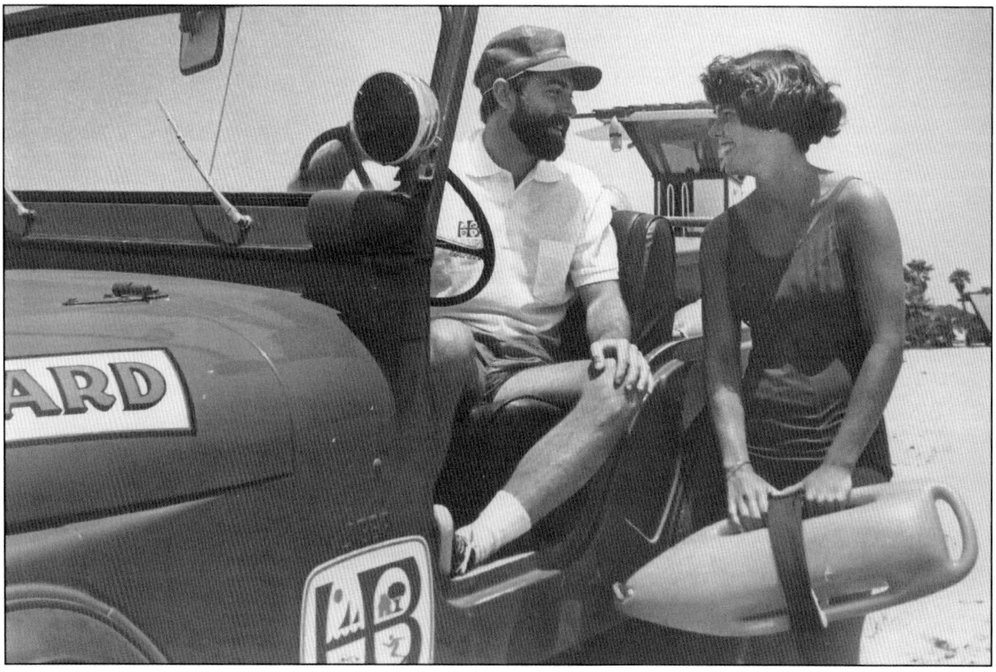

In 1976, Rennie Taylor talks with marine safety officer John Barth during her first summer as a beach lifeguard and later junior lifeguard instructor. She was the city's first female lifeguard in 20 years since Darla Austin and Stephanie Belcher guarded the Sunset Beach area and Huntington Harbor bay beaches. In 1997, Taylor, the Newport Beach junior lifeguard coordinator ,was appointed the chairperson of the California and National Junior Lifeguard Committees.

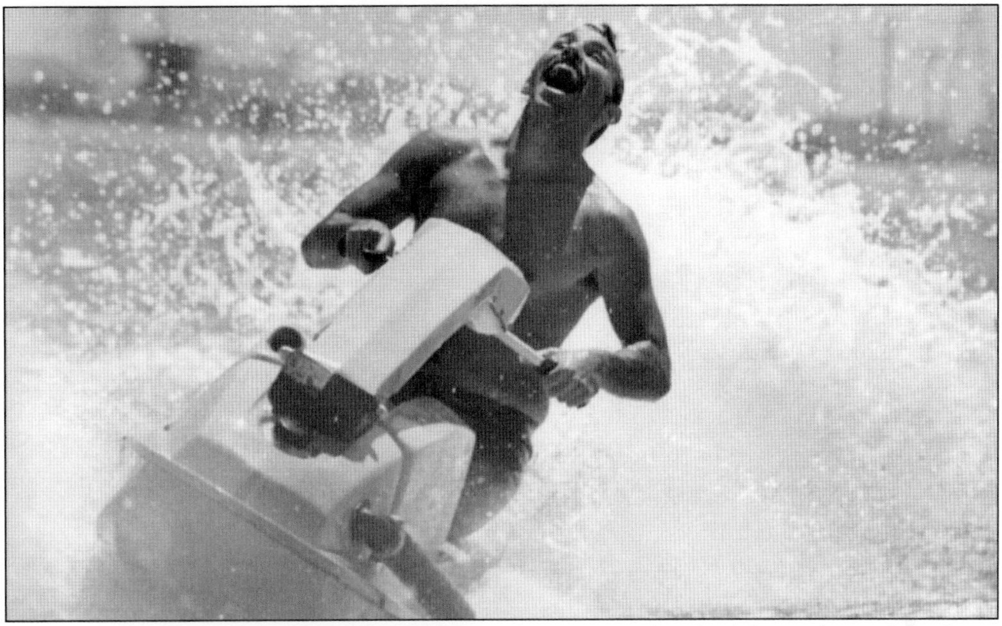

In June 1974, Brian Gerold displays the smile that says it all. The lifeguards purchased two Kawasaki jet skis and test drove the new machines, which helped modify the later model. The new to the market water toy was advertised by Kawasaki as more exciting than Raquel Welch. In early 2000, the lifeguards began to operate the corporate-sponsored Honda PWC, four-cylinder, 746-pound AquaTrax.

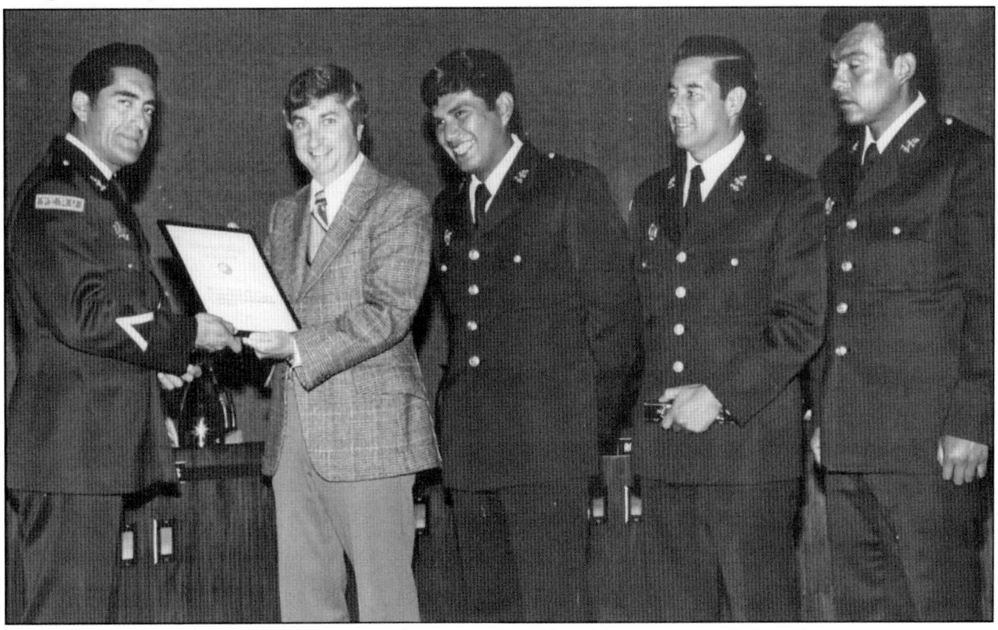

On October 16, 1978, Huntington Beach mayor Ron Shenkman received this plaque as a memento from the Peruvian Lifeguard Team's visit to the United States. In 1990, Shenkman was chairman of the Special Gifts Committee for the successful Landmark Campaign to rebuild the Huntington Beach Pier. His son Dave Shenkman is the owner-operator of the successful Kite Connection and Kites for Kids on the pier.

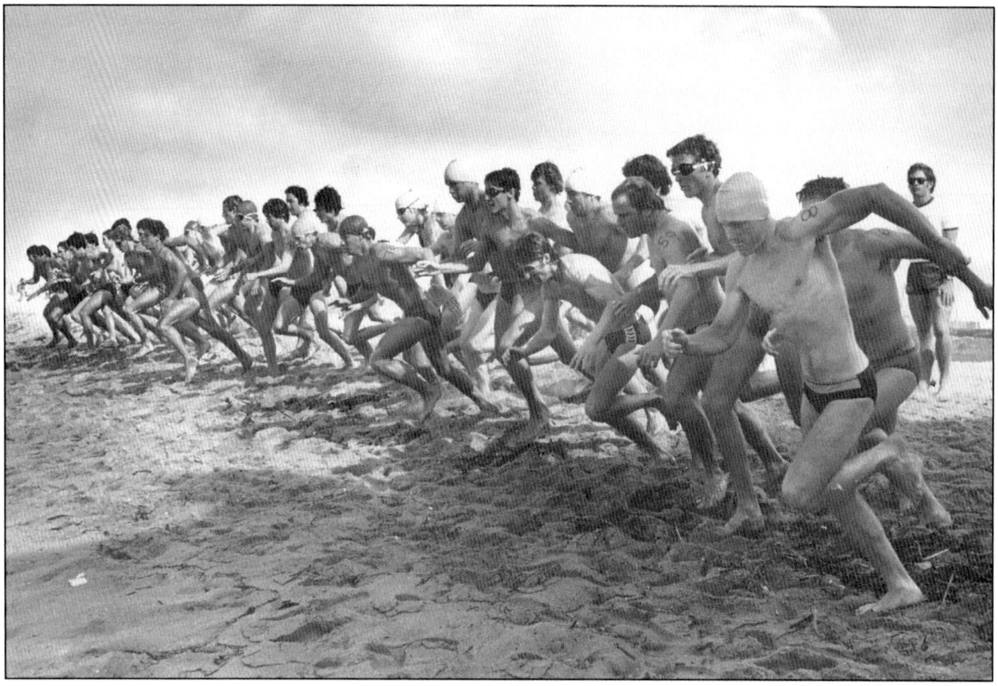

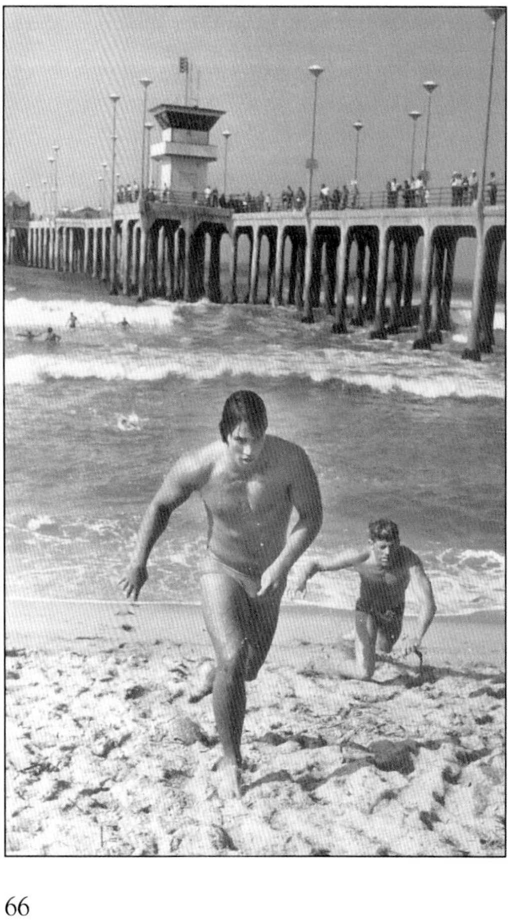

Lifeguard tryouts begin on the west side of the pier each year, sometimes with well over 100 applicants. In 1981, lifeguard and junior lifeguard instructor Mike Eich stands behind the start line as they head out and swim around the pier. Pictured left, the finish line includes a run up the steep berm, sometimes difficult for wobbly legs after the swim. First-place finisher is Randy Gates followed by Todd Picket under the watchful eye of Tower Zero and the crowd on the pier.

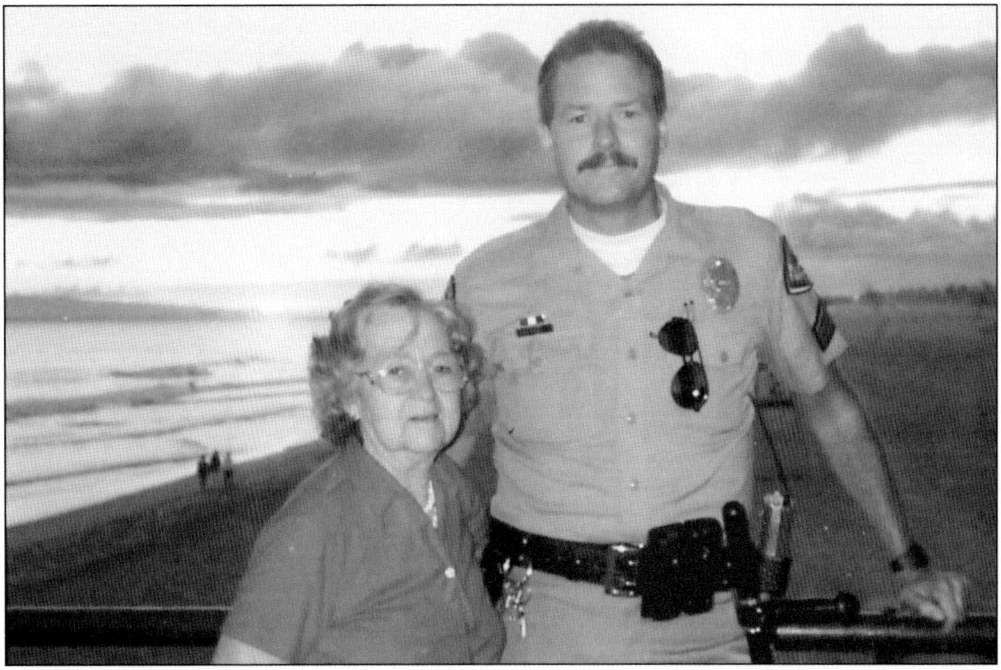

Ella Christensen first opened business on the pier in 1950 and operated Neptune's Locker, the Captains Galley, and the Tackle Box. She was a friend to the lifeguards, the "mom" to the police department's men and women, and the public called her "The Queen of the Pier." Here Sgt. Ed Deuel stands with Ella on the pier in the early 1980s.

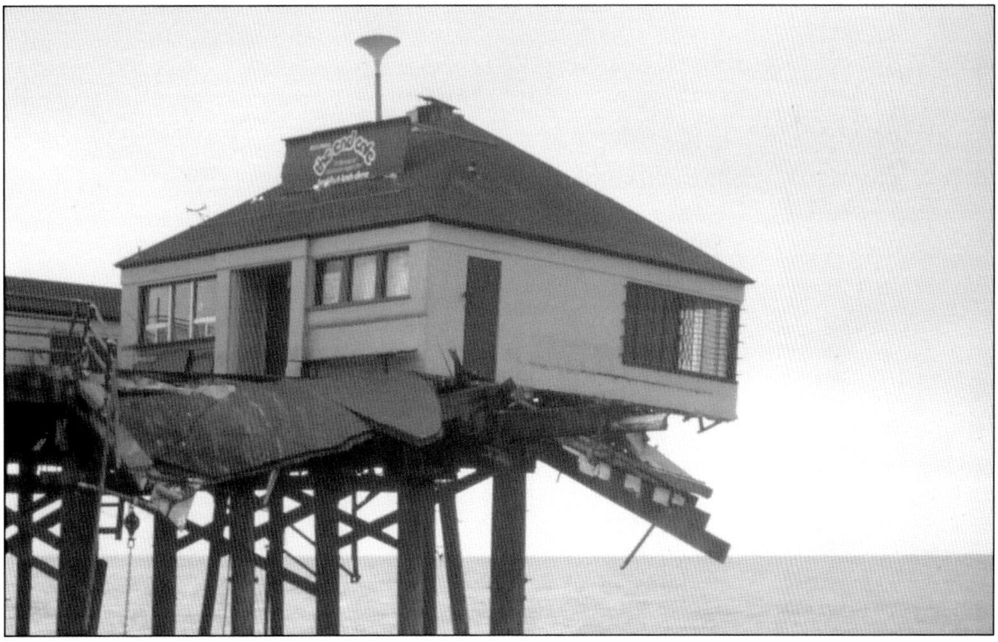

In March 1983, the End Café was destroyed by a strong Pacific Northwest storm. Only days after, the lifeguard tryouts were held, and this photograph was taken by the *Sentinel* 5240 deckhand. In 1939, Jimmy's (DeGualle) Little Café at the end of the pier met the same demise. It was rebuilt and used by the U.S. Army during World War II. After the war, "Pop" Allen operated the little café.

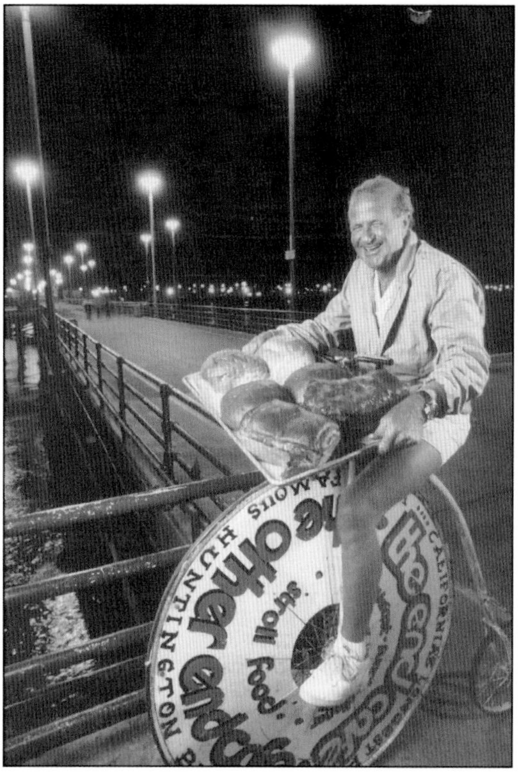

In 1976, John Gustafson purchased the small building at the end of the pier from the McCullough family and renamed it the End Café. Here, in the early 1980s, Gustafson made this ritual bike ride to End Café to deliver warm loaves of bread.

The newly rebuilt and much larger two-story End Café opened in September 1985. The night of the January 17, 1988, storm, John and his customers were asked to evacuate the building and pier by the lifeguards. Shortly afterward, eye-witness reports had the pier end collapse and the new End Café floating east an estimated 100 yards. Here the surf pounds the pier the day after the storm.

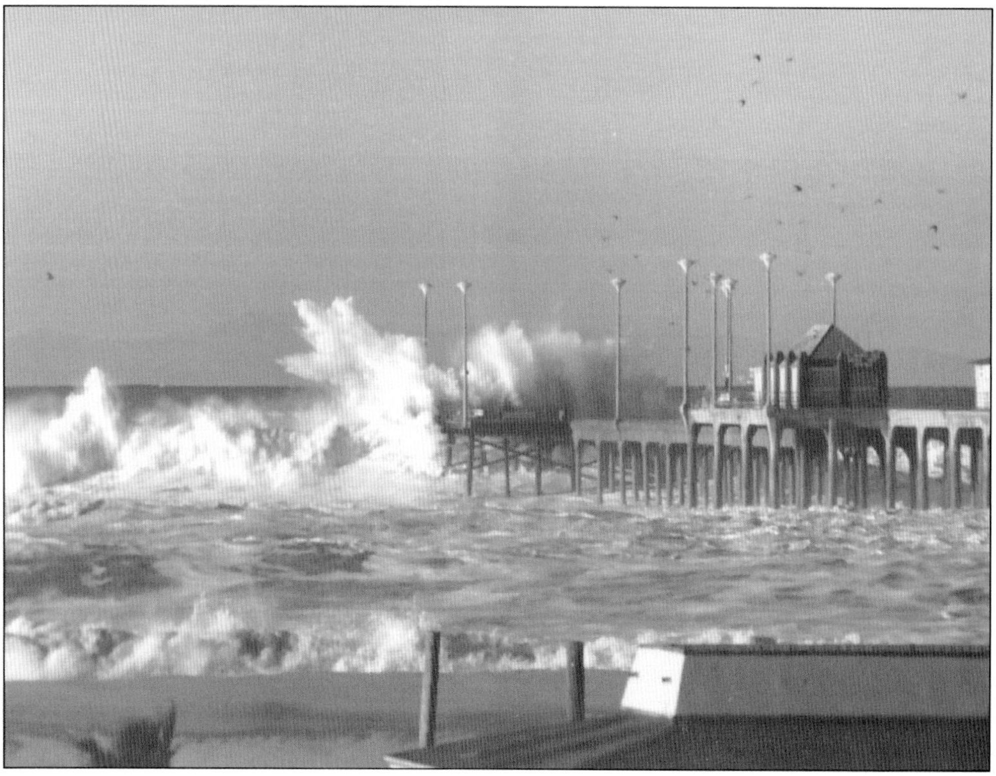

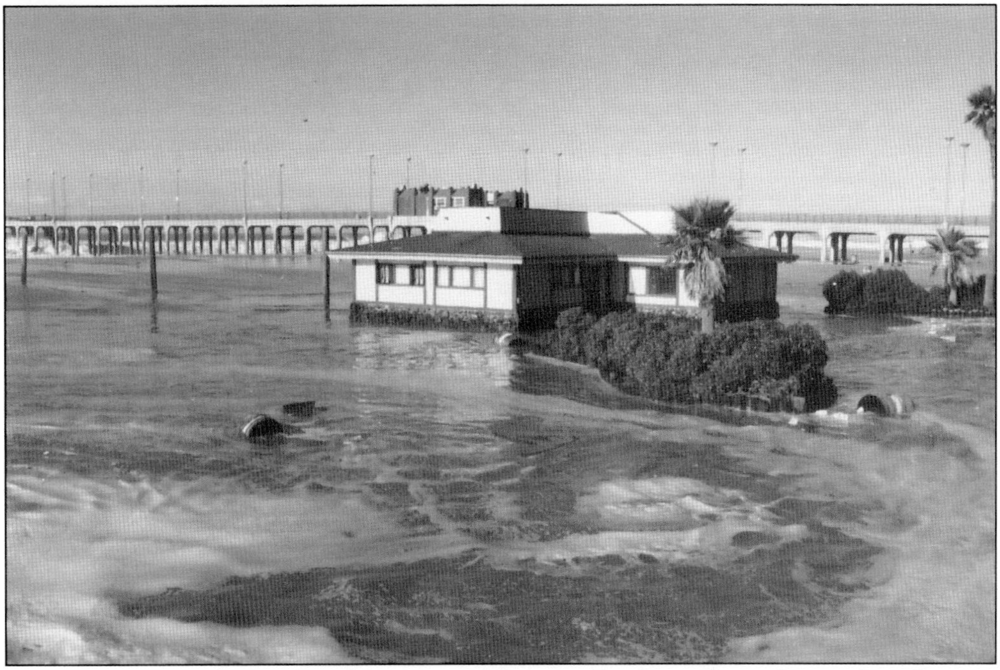

Whoever said that the beach and service road does not flood was obviously mistaken. Here, in January 1988, the junior lifeguard headquarters, the bike path, and nearly the entire beach was under storm water. This was during the same storm that finished off the pier and the End Café.

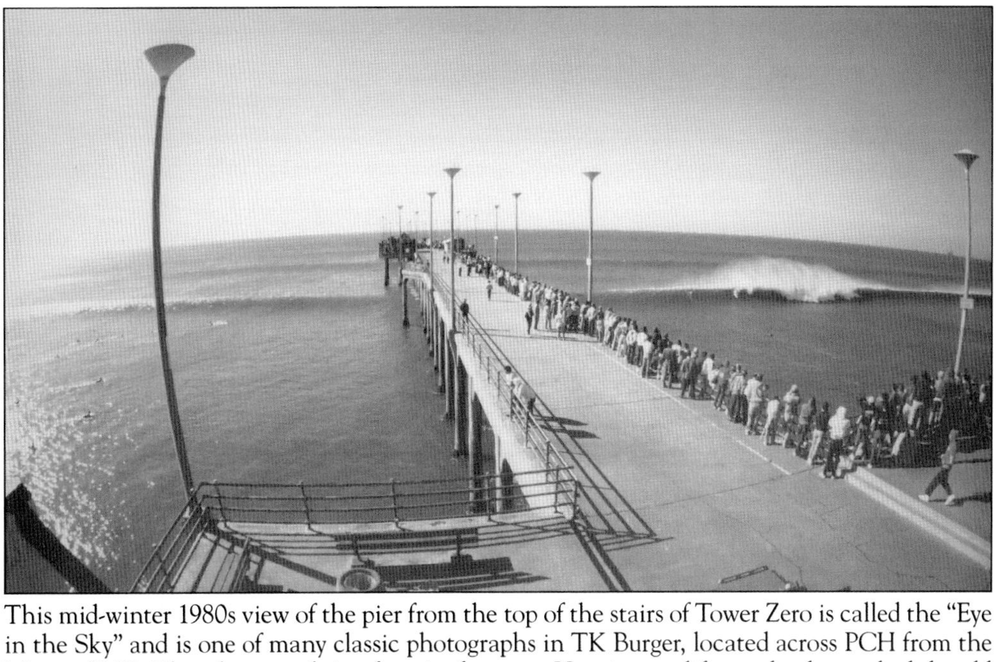

This mid-winter 1980s view of the pier from the top of the stairs of Tower Zero is called the "Eye in the Sky" and is one of many classic photographs in TK Burger, located across PCH from the lifeguard HQ. This photograph is a favorite for many Huntington lifeguards who worked the old tower, which is now long gone but sometimes referred to as the best office in the city.

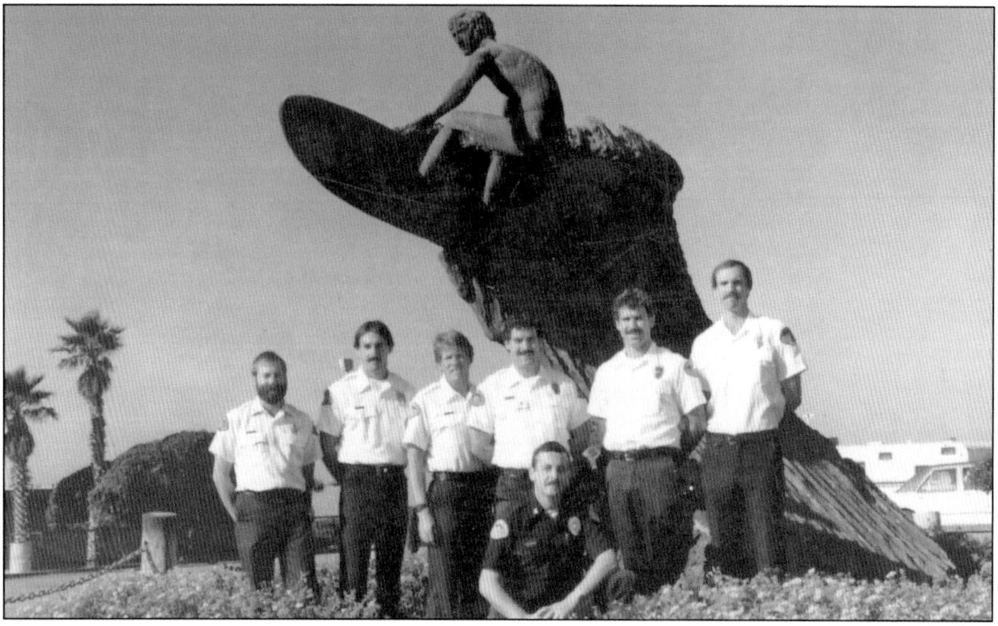

In 1985, the lifeguard staff shrunk to its lowest level in decades with the loss of the west side of the pier (Area Two) to the State Beach (New Beach) and the Orange County contract for Sunset Beach (Area Three), west of Bolsa Chica. In front of the *Ultimate Surfer* statue are, from left to right, John Barth, Steve Seim, Steve Davidson, Steve Reuter, Mike Gifford, Greg Crow, and Capt. Bill Richardson (kneeling).

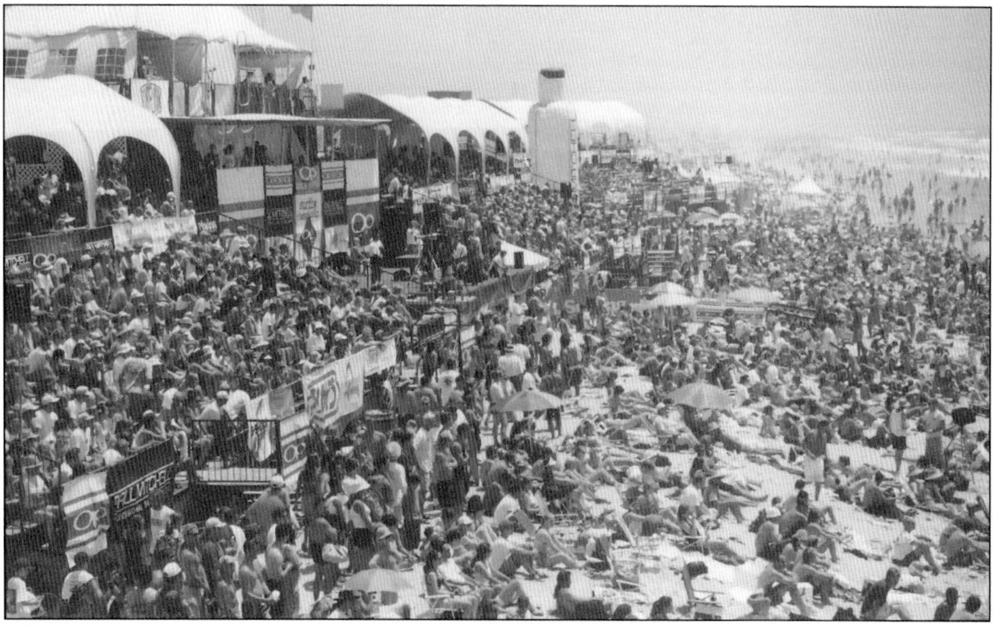

The year 1982 was when the first Ocean Pacific (OP) Pro was held at the Huntington Beach Pier. The next year, ESPN, then a fledgling cable network, saw the crowds top 100,000 for the first time. Past OP Pro winners include Cheyne Horan (1982), Mike Cruickshank (1983), Tom Curren (1984 and 1988), Mark Occhilupo (1985 and 1986), Barton Lynch (1987), Richie Collins (1989), and Todd Holland (1990).

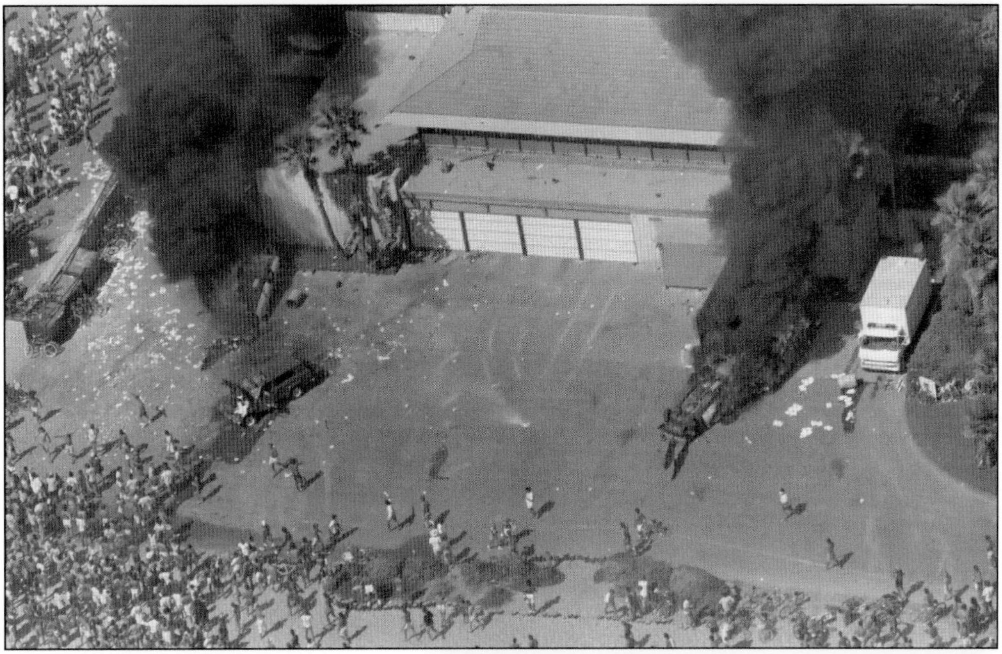

The August 1986 OP Pro riot was the worst in Orange County history. Police and lifeguard vehicles were torched, and the lifeguard headquarters was briefly evacuated. Capt. Bill Richardson fired the shot that sent the insane crowd out of the building. In the same day, the city of Cerritos witnessed the Air Mexico midair collision. This disaster killed 65 passengers and 15 people on the ground, and destroyed 10 homes.

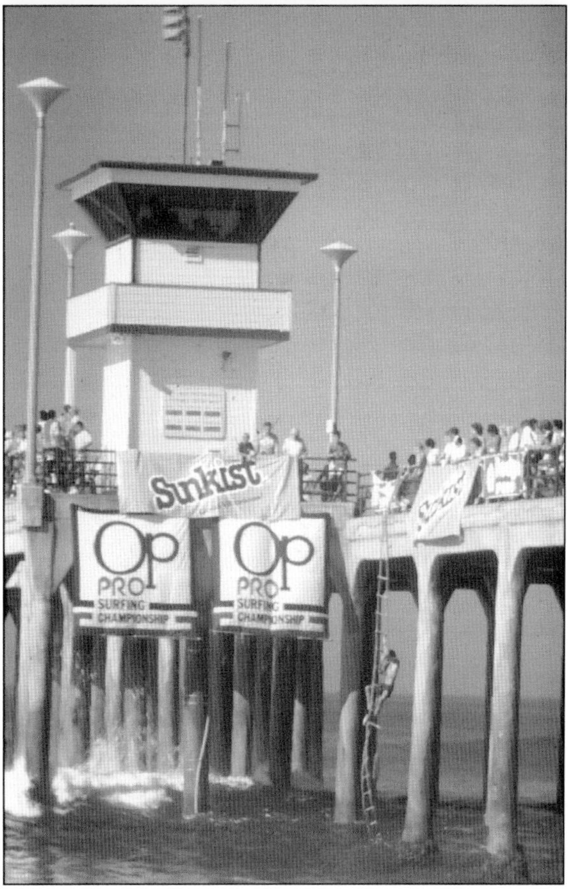

The OP Pro banners and other sponsor banners that hang from the pier are a huge marketing success. On occasion, a surf competitor may get injured and require assistance. Here a lifeguard returns to Tower Zero and climbs the rope ladder after responding to a call in the contest area. The OP Pro changed its name to the U.S. Open of Surfing in 1994.

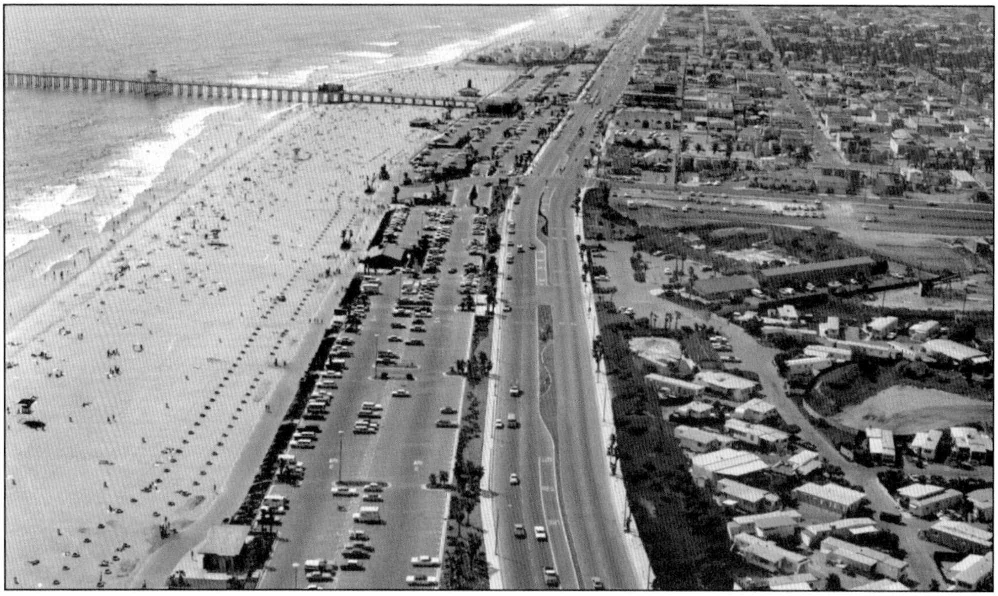

This 1971 view of the south side of the pier shows a few landmarks that are now long gone. The Huntington Shores Motel, Driftwood Mobile Home Park, and nine-hole golf are a few. In their place is the 31-acre parcel, a future mixed-use development named Pacific City and owned by Makar Properties. Adjacent to this property are the Hilton Waterfront Beach Resort and the Hyatt Regency Resort and Spa.

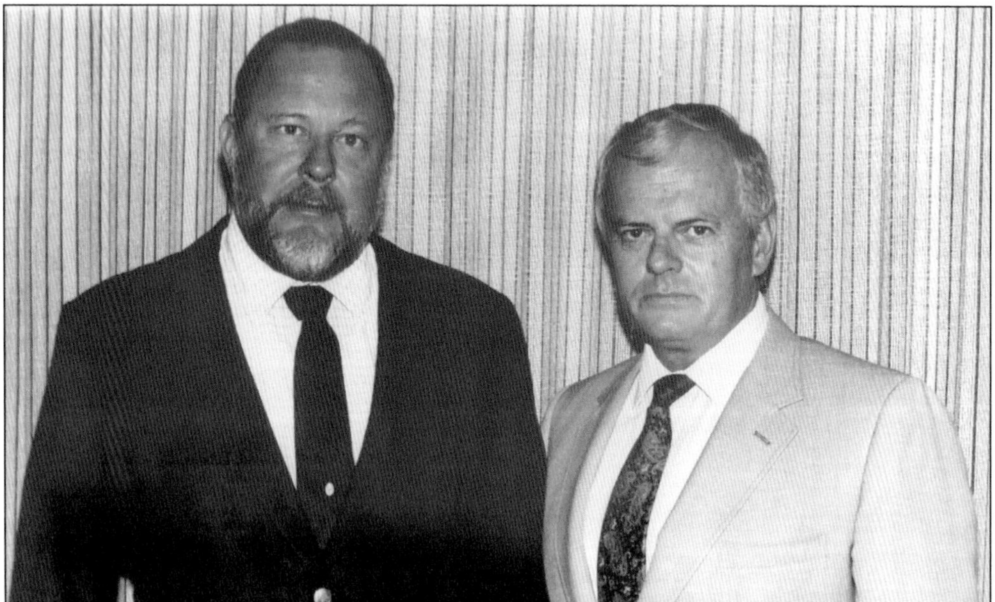

In this 1988 photograph are, from left to right, World Life Saving secretary general Doug D'Arnall and Pres. Max Bowman. Both were active leaders in the surf lifesaving movement on the local, regional, national, and international level. The United States Lifesaving Association (USLA) published the first book of its kind, *Lifesaving and Marine Safety*, in 1981 with committee chairman D'Arnall and members Don Rohrer, Richard Mark, and Bob Shea.

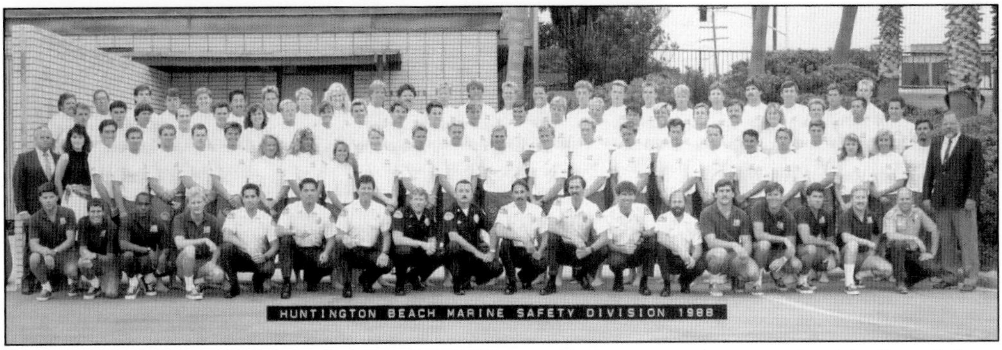

Here is the 1988 annual Huntington Beach Marine Safety crew photograph with, from left to right, (front row) Mike Beuerlein, Robert Thomas, Kyle Lindo, Doug Bloom, Claude Panis, Marc Panis, Kai Weisser, Steve Davidson, Bill Richardson, Steve Seim, Greg Crow, Mike Gifford, John Barth, Mike Gifford, Dan Hoffman, Matt Karl, Mike Baumgartner, and Dave Winkler, the park ranger naturalist. On the far left is Max Bowman, and on the far right is Doug D'Arnall.

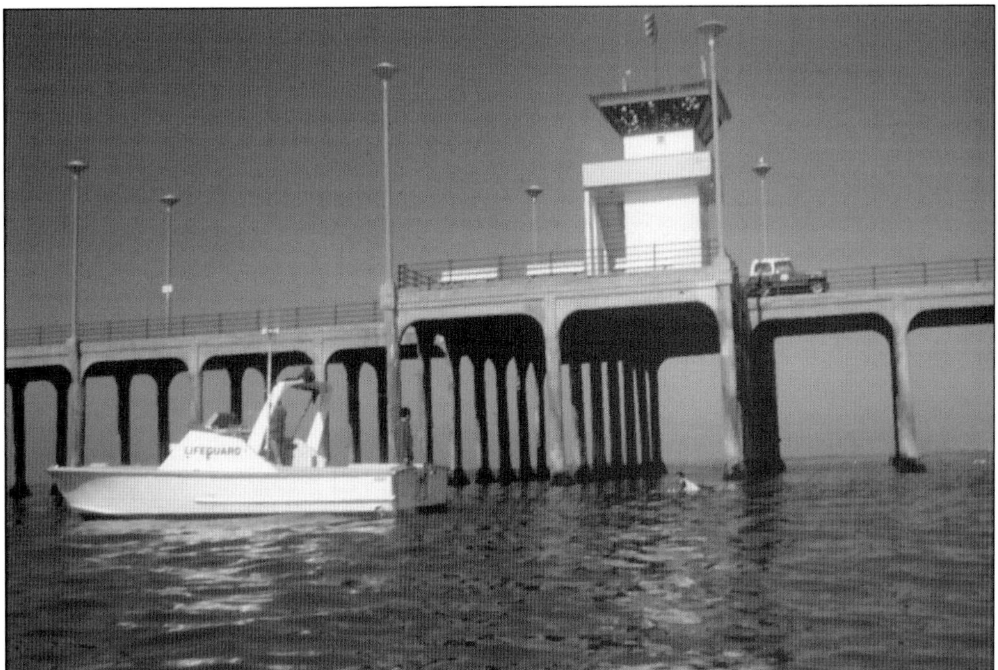

Sentinel 5240 parks here, seemingly just under Tower Zero, during the 1992 lifeguard tryouts. With twin rudders, 5240 has a draft of about three feet, and the deckhand here carefully checks the depth of the water for the skipper. Clearing anything less than three feet would damage the rudders, a costly proposition.

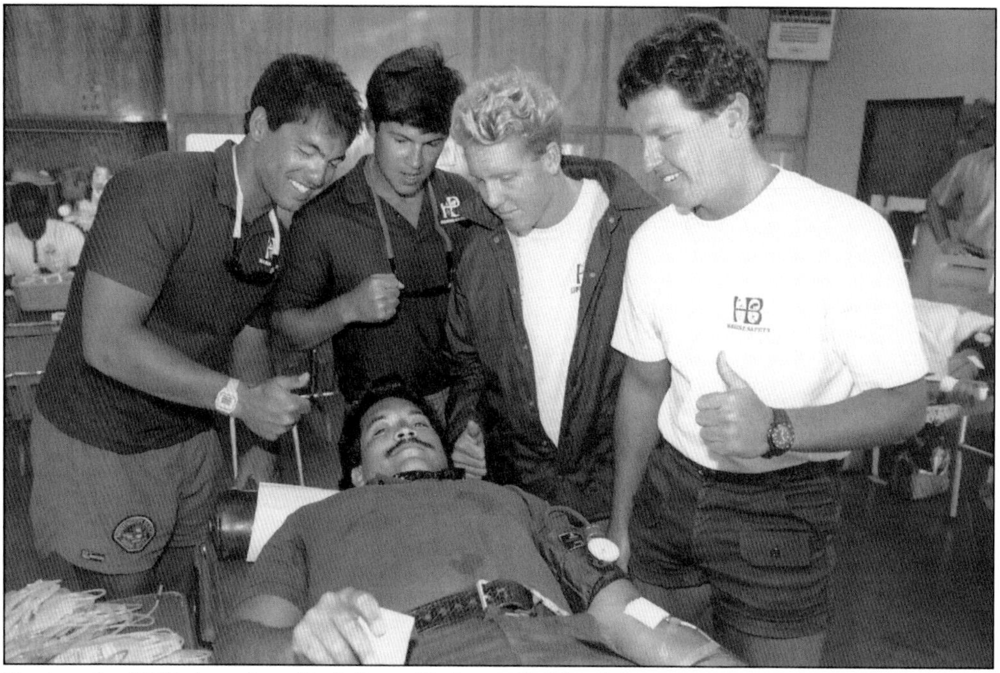

During the 1987 American Red Cross "Lifeguard" Blood Drive, marine safety officer Claude Panis gets comfort and reassurance after donating blood from, from left to right, Marc Panis, Mike Beuerlein, Scott Ferry, and Kai Weisser. Today the American Red Cross "Lifeguard" Blood Drive includes lifeguard departments across the United States.

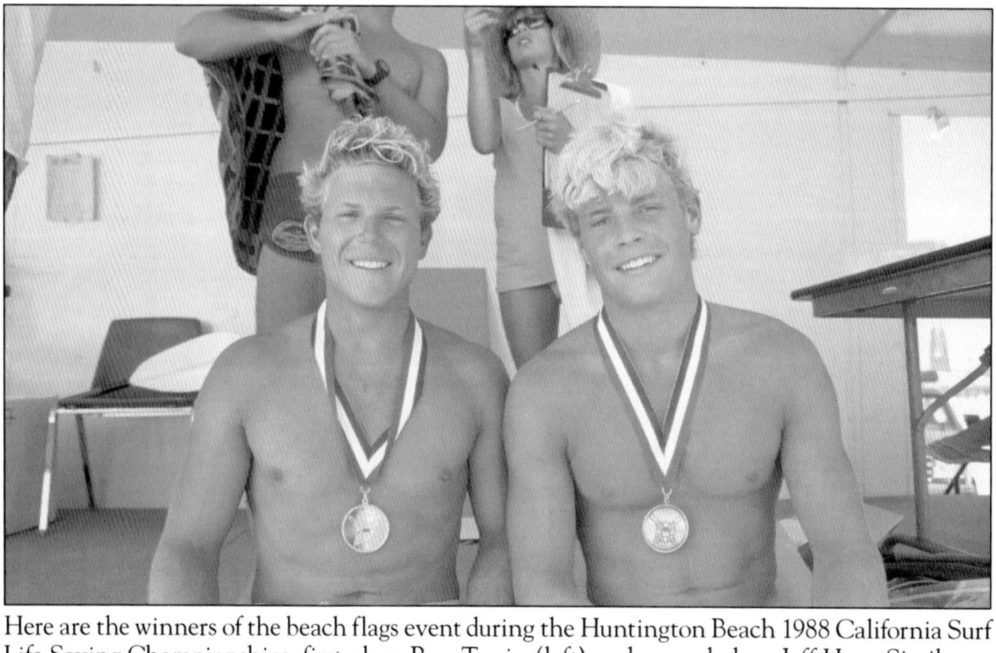

Here are the winners of the beach flags event during the Huntington Beach 1988 California Surf Life Saving Championships: first place Ron Tassin (left) and second place Jeff Hoss. Similar to musical chairs, beach flags eliminates one competitor per heat at a time, and the last heat has only two competitors. Contestants must lie down in the sand, and upon the whistle get up, turn around, and sprint to any available flag.

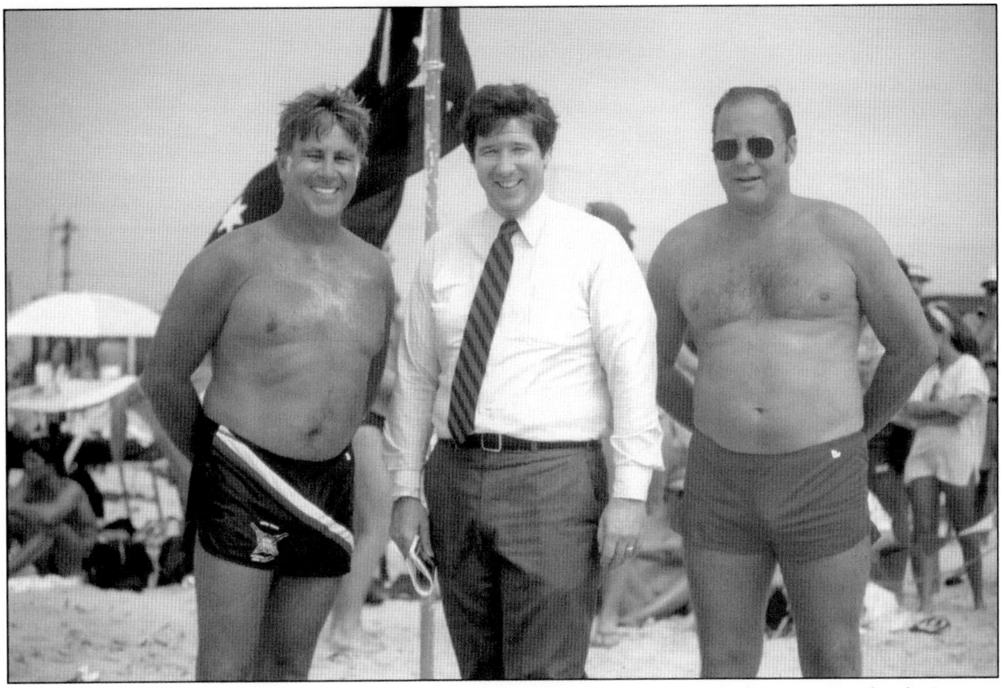

Official guests and spectators during the Huntington Beach 1989 California Surf Life Saving Championships are, from left to right, Long Beach lifeguard chief Dick Miller, Huntington Beach city administrator Charles Thompson, and Beach Services manager Doug D'Arnall.

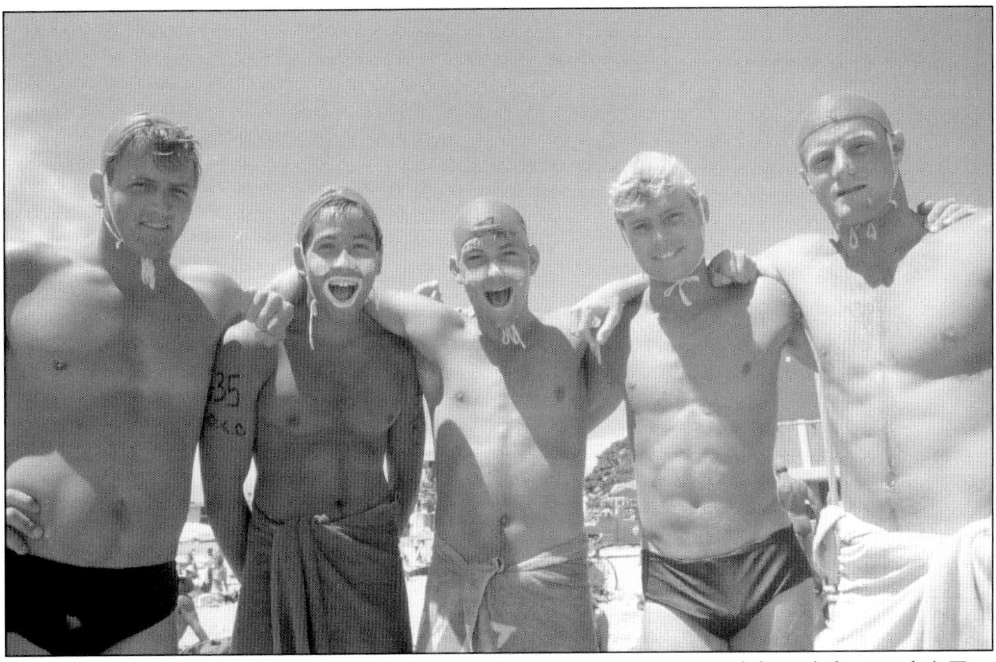

Team Orange County, made up of city and state lifeguards, (pictured from left to right) Tim Stanford, Eric Ching, Jay Miller, Jeff Hoss, and John Beebe share a fun moment during the 1989 Bud Light Ocean Festival Lifeguard series.

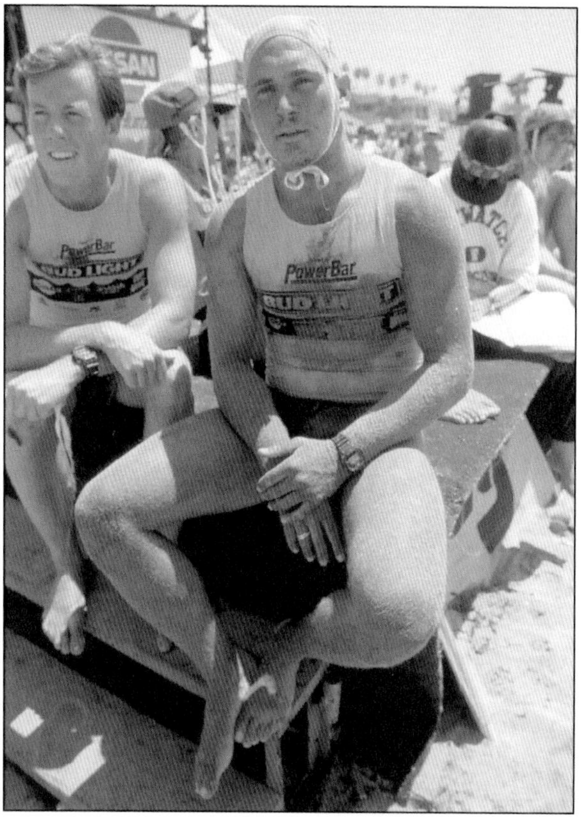

Bill "the Squirrel" Swearingen (right) is seen here in 1992 after he just finished the beach flags event and has collected a typical amount of sand during another Ocean Festival in HB. Swearingen was also an excellent rowing partner and a member of the National Doryman's Association (NDA). Next to him is Tim Hinchey.

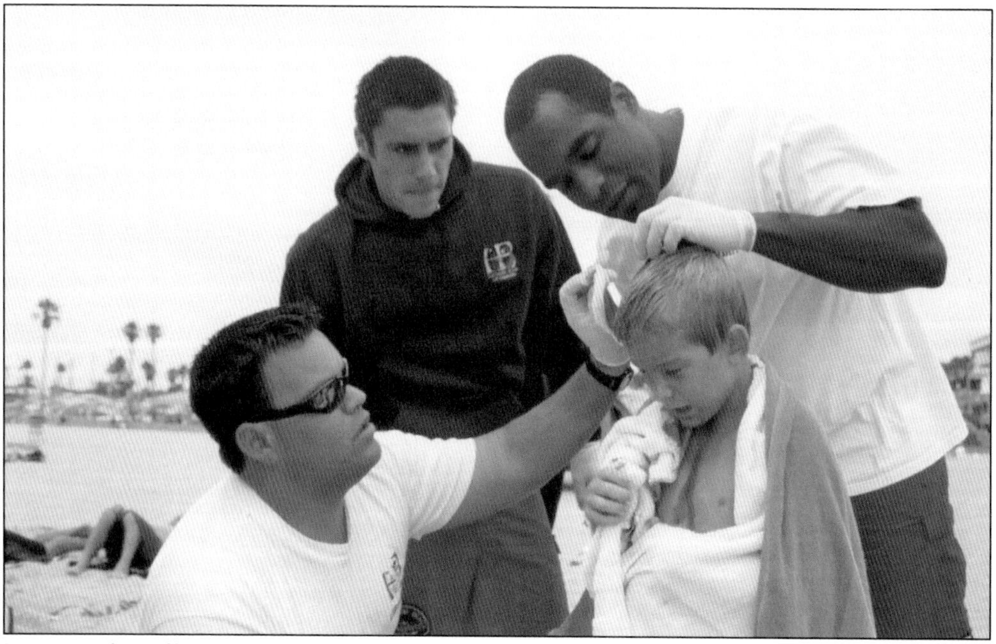

Marine safety officer Kyle Lindo and Tony Villalobos in this 1990 photograph provide first aid to an injured junior lifeguard while instructor Matt Elser stands by. In 2002, Lindo was promoted to marine safety chief.

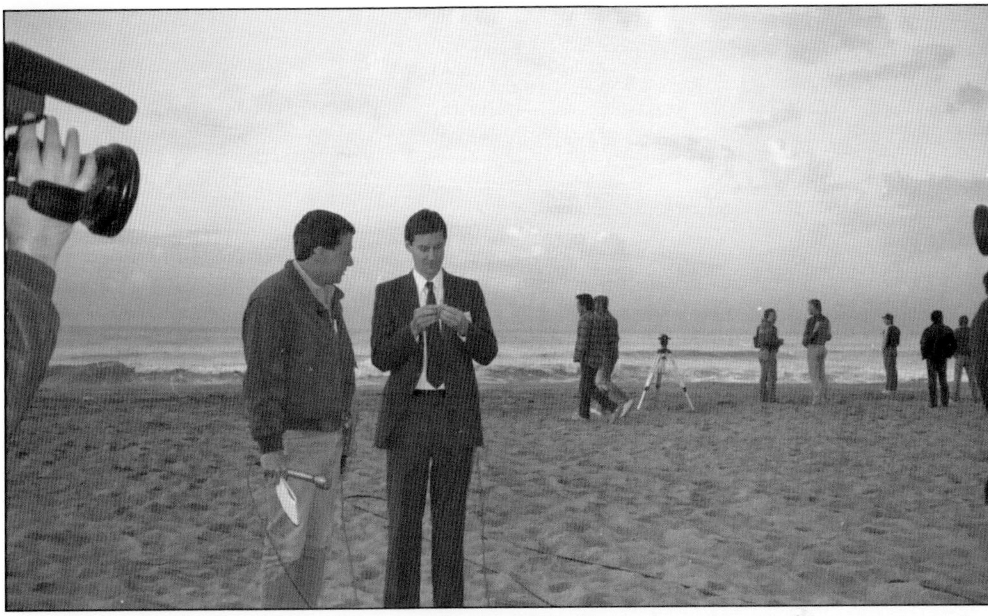

Huntington Beach mayor Tom Mays, newly elected in December, prepares for a press interview after the disastrous February 7, 1990, tanker *American Trader* oil spill. The oil tanker ran over its anchor and spilled 416,598 gallons of crude oil, mostly landing in Huntington and Newport Beaches. Mays recalled meeting the U.S. Coast Guard admiral; many federal, state, county, and local officials; and the Huntington Beach lifeguards, who offered gracious logistic support and professionalism.

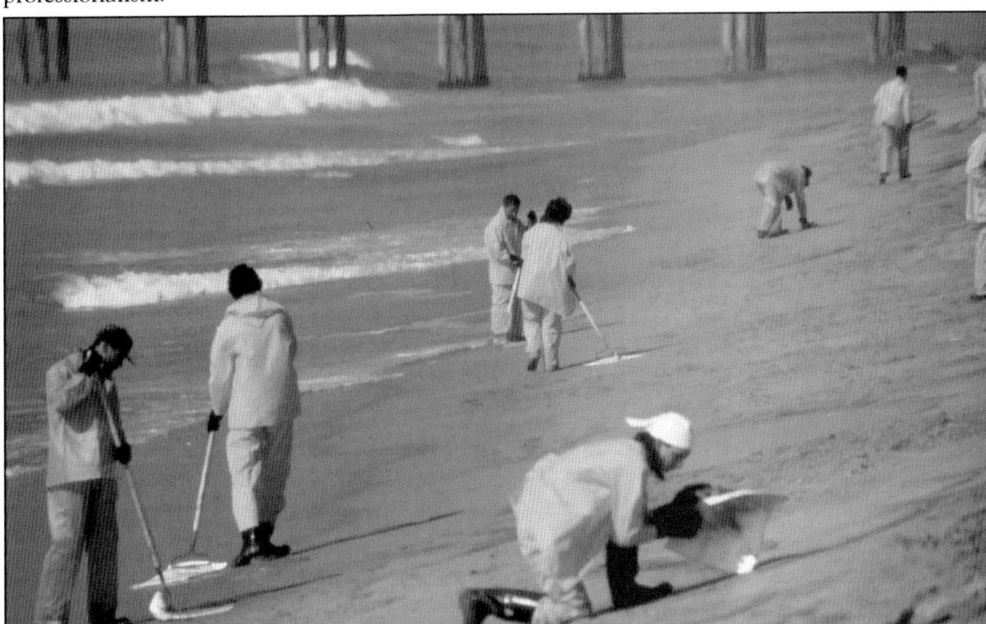

During the 1990 cleanup after the tanker *American Trader* oil spill, the largest in Orange County history, the beaches were closed for nearly three weeks. The case and settlement of the recreational component went to trial and awarded the trustees $13.2 million. The biological component settled out of court for $2,884,566 for bird- and fish-related injuries.

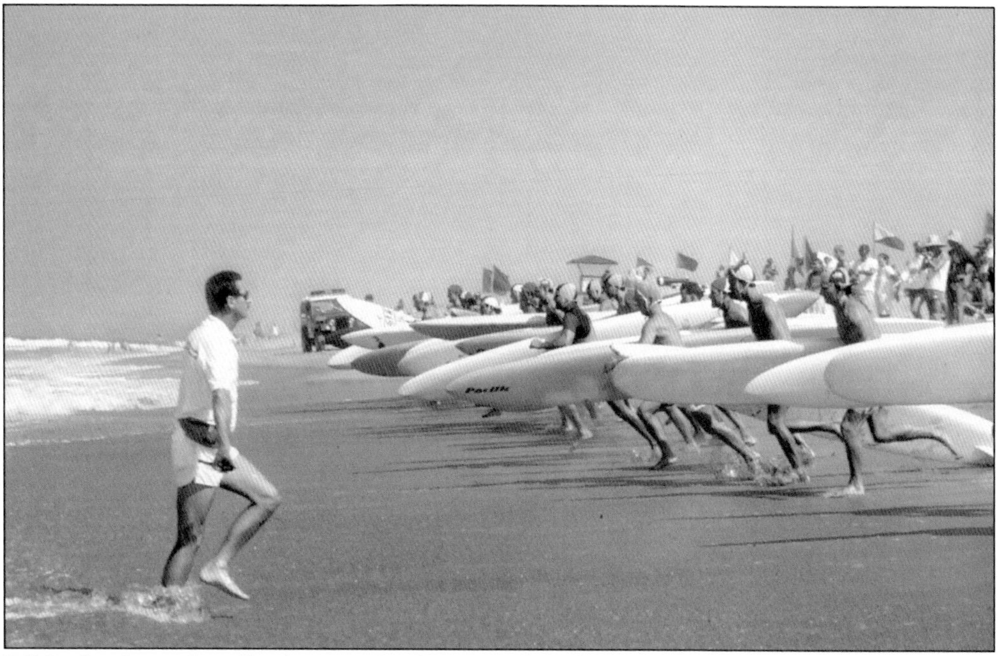

Bill Richardson, the official starter for the event, lets the paddleboard race begin on the north side of the pier for the 1989 California Surf Life Saving Championships. Richardson continues to volunteer for regional and national lifeguard competitions throughout the United States.

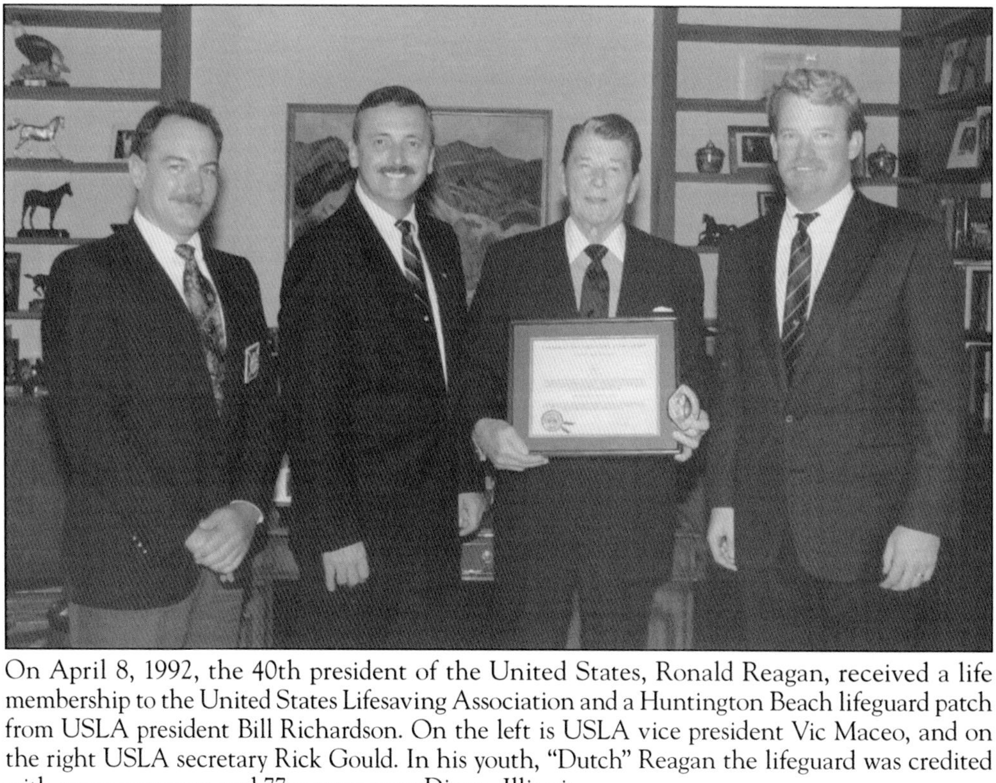

On April 8, 1992, the 40th president of the United States, Ronald Reagan, received a life membership to the United States Lifesaving Association and a Huntington Beach lifeguard patch from USLA president Bill Richardson. On the left is USLA vice president Vic Maceo, and on the right USLA secretary Rick Gould. In his youth, "Dutch" Reagan the lifeguard was credited with seven summers and 77 rescues near Dixon, Illinois.

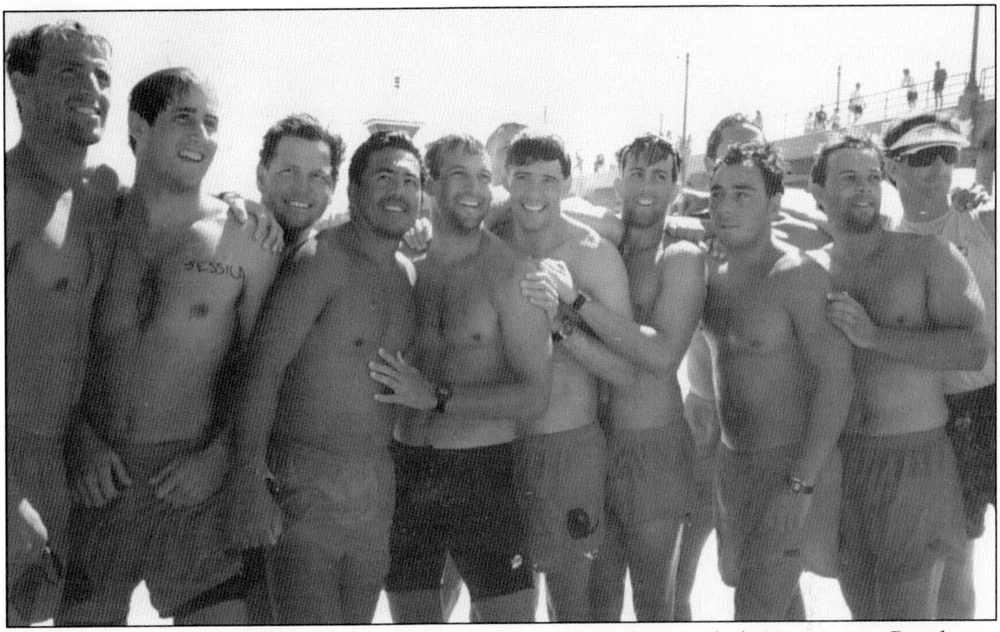

The 1993 Coastal Crusade run-swim-run participants shown here include Huntington Beach city and state lifeguards and Santa Ana firemen. The Coastal Crusade started at the U.S.–Mexico border and finished at the pier during Memorial Day weekend. Pictured from left to right are Mike Bartlett, Steve Addleman, Kai Weisser, Al Pepito, Dan Moorhouse, Fin McClafferty, Grady Howes, Steve Mataviesko, Jeff Koller, and Dick Deboer (not visible in the photograph are Brian Hopp and Marc Struwig from South Africa).

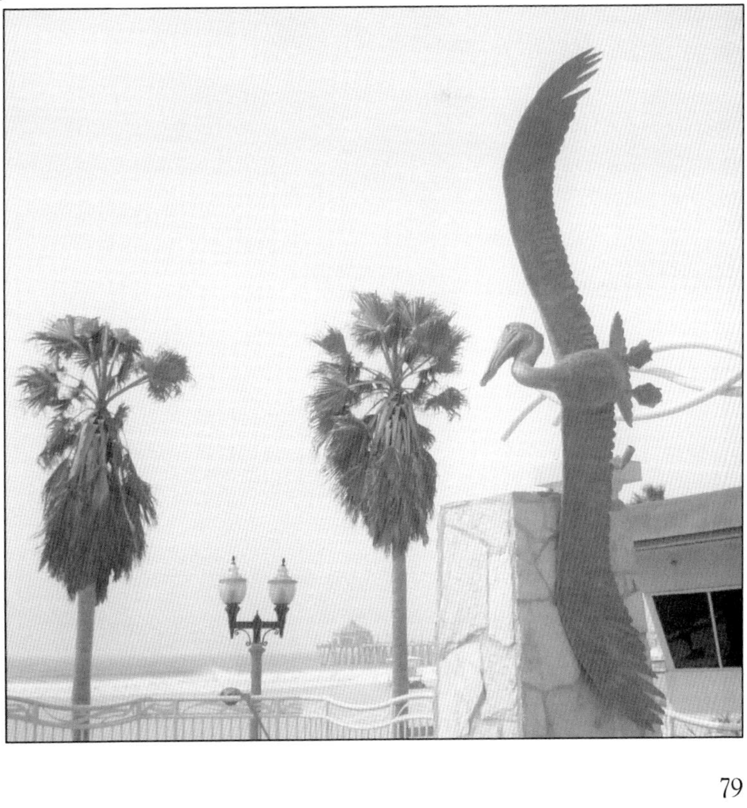

The Coastal Crusades of 1993, 1994, and 1997 were tests of amphibious physical endurance. Equally impressive, the events raised money to purchase the monument of a large bronze pelican called *Endless Flight* by artist Terry Thornsly. The monument, shown here in 2007, was dedicated to late lifeguard chief Vince Moorhouse on August 30, 1998.

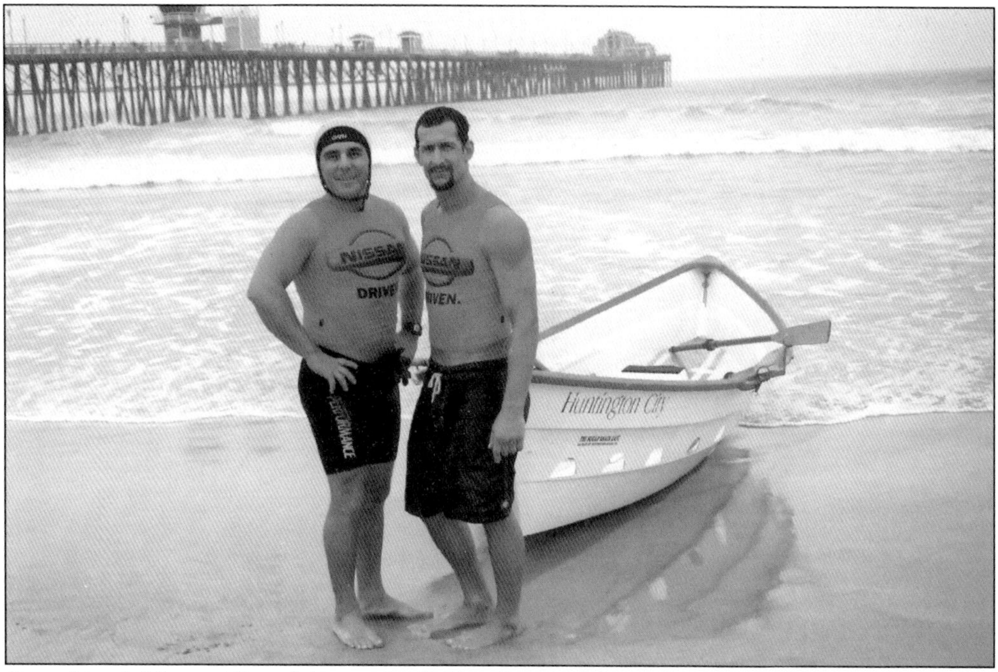

Great friends lifeguard Steve Matavieskо (left) and junior lifeguard instructor Alex Arie prepare for the always exciting three-lap dory race in 1990. In 1993, with strong dory crews, Team Huntington City finished a strong third place in the Los Angeles County Lifeguard Taplin Relays.

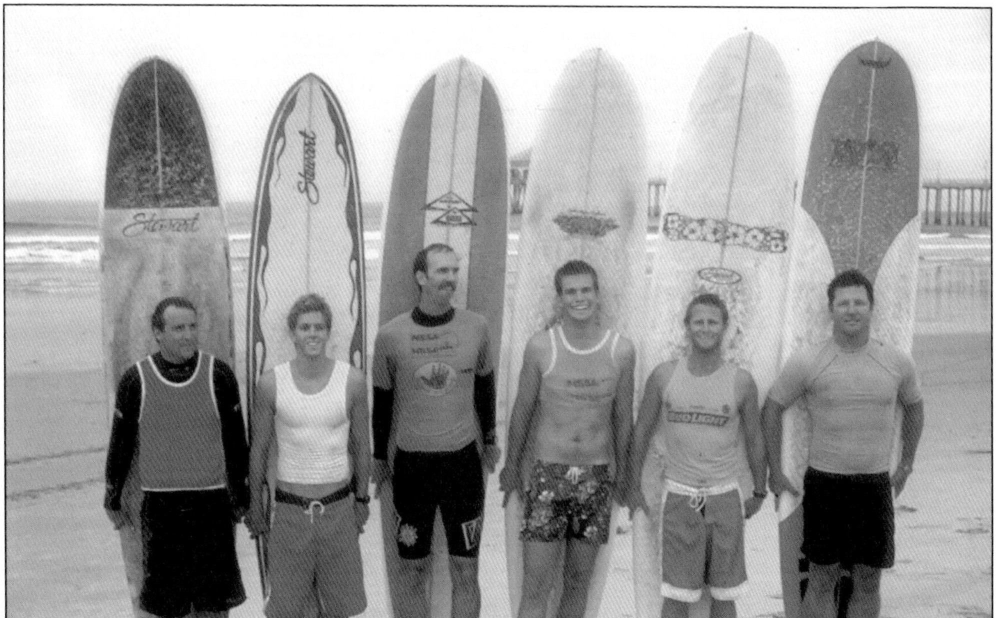

The Huntington Beach Surf Life Saving Association hosts several summer events, including softball, basketball, volleyball, bodysurfing, surfing, and this lifeguard long board contest in 1997. Finalists are, from left to right, Todd Bartlett, Blaine Morgan, Greg Crow, Eric Tucker, Greg Eisele, and Kai Weisser.

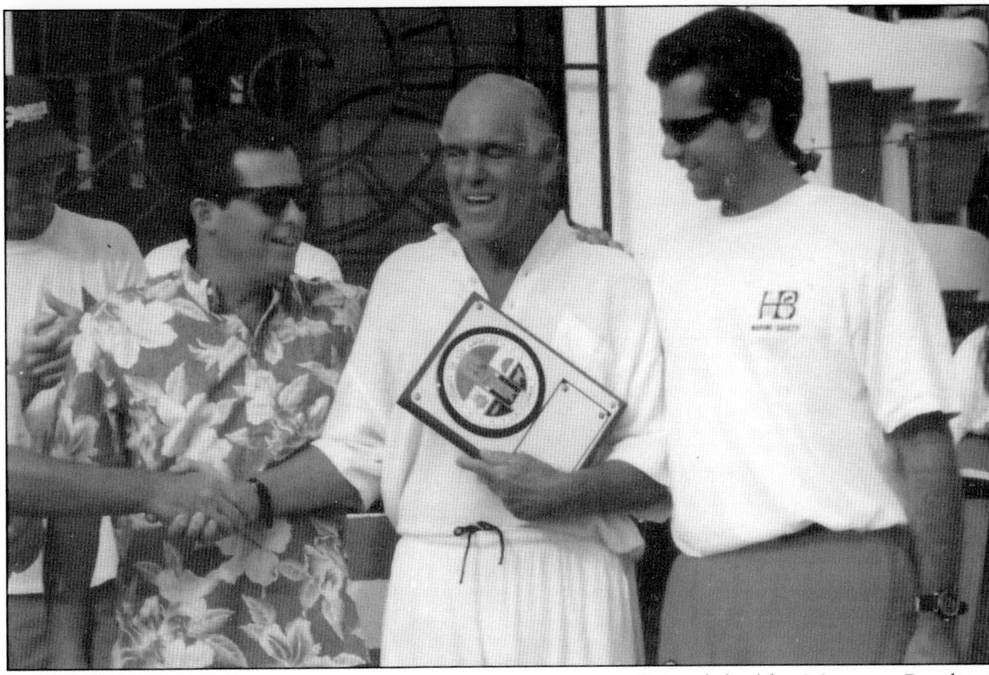

The First Mexico USLA Lifeguard Exchange with Puerto Escondido (the Mexican Pipeline) and Huntington Beach was in July 1996. For several years, the USLA raised funds for a new lifeguard headquarters at Zicatella playa in Puerto. The 1997 ceremony and dedication had USLA representatives, from left to right, Rob Webb, a Long Beach City councilman; Bob Burnside; retired Los Angeles County lifeguard chief; and Huntington Beach marine safety officer Matt Karl.

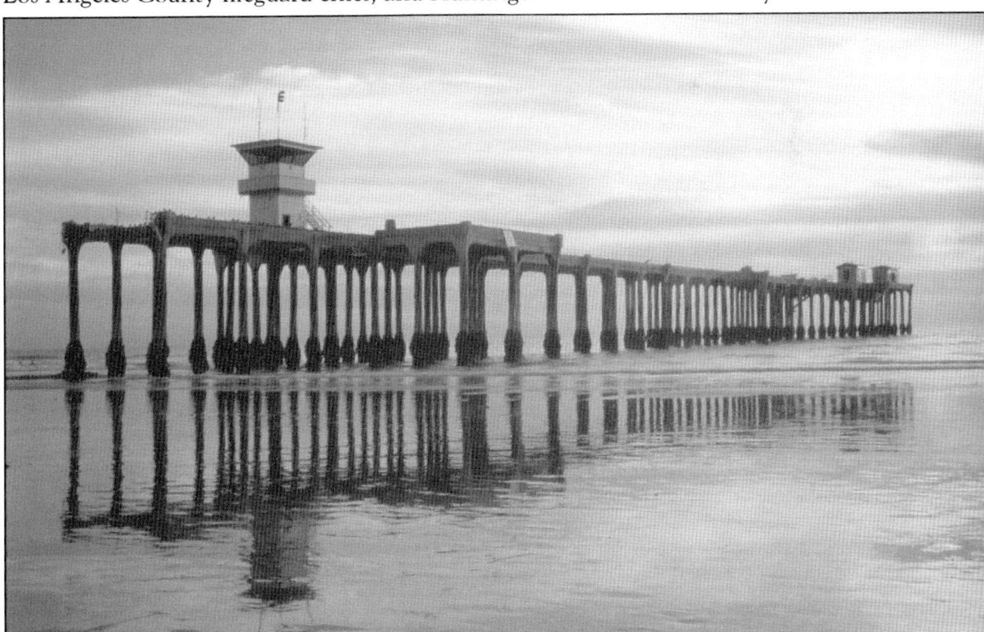

This 1990 photograph shows Huntington Beach Pier being deconstructed, which left Tower Zero an island. As reported on CNN, Tower Zero was still in operation, and lifeguards with their gear in dry bags paddled to a ladder near the end of the pier.

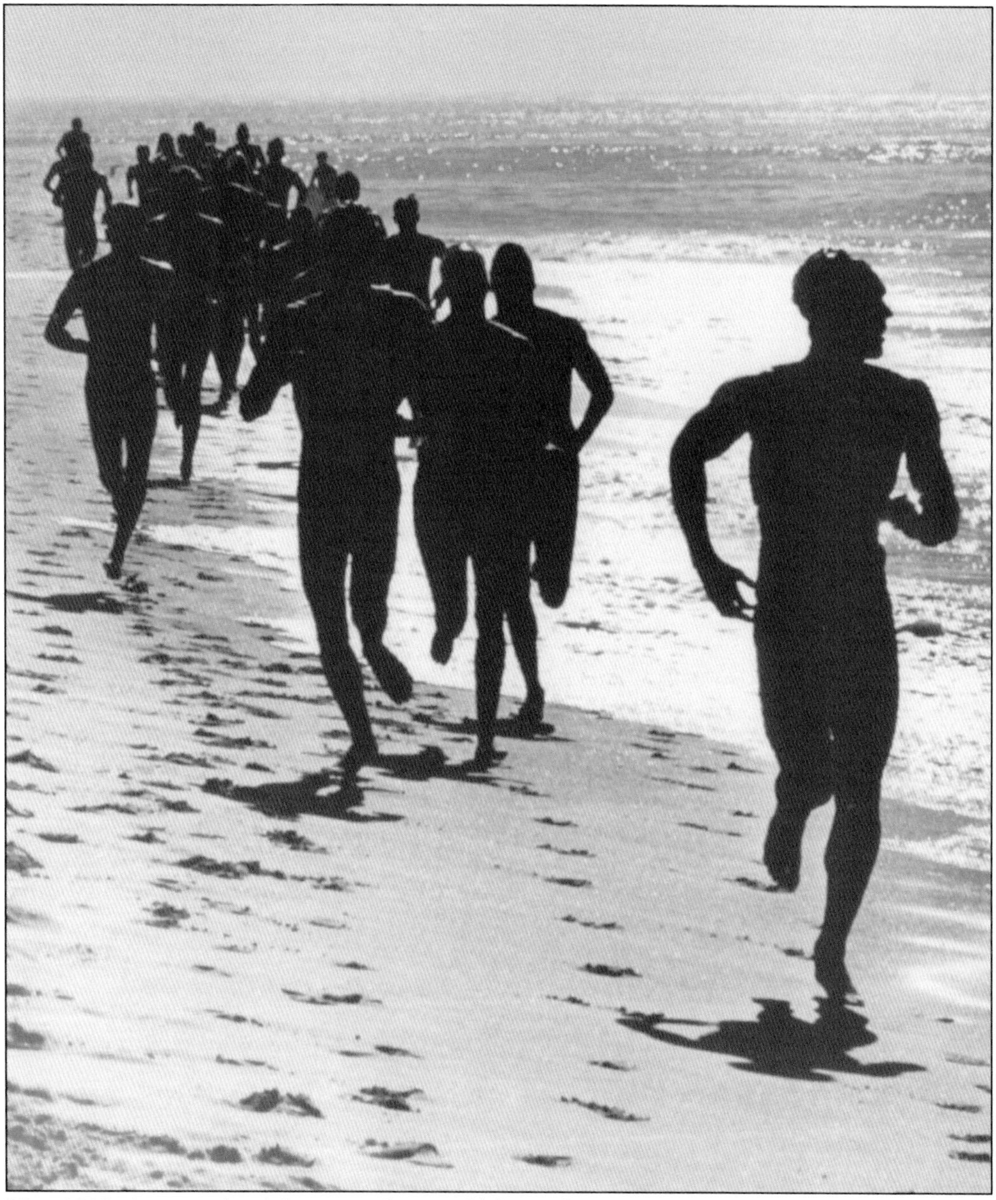

This 1980 photograph of the second part of lifeguard tryouts, the run-swim-run, qualified up to 30 hopefuls for lifeguard cadet school. The cadet school typically runs through the week of Easter school break and two weekends, concluding with rigorous written and practical exams and an interview.

Four

California State Park Huntington Beach 1950–2007

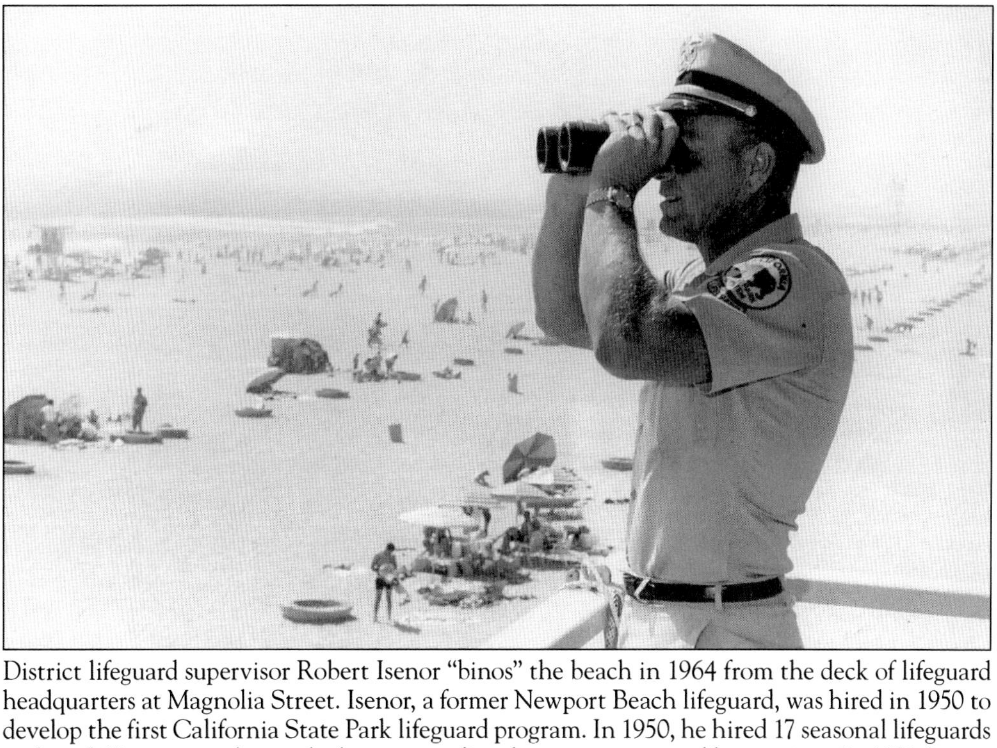

District lifeguard supervisor Robert Isenor "binos" the beach in 1964 from the deck of lifeguard headquarters at Magnolia Street. Isenor, a former Newport Beach lifeguard, was hired in 1950 to develop the first California State Park lifeguard program. In 1950, he hired 17 seasonal lifeguards and used 10 towers with no telephones or radios that were supported by one jeep. In 1951, Isenor also hired the seasonal lifeguards for Silver Strand State Beach in south San Diego County.

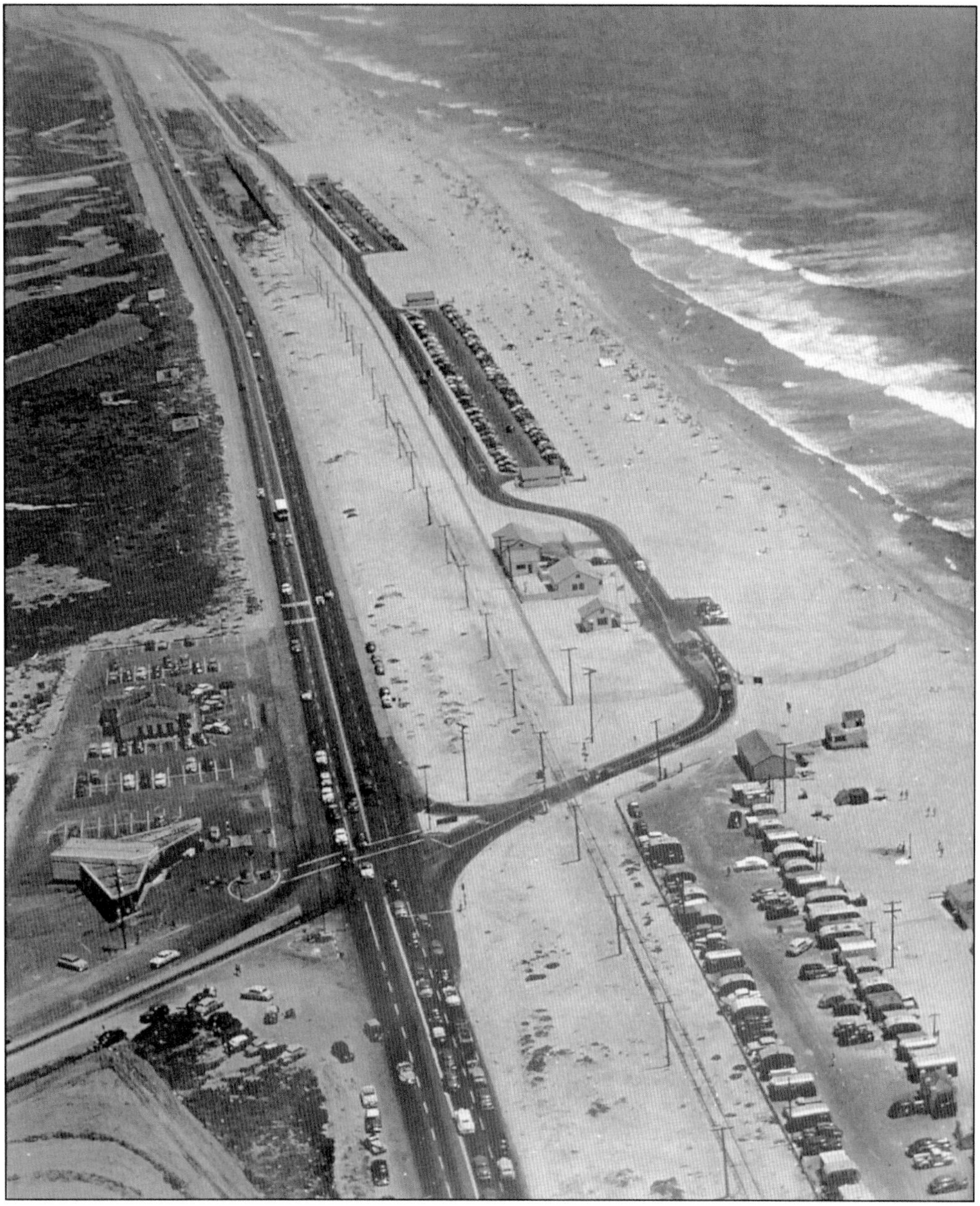

This 1952 view is of the west end of the state park entrance at Beach Boulevard and PCH. After many years of planning and negotiating, in 1948, the state parks commission purchased 11,000 feet of beachfront east of the Municipal Trailer Park to the Santa Ana River jetty. In 1950, Eugene Velzy, assistant superintendent of parks, and Frank Davies, assistant ranger and first park resident, organized the opening of the park. District lifeguard supervisor Robert Isenor became the first lifeguard peace officer in July 1954. On August 20, 1958, the resident chief ranger William Reinhart officially recognized the millionth car to enter the park since its opening. Soon after the launch and success of *Surfwatch* in 1964, the second state lifeguard rescue boat *Sea Ranger* was launched at Salton Sea. In 1973, the California State Parks Commission became the first agency in the nation to include peace officer training and have armed lifeguards with full peace officer powers. After 33 years of directing the lifeguard services, Isenor retired in 1983.

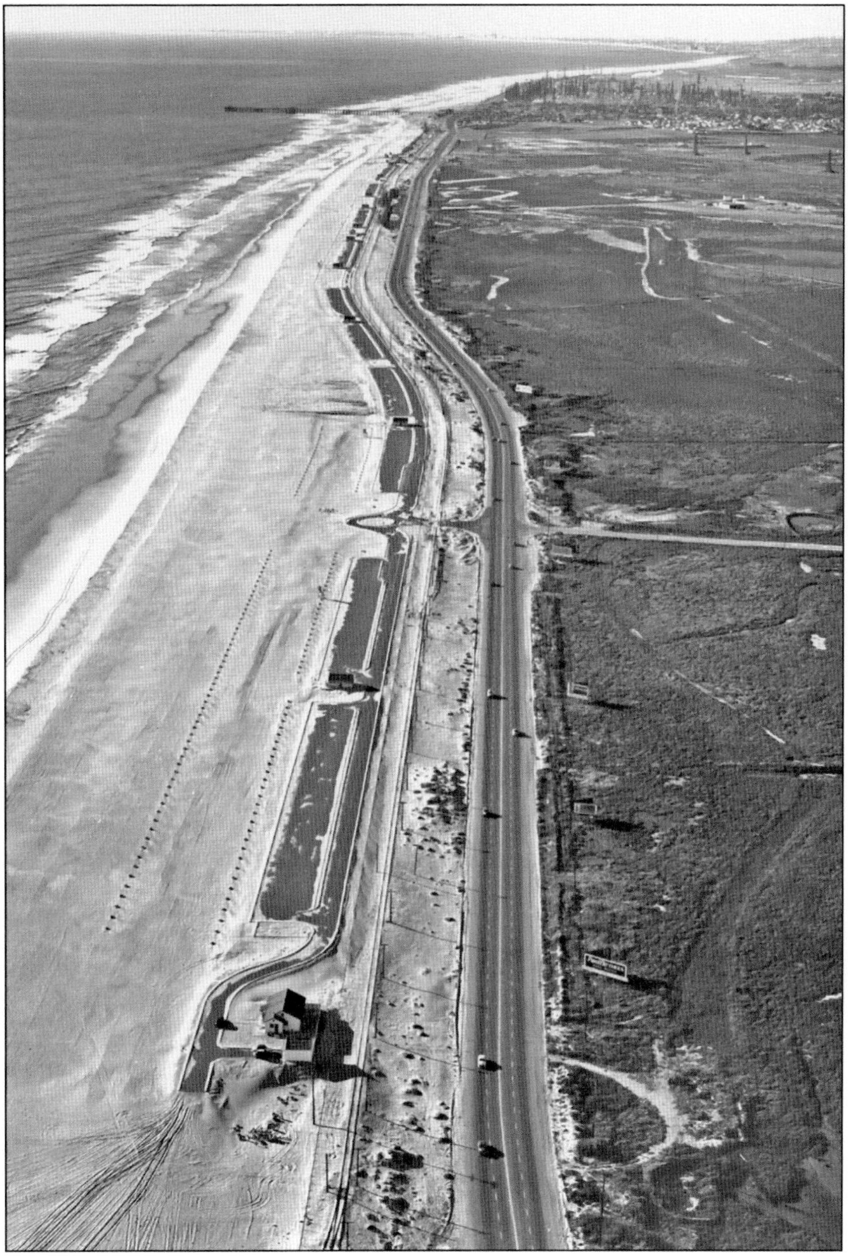

This 1951 view is of the east end of the state park near the Santa Ana River jetty, which creates the border between Newport Beach and Huntington. Only two miles west of the Huntington pier was Tin Can, or Beer Can, Beach. The *Orange County Register* wrote in 1960: "Long a no-man's land, 'Tin Can Beach' was a dirty, cluttered 'hell's half acre' ruled over by self-styled 'kings' and 'mayors' who erected tar-paper and burlap covered shacks with 'property lines' outlined in rusty cans. There wandering, beachcombers and weekend party groups held forth for years with no one to tell them to move on or clean up the surroundings. After nearly ten years of negotiating with up to 300 individuals and property interests," California officially dedicated the opening of Bolsa Chica State Beach on October 1, 1960. The first Bolsa Chica State Park supervisor was Huntington Beach resident Jack Welch.

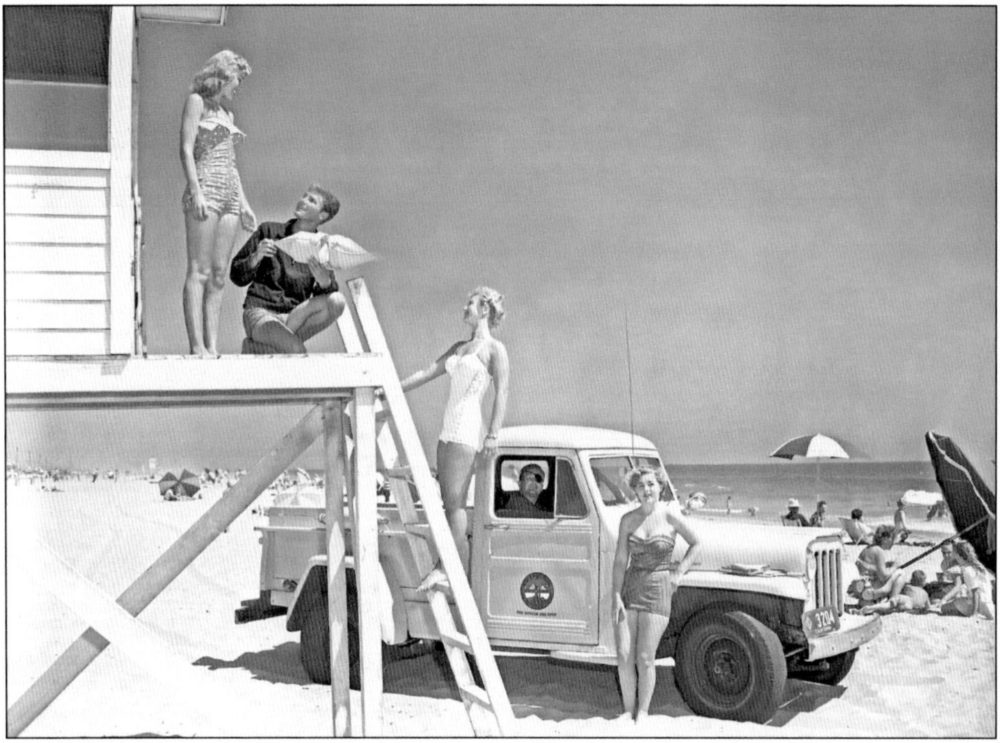

Another classic Robert Geivet photograph from the Old Courthouse Museum is a Huntington State Park publicity shot from July 1, 1952. Unfortunately, the names of the lifeguard, girls, and the eye-patched man in the truck were not recorded.

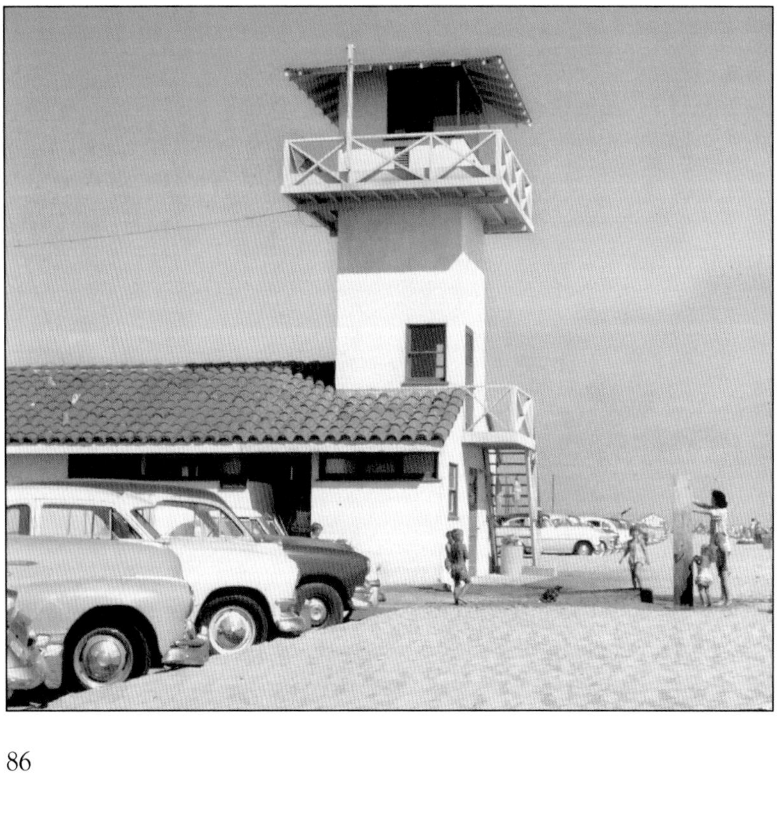

This 1960 photograph was taken at the Magnolia Lifeguard Tower at Huntington State Beach. The elevated view of the lifeguard tower was critical to operations and was placed in the middle of the two-mile park. The building offered a small storage room for the lifeguards below and public restrooms.

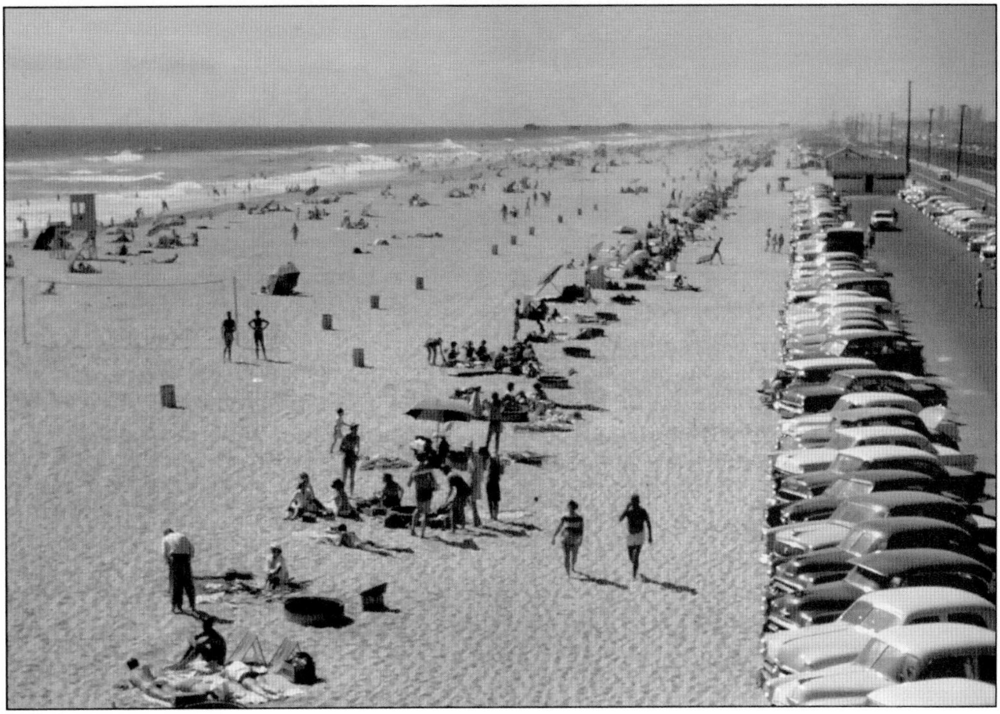

This photograph was taken on the same day as the previous photograph from the deck of the Magnolia Lifeguard Tower. The full parking lot with now-classic cars and the pier in the distance made a great view for the lifeguard on duty.

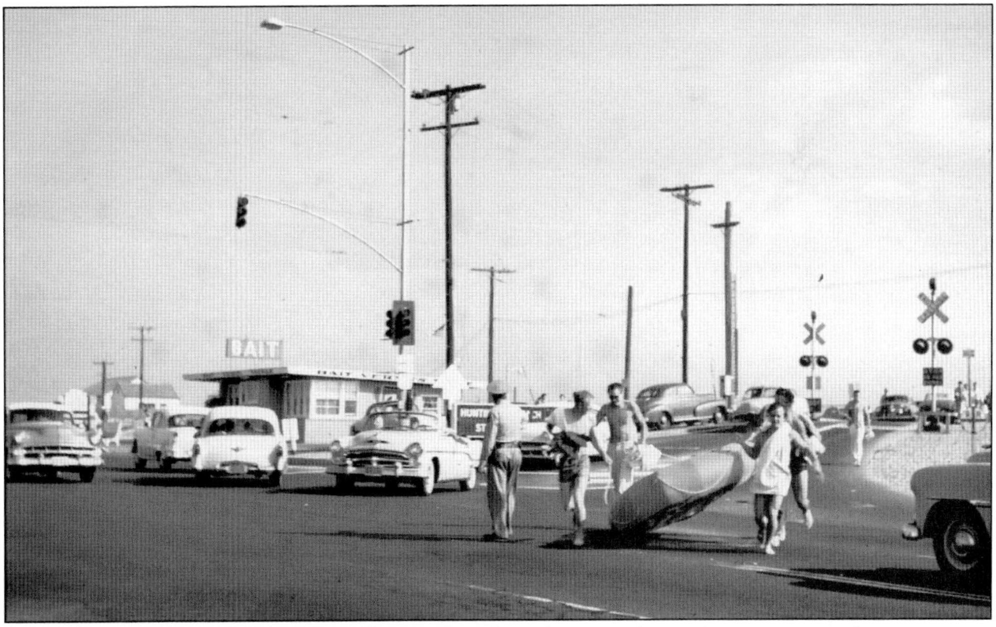

On this 1957 summer day, the traffic cop was kept busy at the park entrance and intersection of Beach Boulevard and PCH. The railroad tracks and bait shop are long gone, but the people with all their stuff and various flotation devices are not. The lifeguards along the coast would call this scene job security.

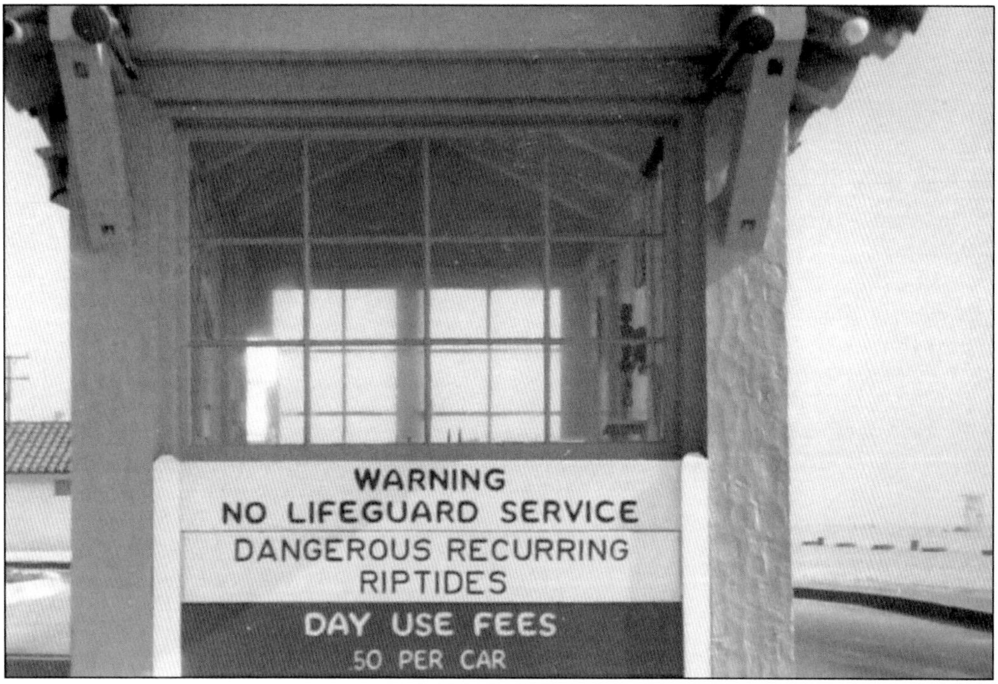

The Huntington State Beach entrance kiosk and park staff welcomed visitors. The first several years the park was open, lifeguards were scheduled for only six months of the year starting the week before Easter Sunday. In 1957, the park employed a lifeguard staff for the whole year. Lifeguards and the public now refer to riptides as rip currents, or just "rips."

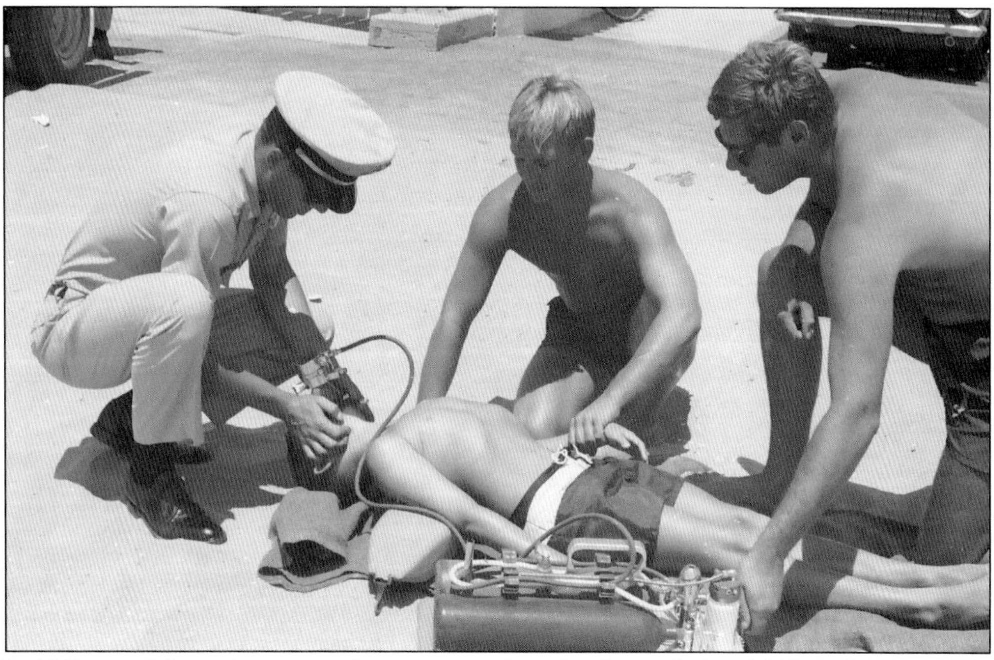

In 1962, state lifeguard testing and training was formalized to include a 1,000-yard swim, a 600-yard run-swim-run, and 20 hours of in-service first aid and rescue instruction. With the oxygen resuscitator, Jack Buck demonstrates and trains seasonal lifeguards.

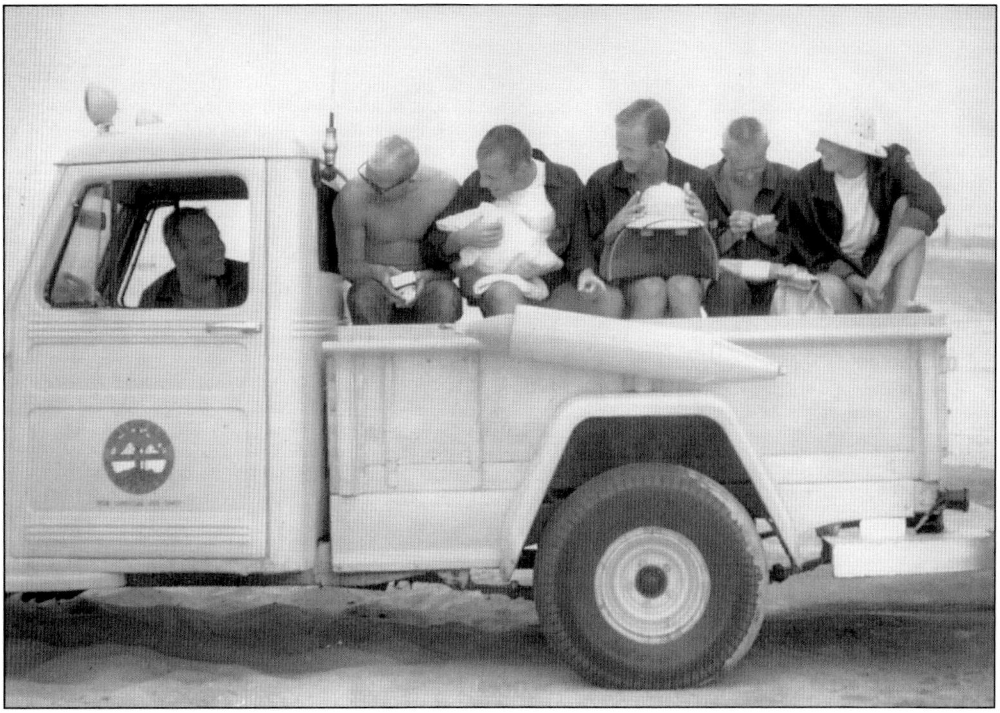

This 1963 photograph, called "Truck Ride," shows the lifeguard crew ready for deployment to their assigned towers. Mounted on the truck is an old lifeguard torpedo buoy holder; the pith helmets add character too.

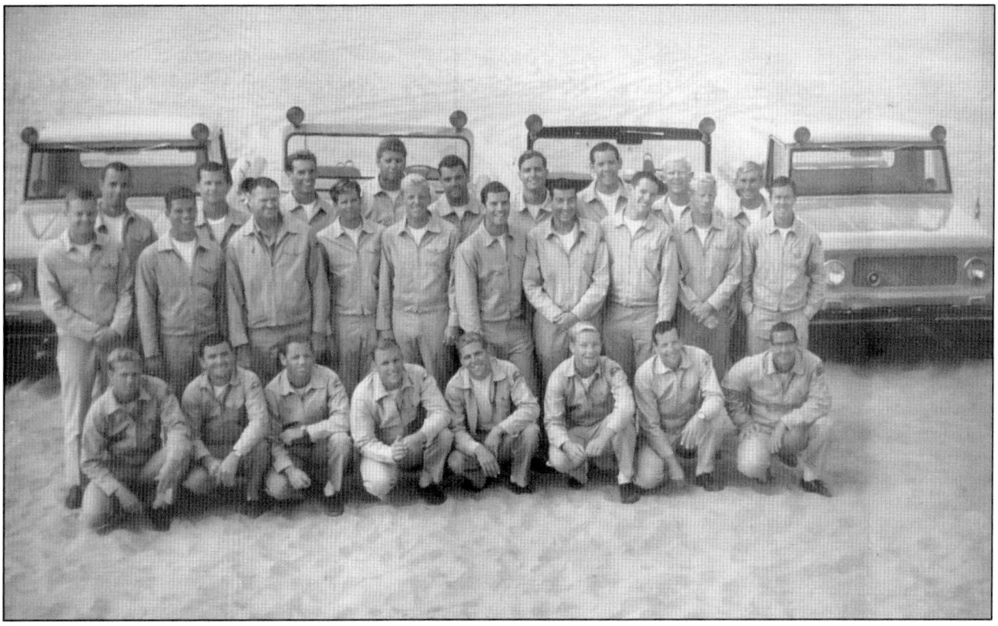

The 1964 Huntington State Beach crew took this photograph with these lifeguard vehicles. In the same year, the Huntington State Beach Lifeguard Association was formed and later successfully lobbied for safety retirement. The state also created the positions of aquatic specialist and lifeguard supervisor.

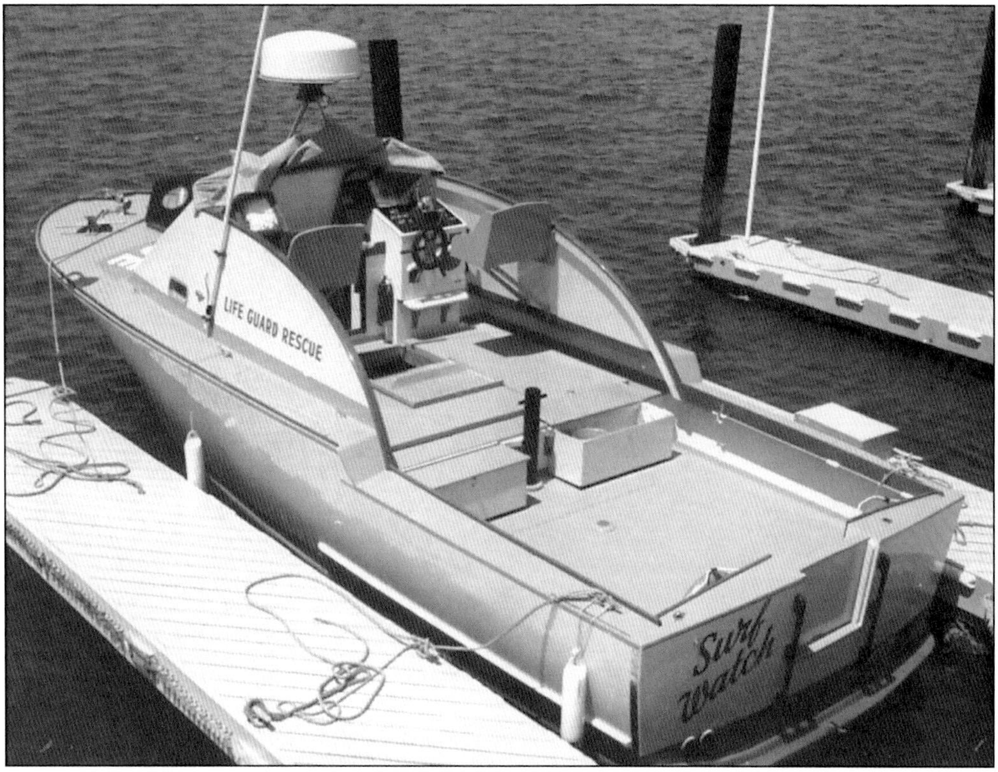

The rescue vessel *Surfwatch* rests quietly in her slip after her maiden voyage in 1964. Soon after, *Surfwatch* and its crew made a dramatic mass rescue of 36 people from a single monster rip current. *Surfwatch*'s home port is Newport Harbor next to the Newport lifeguard rescue vessels, Harbor Patrol, and a U.S. Coast Guard cutter.

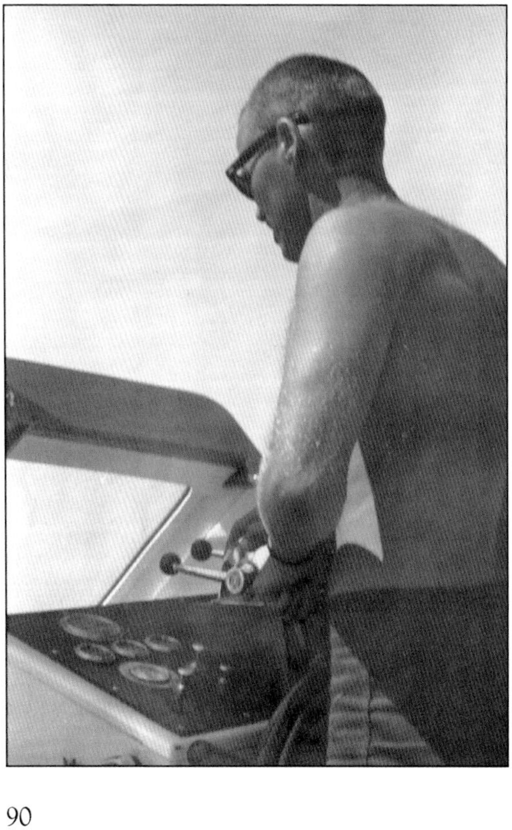

Surfwatch skipper Mell Tubbs stands ready at the helm, checking the gauges and handling the twin engine controls. The daily voyage from Newport to Huntington and back must have been a nice one. Tubbs also became the first department-sanctioned scuba diver at Huntington State Beach.

With the power plant at Newland Street and PCH in view, Zack the boat deckhand prepares to exit the stern of *Surfwatch*. Looking for the victim or victims and the beach lifeguard in the water somewhere in the surf-line, Zack waits for the skipper's command to "Go!"

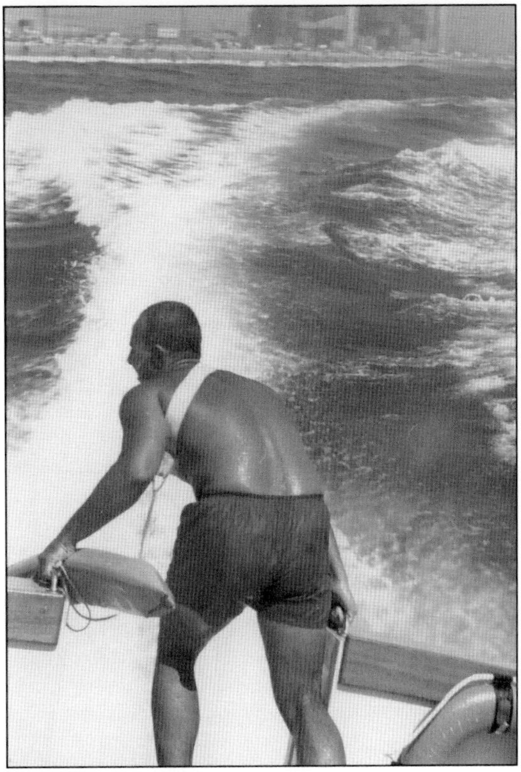

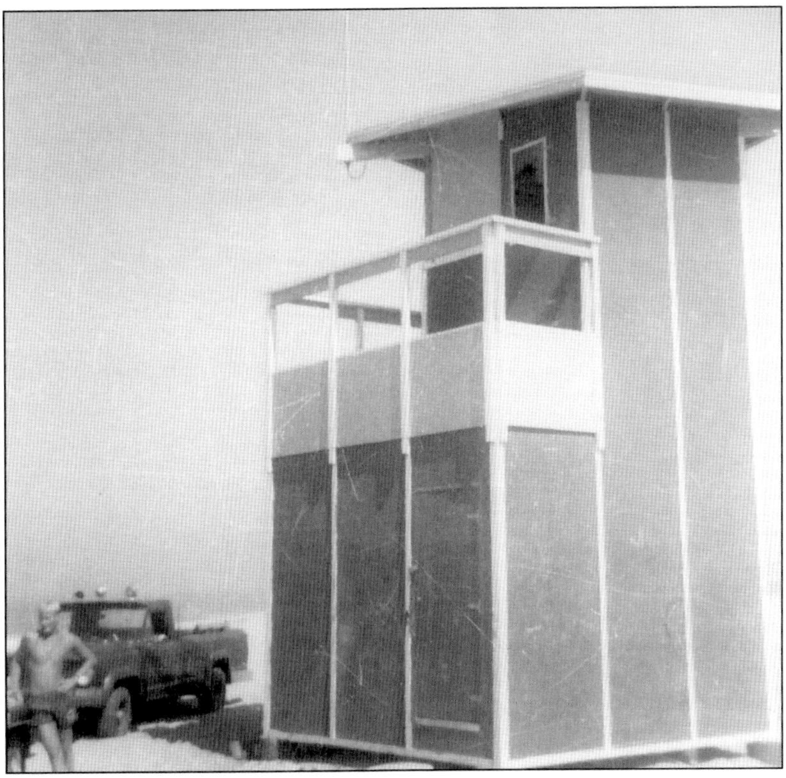

Bolsa Chica State Beach in 1960 did not receive the same kind of initial capital investment Huntington State Beach did in 1950. This rough-looking structure was the first Bolsa Chica lifeguard headquarters with an elevated observation deck.

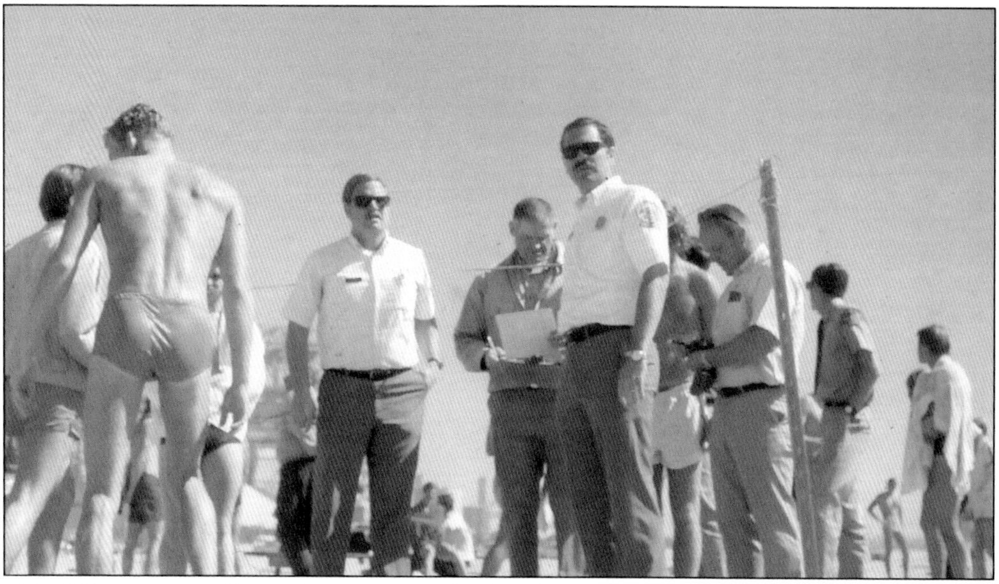

This 1973 state beach lifeguard tryout and recheck with a large turnout was for the southern district. In uniform are Bill Kramer (left) and Kirby Temple, and in the background is a Huntington City lifeguard. Lifeguards from other agencies were often seen at tryouts up and down the coast.

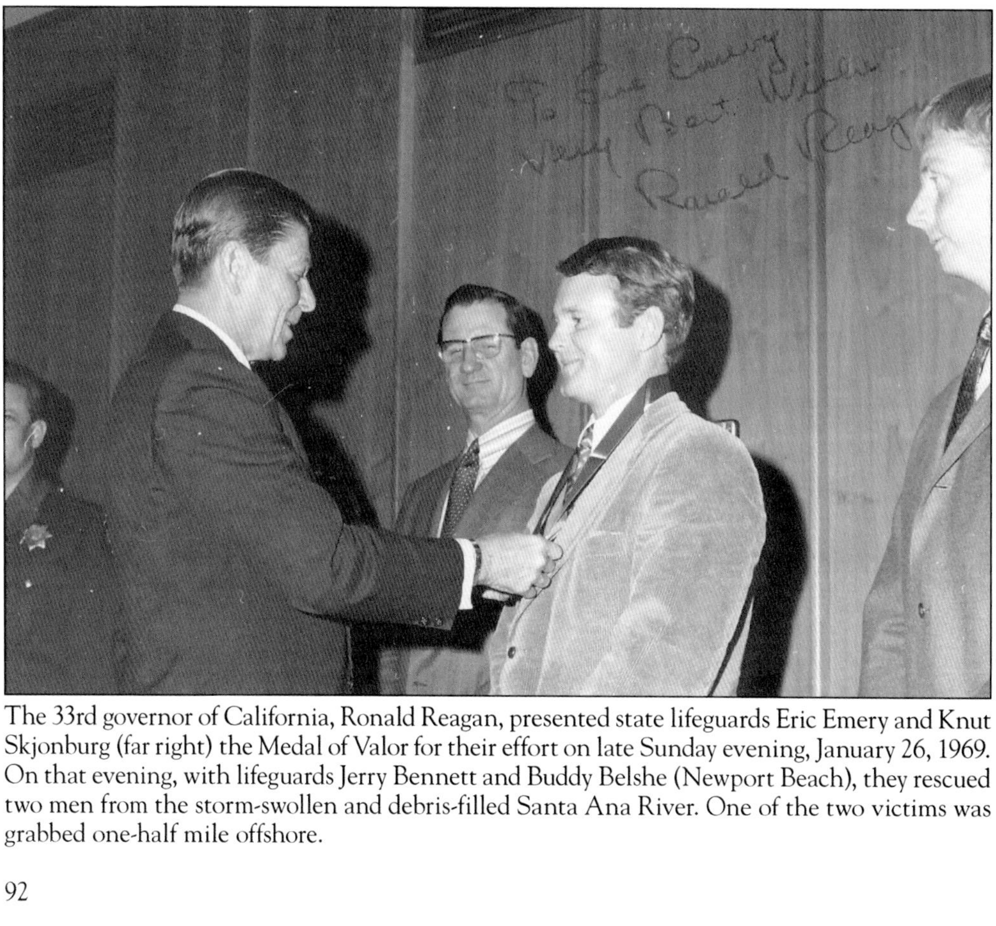

The 33rd governor of California, Ronald Reagan, presented state lifeguards Eric Emery and Knut Skjonburg (far right) the Medal of Valor for their effort on late Sunday evening, January 26, 1969. On that evening, with lifeguards Jerry Bennett and Buddy Belshe (Newport Beach), they rescued two men from the storm-swollen and debris-filled Santa Ana River. One of the two victims was grabbed one-half mile offshore.

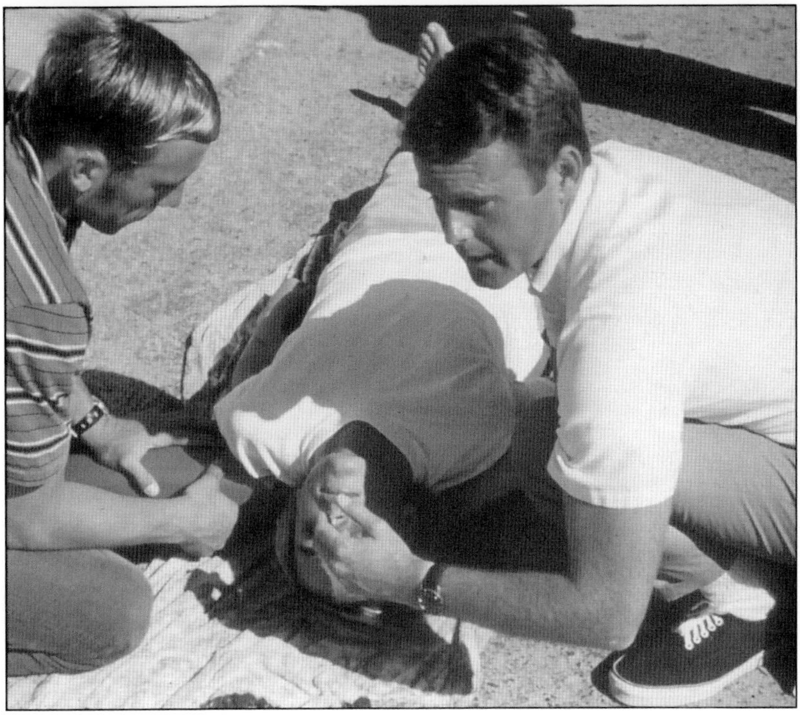

This 1977 annual state lifeguard training and skills review was led by Eric Emery (right). Lifeguard sections from the Southern District combined their efforts and met at Huntington. Emery also taught English and retired from nearby Edison High School.

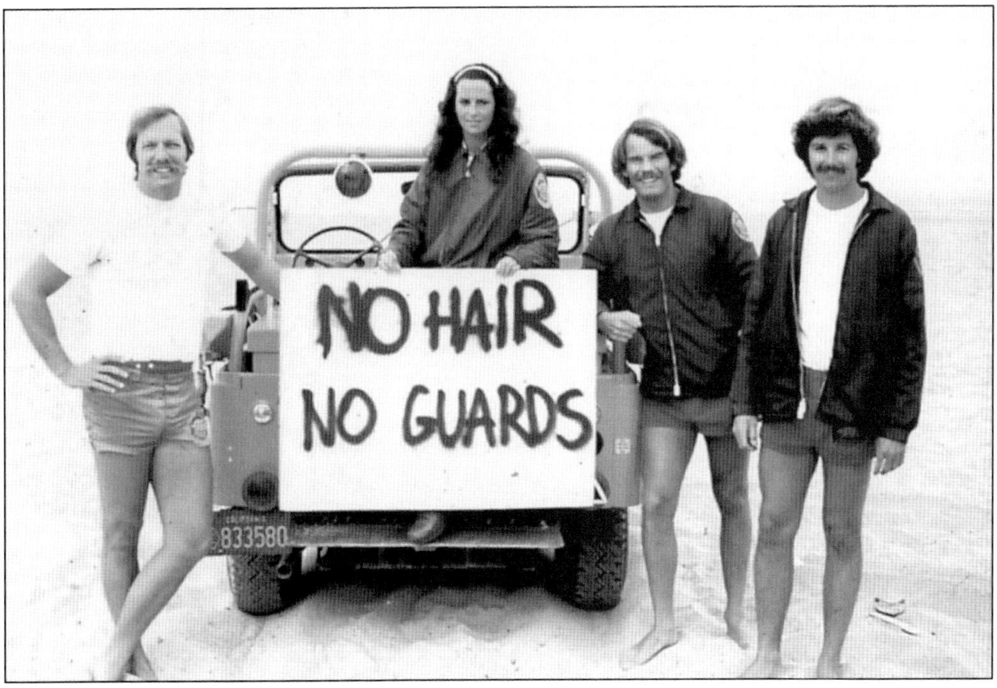

"No Hair, No Guards" protest says it all for the high and tight hair policy in 1974. Marty Armstrong remembers the grievance with the California State Employees Association (CSEA) that led to management changing the regulations. With lots of hair are, from left to right, Dan LaFlamme, Colleen Donneley, Ralph Cross, and Armstrong, who said, "Funny the things that were important when you were young."

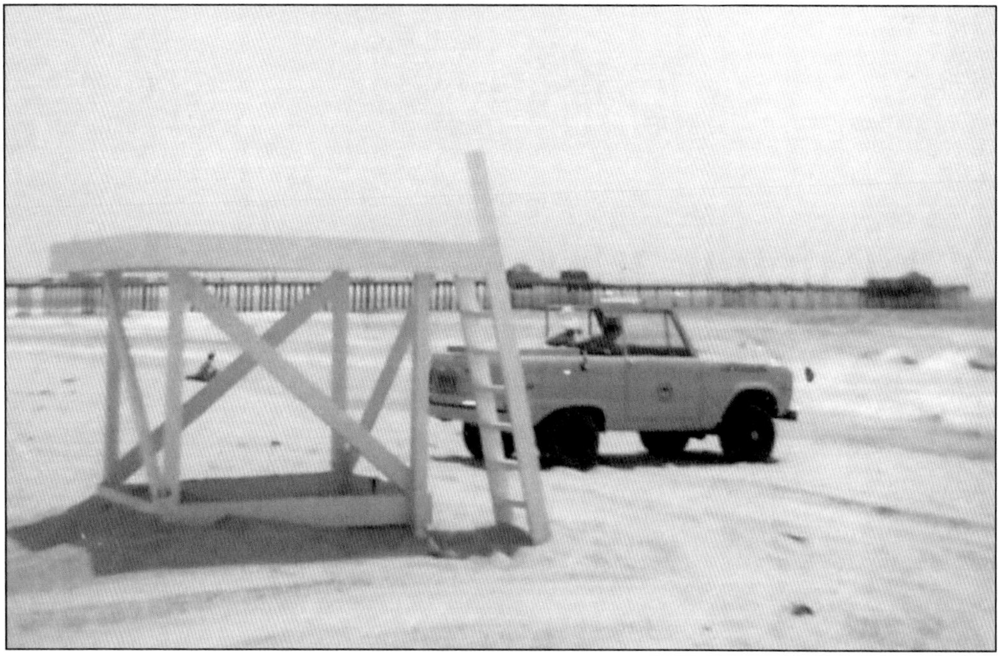

In the early 1970s, the ownership of the beach west of the pier was in conflict between the City of Huntington Beach and the State of California. In 1973, the Huntington State Beach lifeguards began their patrol of what was then called "New Beach," and in this photograph one of the new towers is visible. In 1983, the city regained control of the area to the Bolsa border, now Seapoint and PCH.

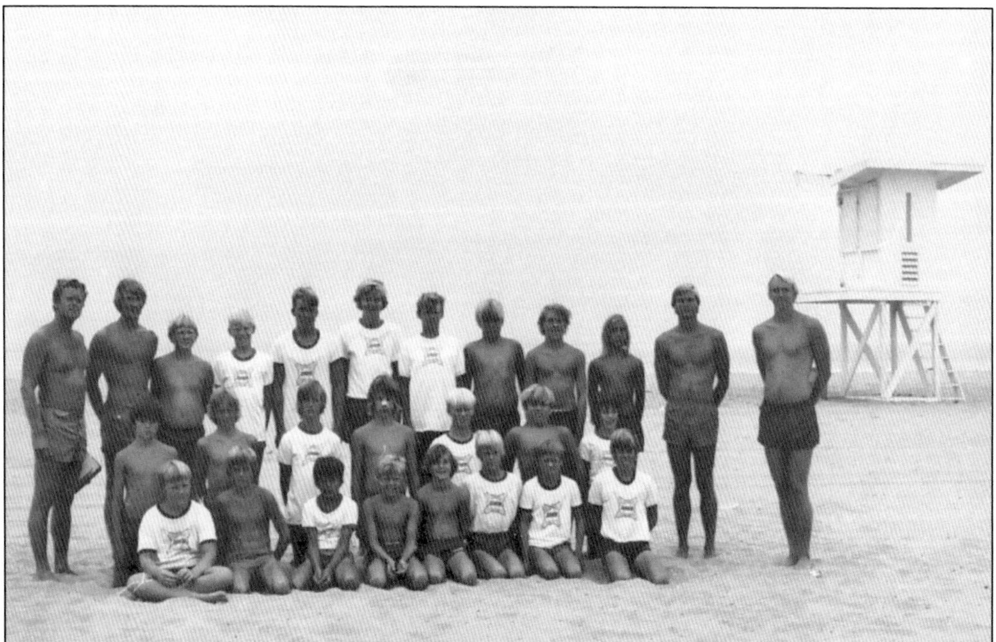

The 1974 state beach junior lifeguards met for this group photograph near the river jetty and Lifeguard Tower No. 1. The junior lifeguard instructors are, from left to right, Eric Emery, Mike Beale, Doug Wurster, and Lee Graham.

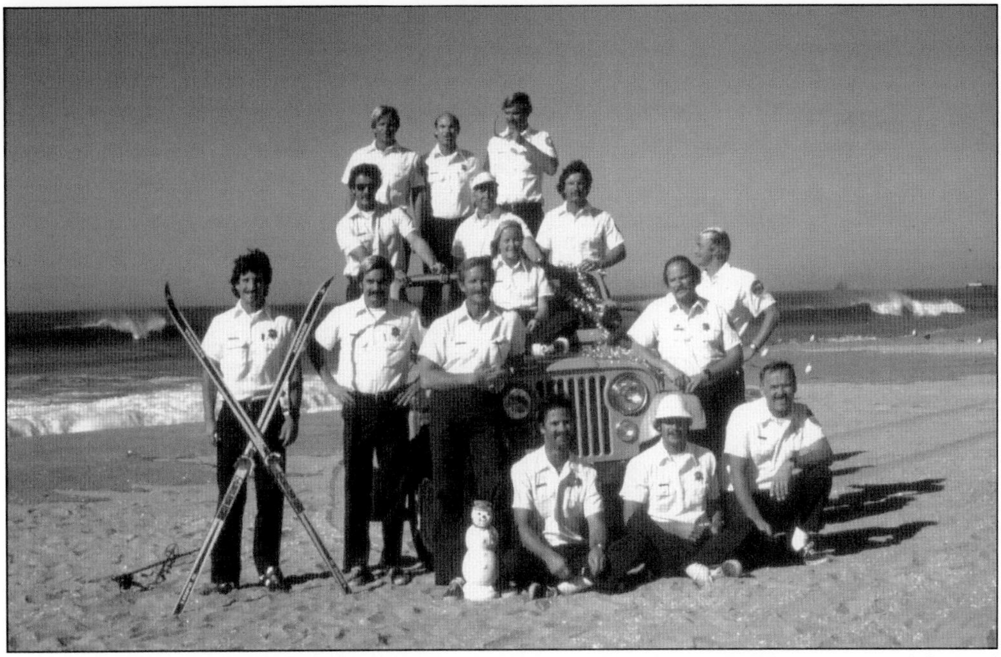

This 1981 Christmas card and photograph of the Huntington State Beach permanent lifeguard crew was a popular one. From top to bottom and from left to right are Tom Baylock, Doug Harding, unidentified, Brett Ross, unidentified, John Topar, Dave Perry, Steve Rogers, Paul Frost, Debbie Freedman, Bill Kramer, Lee Graham, Rick Campbell, Greg Tice, and Mell Tubbs.

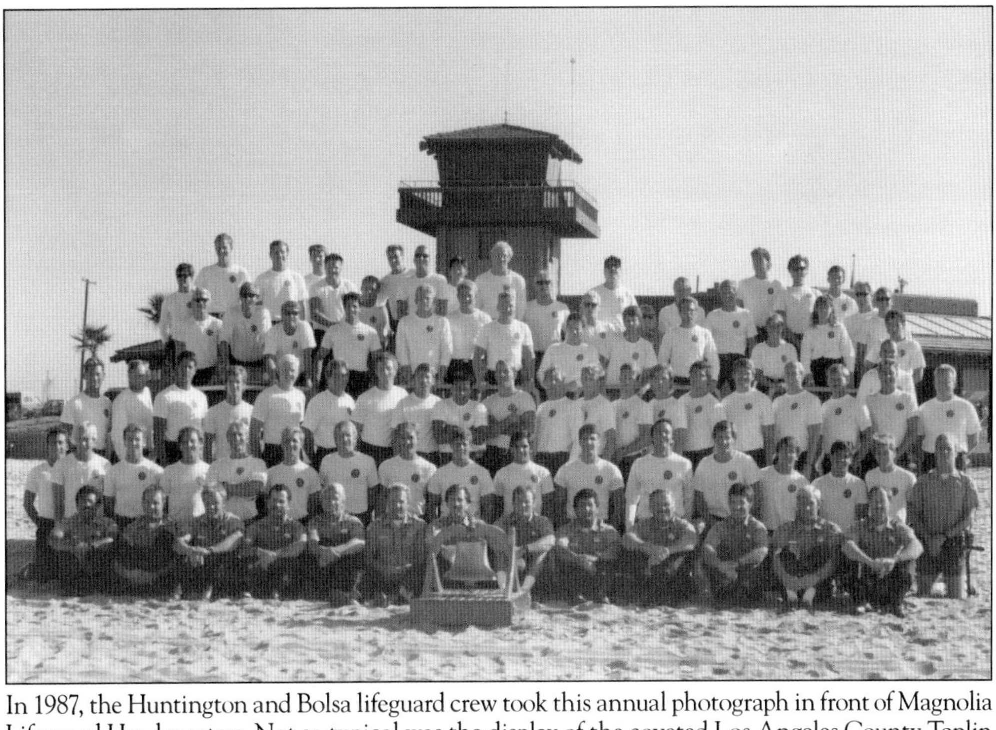

In 1987, the Huntington and Bolsa lifeguard crew took this annual photograph in front of Magnolia Lifeguard Headquarters. Not so typical was the display of the coveted Los Angeles County Taplin Relays Bell. The bell rarely leaves Los Angeles County and was kept in Huntington for the year.

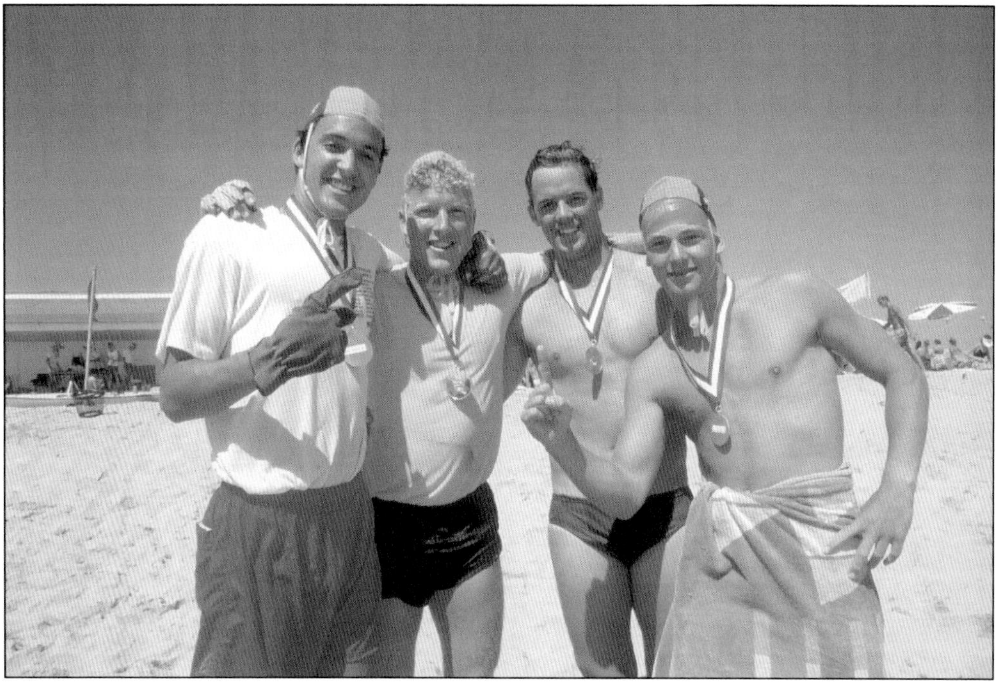

The land line event is a favorite of the Huntington State Beach lifeguards. The 1988 California Surf Life Saving Champions for the land line event were, from left to right, John Hernandez, Jeff Amman, Tom Harrison, and Jay Miller.

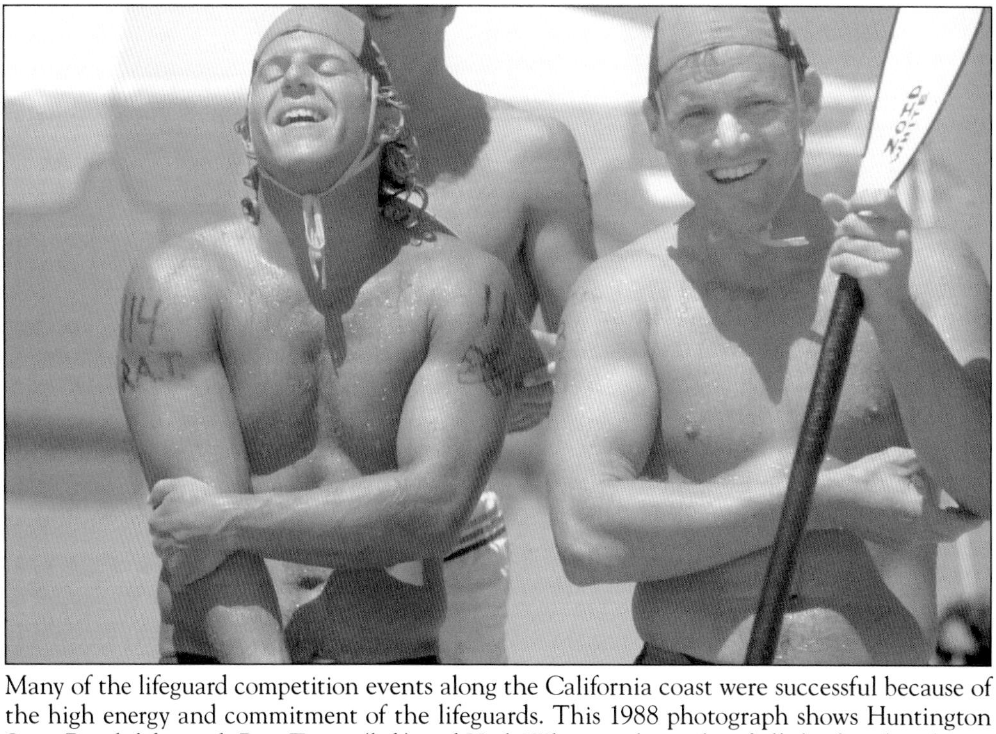

Many of the lifeguard competition events along the California coast were successful because of the high energy and commitment of the lifeguards. This 1988 photograph shows Huntington State Beach lifeguards Ron Tassin (left) and Herb White in the midst of all the fun that day.

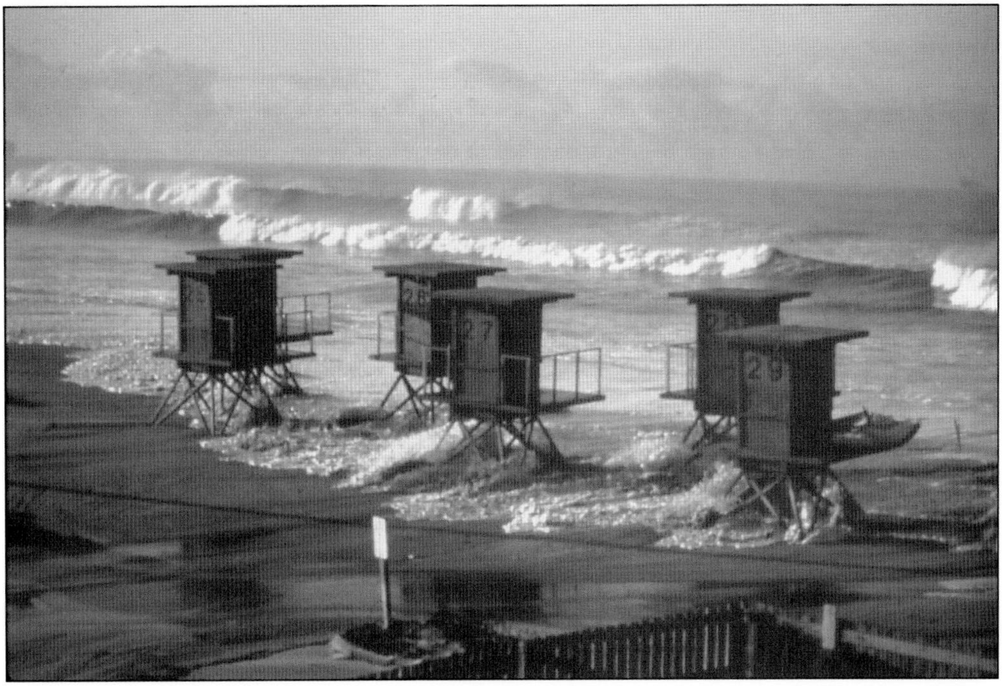

Each year, the Bolsa lifeguard towers are stacked together for the winter and off-season. During this 1988 storm, the combination high tide and large surf gave the towers a heavy saltwater rinse and nearly washed them away. This was the same storm that damaged the old Huntington Beach Pier for the last time.

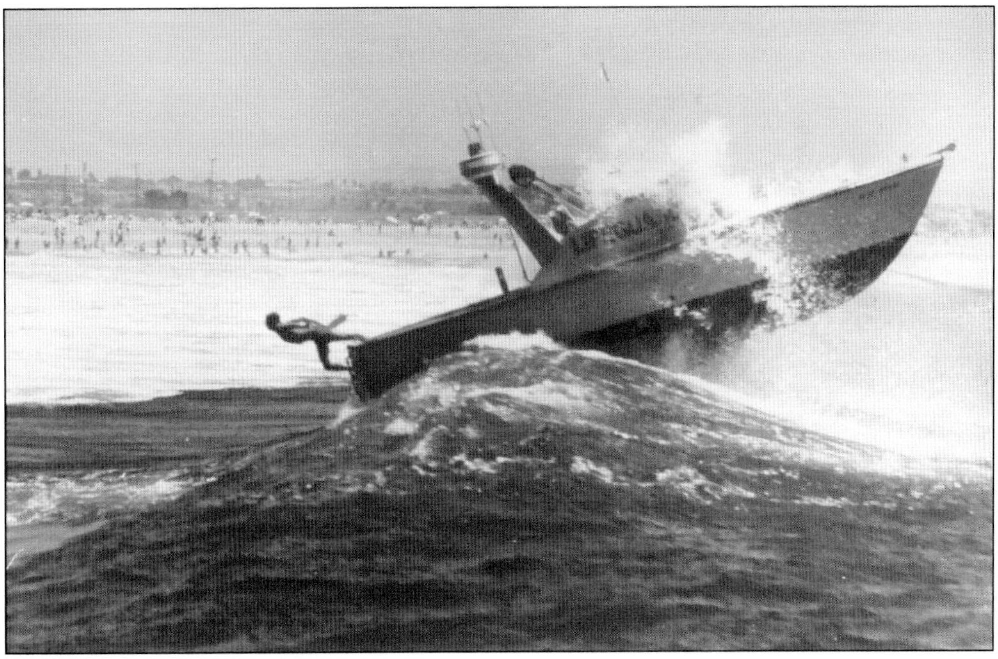

This popular 1992 photograph was taken near Beach Boulevard and demonstrates how close *Surfwatch* can back up to the surf line and drop off the deckhand. Swimmers, boogie boarders, and even surfers in trouble are often surprised by how fast the lifeguard deckhand can meet them.

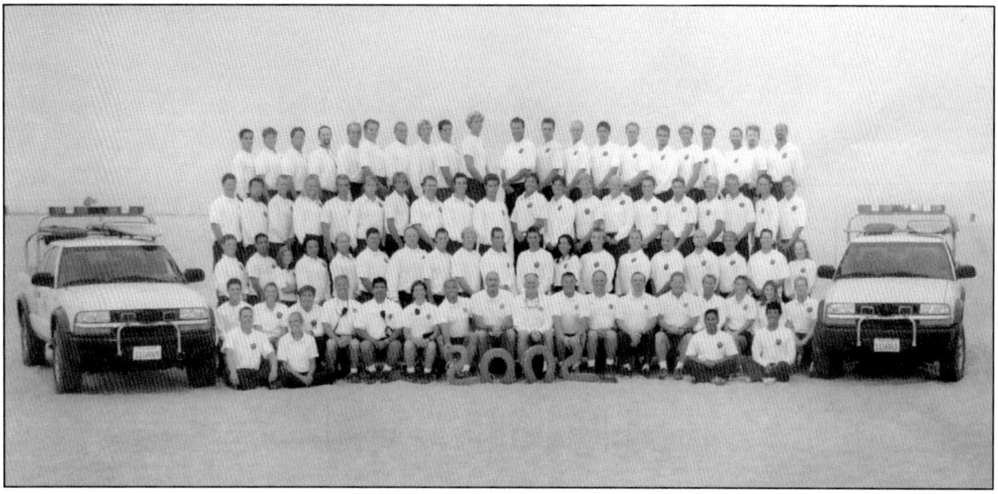

The 2002 Huntington and Bolsa lifeguard crew took this annual photograph in front of Magnolia Lifeguard Headquarters.

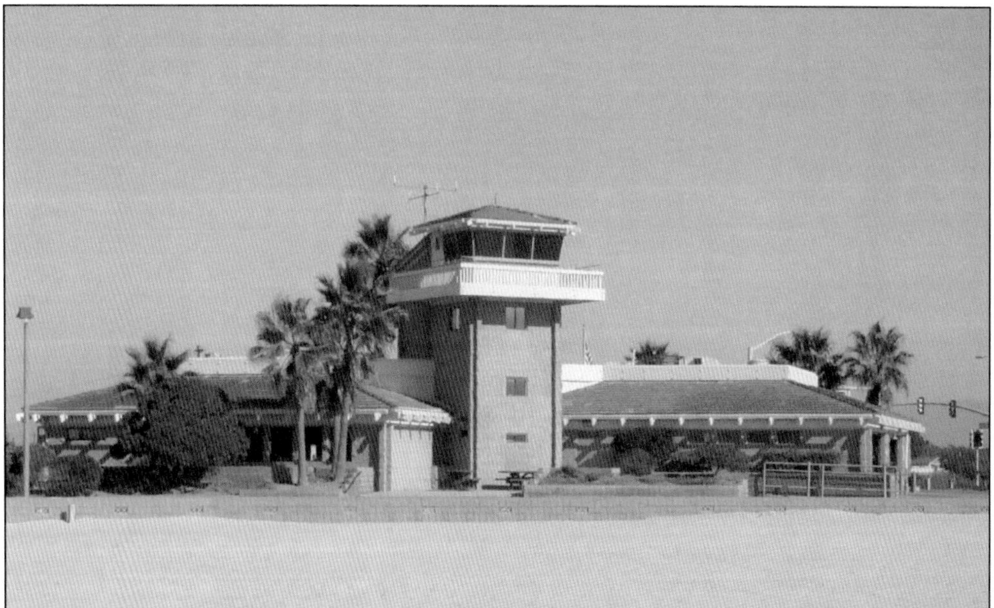

Huntington Beach is by far the busiest California Park State Beach in California based on the number of visitors and the services provided. This 2004 photograph shows the lifeguard headquarters, training facility, and observation tower at Magnolia Street and PCH.

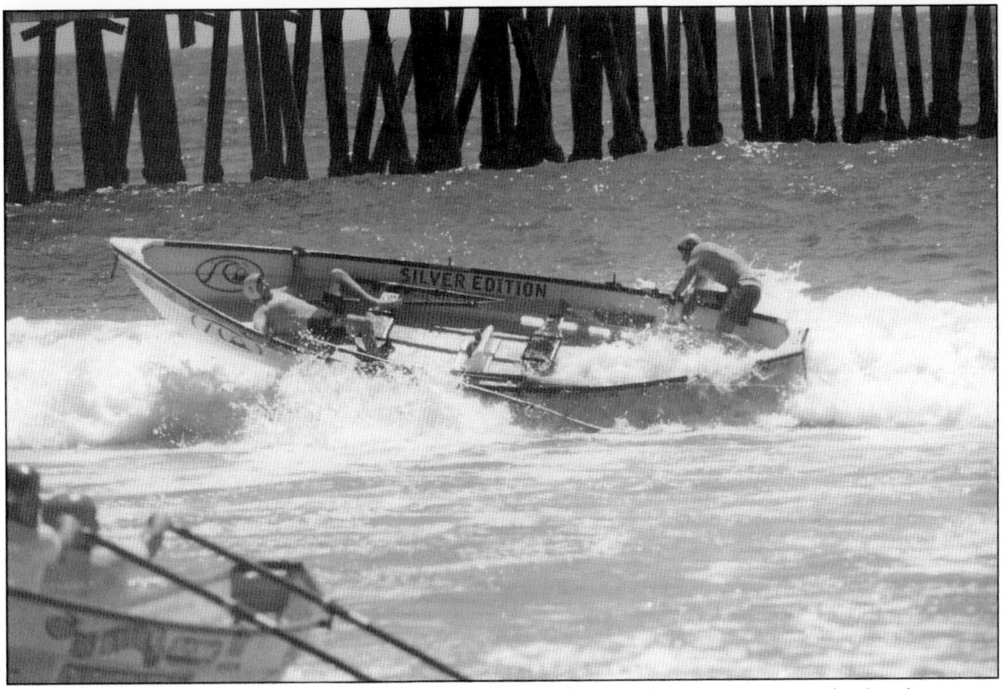

The Deboer brothers (identical twins) show their skill and ability to stay inside the dory near the end of the National Doryman's Association (NDA) three-lap dory race. This race was at the San Clemente Ocean Festival, held each summer in late July.

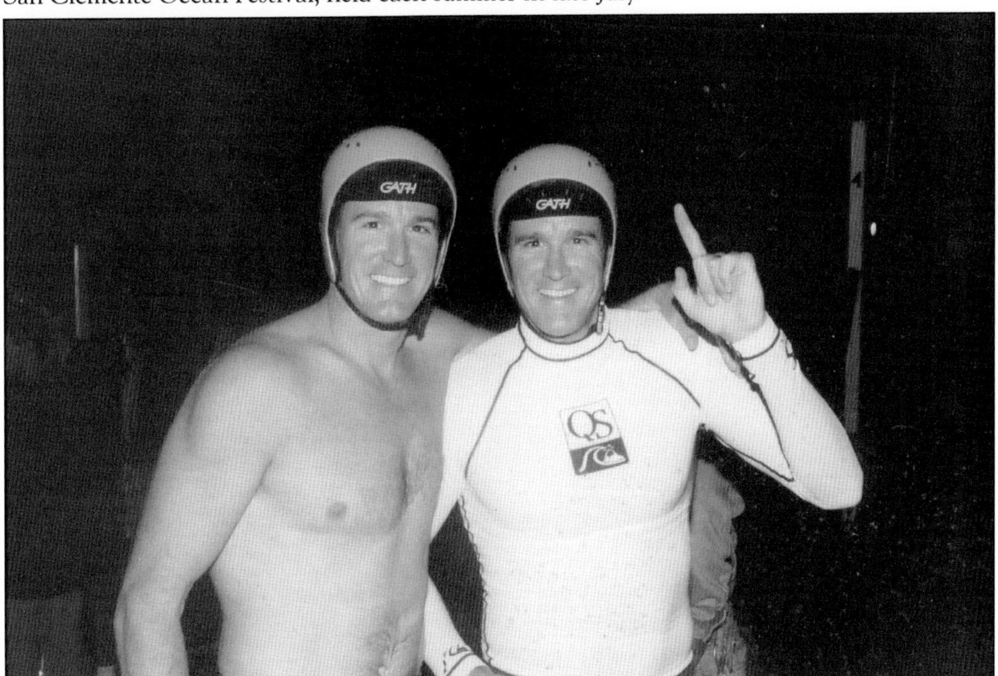

Dick and Dane Deboer (in no particular order) celebrate after a dory race, as they sometimes do. The Deboer brothers have entertained themselves and others at many lifeguard competitions since the early 1980s.

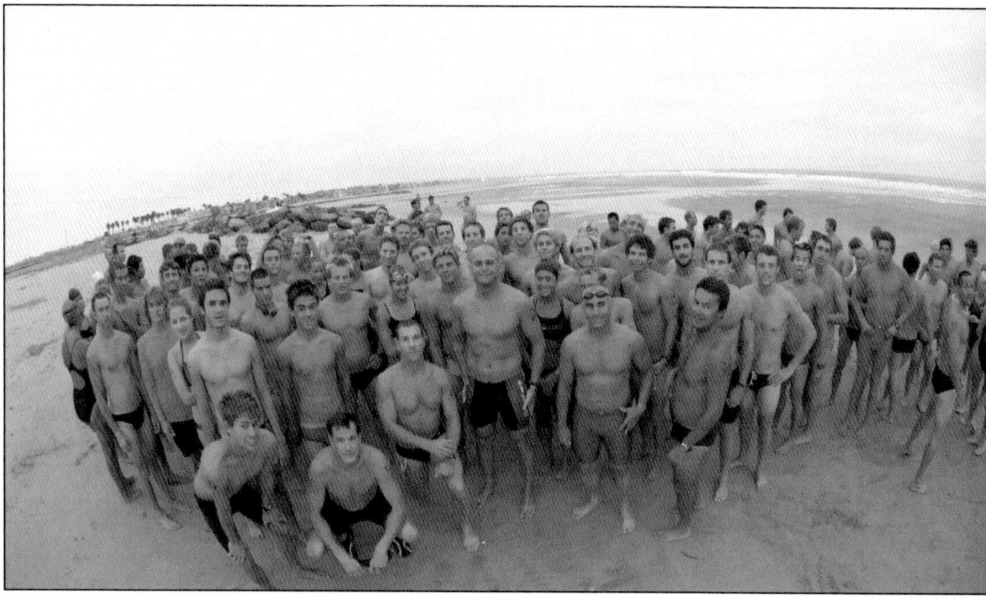

The 2007 Megacolossus, the pride and joy of the Huntington State Beach lifeguards, started at the Santa Ana River jetty. The event includes 4,000 yards of swimming (around the Newland buoy, pier, Twelfth Street buoy, and Bolsa buoy) and eight and a half miles of running. The finish line is at the west end of Bolsa Chica State Beach. The first Mega winner in 1979 was Mike Bartosh, and the current record holder, Marc Rinzler, holds the time of 1:28:15.

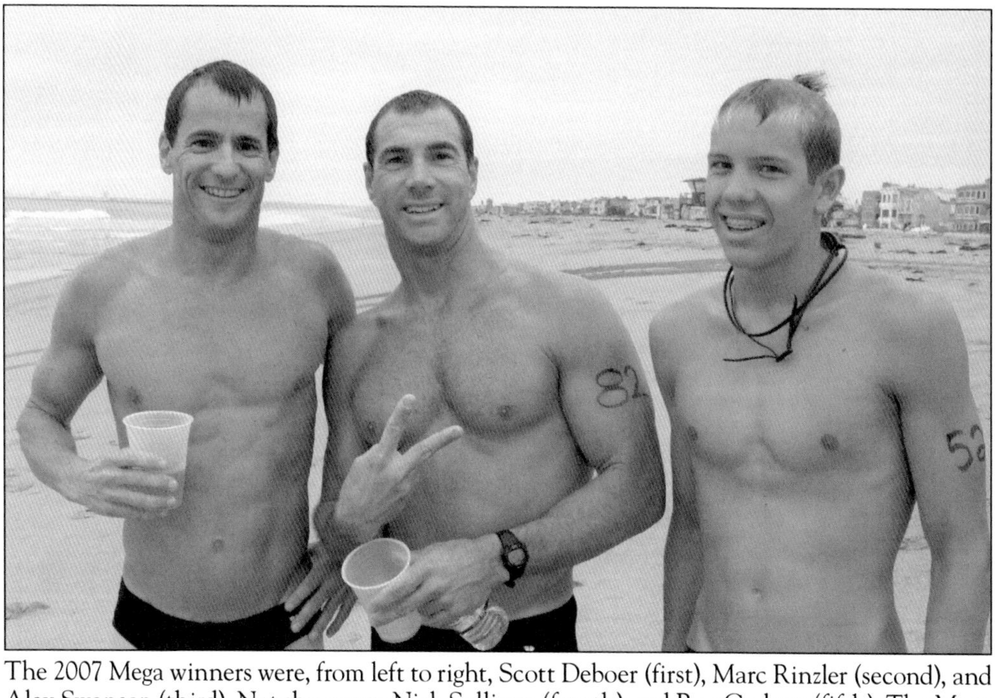

The 2007 Mega winners were, from left to right, Scott Deboer (first), Marc Rinzler (second), and Alex Swanson (third). Not shown are Nick Sullivan (fourth) and Ben Carlson (fifth). The Mega king and seven-time winner is Marc Rinzler. Schyler Kirby has won three times. Past winners include Andy (Miller) Bray, Gordon Duff, and Thomas Gallagher. Past race director Dick Deboer and John Rodgers dedicated the race to the memory of Ronnie A. Tassin in 2005.

Five

The Junior Lifeguard Program 1964–2007

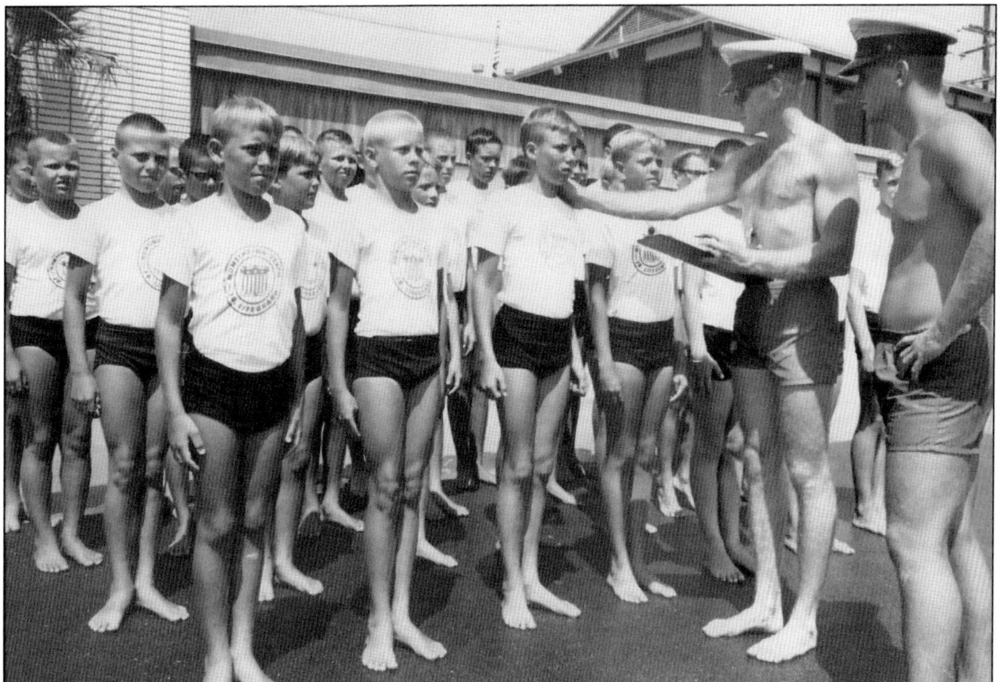

Jack Greenfield and Bill Rose in 1964 inspect the first group of Huntington Beach junior lifeguards who are wearing standard-issue black Speedos and white T-shirts. Push-ups, sit-ups, jumping jacks, and the response "yes, sir" were encouraged each day from the early days of the program.

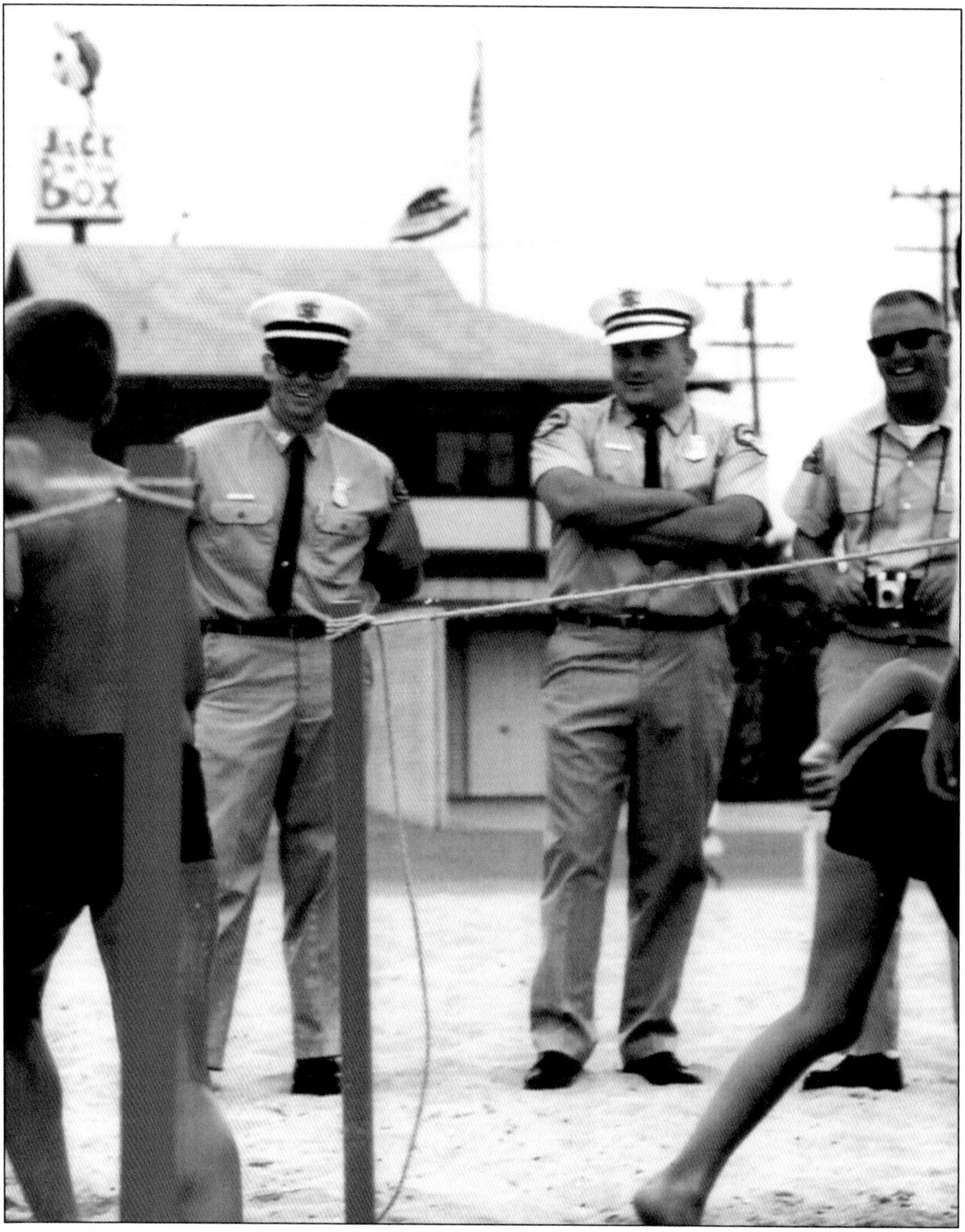

During the first year of the newly organized Huntington Beach Junior Lifeguard Program, other lifeguard agencies became interested in starting their own programs. Here, from left to right, Chief Moorhouse, Max Bowman, and visiting chief lifeguard Dick Hazard of San Clemente enjoy the youthful excitement on the sand.

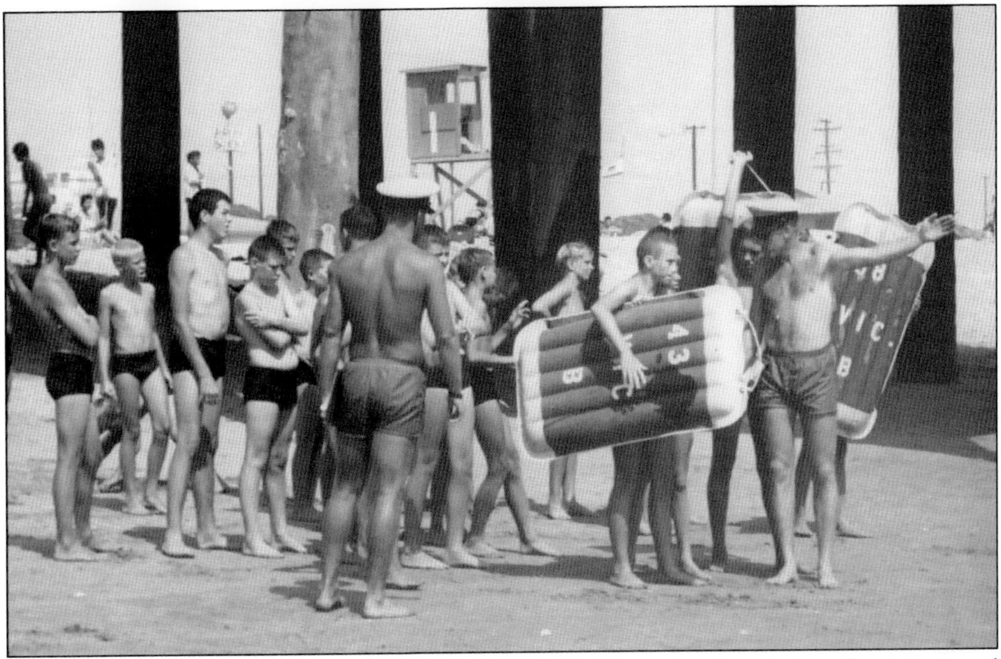

Rock-hard inflated surf mats were popular before the body board, or boogie board, was invented by Tom Morey in 1971. Next to the pier, Jack Greenfield (left) and Bill Rose prepare the boys for the start of a surf-mat relay. Vic's and Dwight's beach concessions provided the mats for several years.

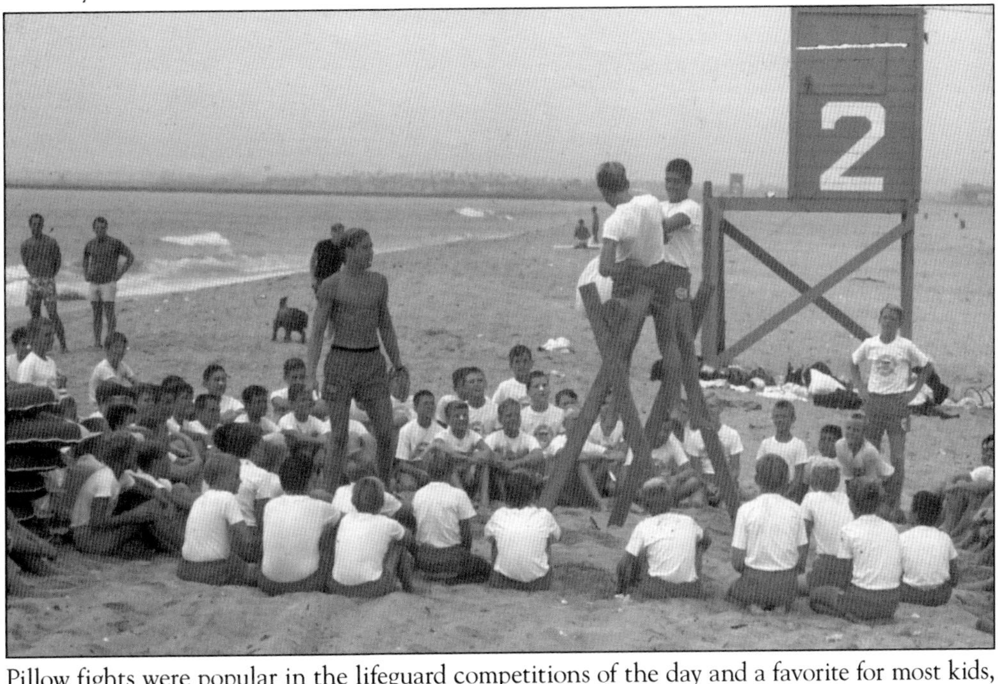

Pillow fights were popular in the lifeguard competitions of the day and a favorite for most kids, except for those with sunburned lips and noses. Sunset Beach was a county beach protected by Huntington lifeguards until the mid-1980s, and it was here on this day in 1968 that junior lifeguards took turns on the pillow-fight pole.

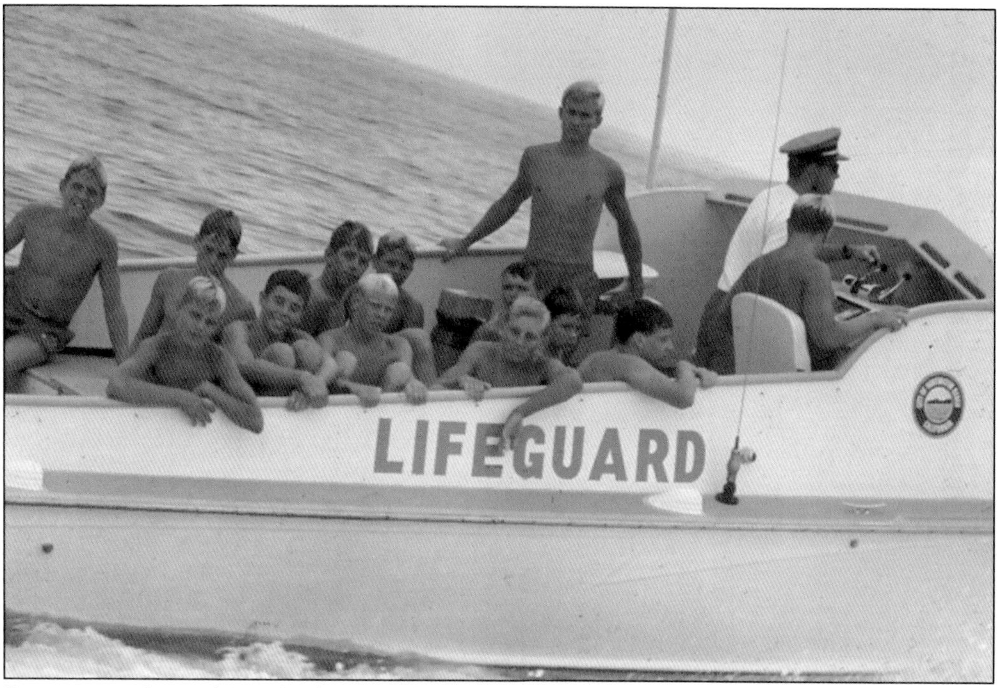

Swims out to *Sentinel* 5240 for the junior lifeguards were special occasions and carefully organized. This 1968 photograph has skipper or rescue boat operator Lyn Lockyer with a boat full of kids taking a run outside the surf line on the south side of the pier.

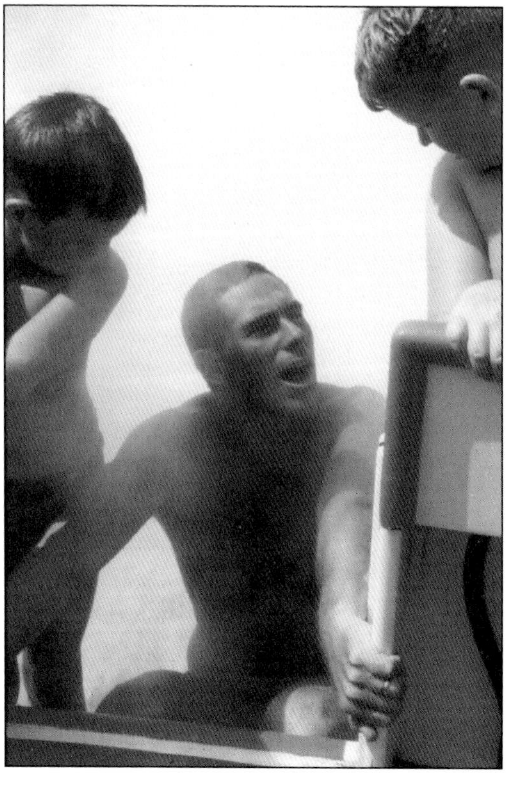

Junior lifeguard instructor Raymond Bray in this 1966 photograph helps prepare the two boys for what is likely their first speed drop from the stern of *Sentinel*. The drill goes like this: Walk or crawl out to the stern of the boat, step down to the swim step, hold on to the rail, sit, squeeze your buns, and let go when the deckhand says, "Go!"

The beautiful Pismo clams off the Huntington Beach shores disappeared in the late 1980s. On this day in 1975, however, Bray returned to the beach with his wet suit full of Pismo clams. He was so weighted down by clams that he bounced off the bottom and then to the surface to get a breath, all the way back to shore. The clam chowder, like Bray, was legendary.

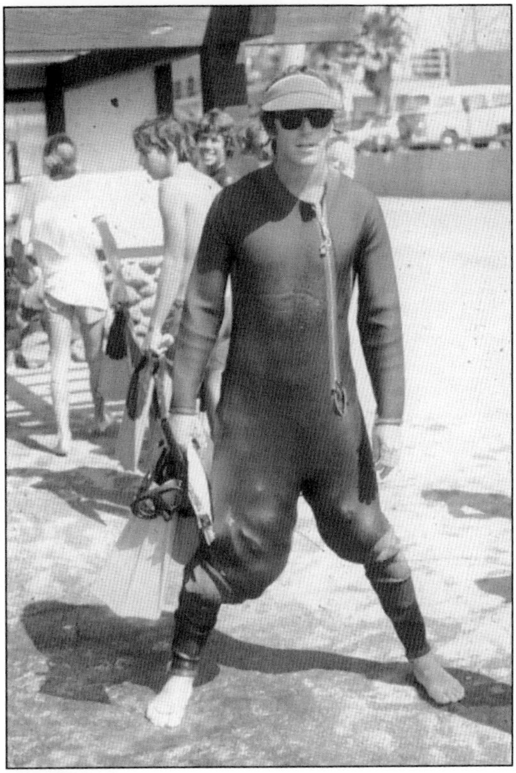

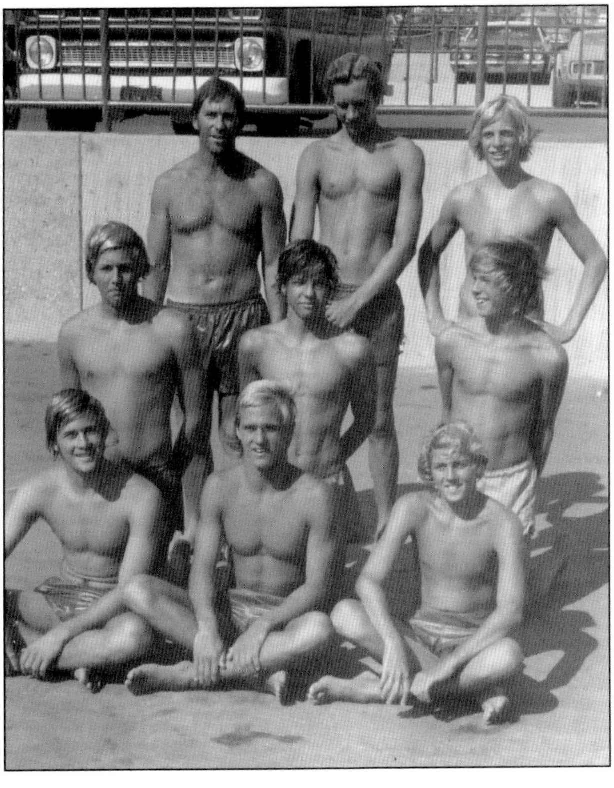

The first of many unbelievable Bray events was this 1975 U.S.–Mexico border coastal run-swim-run to Huntington Beach, swimming around every pier along the way. Hungry and tired are, from left to right, the following: (first row) Mike Brayman, Andy Miller, and Mark Reddick (age 14); (second row) Bill Taylor, Kai Weisser, and Tom Taylor; (third row) Ray Bray, Ron Lade, and Howard Furlong. Each year the distance increased until it was agreed Point Conception was far enough.

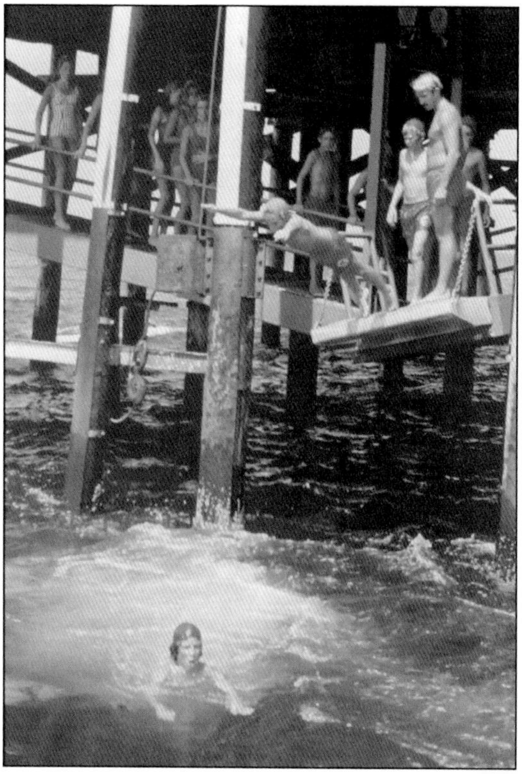

Junior lifeguard instructor Brian Gerold in 1975 took his group to ramp at the end of the pier. This, too, was a favorite event where the lifeguard rescue vessel sometimes would be waiting to pick up the junior lifeguards for speed drops.

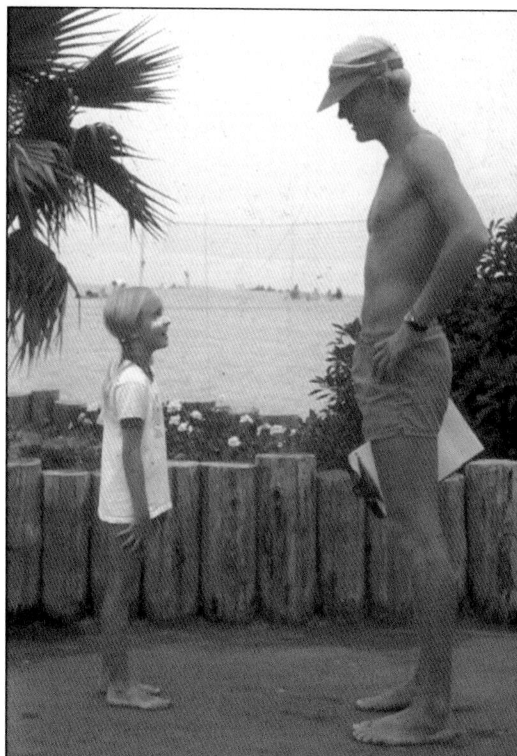

The year 1975 was a good one for photographs of the HB Junior Lifeguard Program, such as this image, simply called "Little and Big." A very small Tracy Melvin and "C" junior lifeguard looks up to very big junior lifeguard instructor Bruce Cleeland.

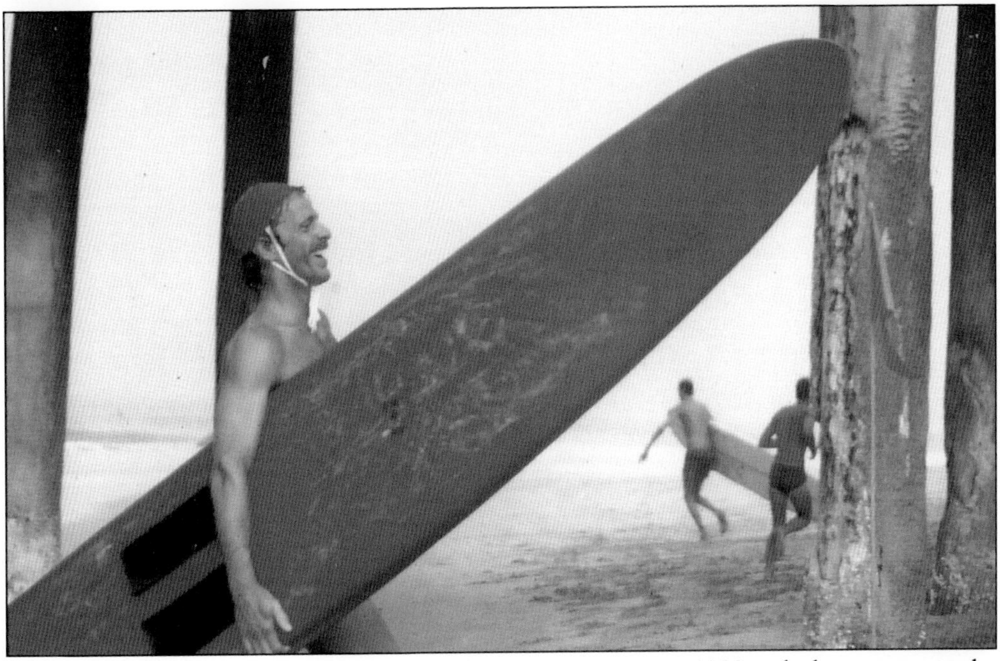

Junior lifeguard "B" group instructor Howard Furlong competes in 1980 with the captains in the traditional lifeguard iron man event. This event's focus is the pier and includes the distance of a two-mile run, pier swim, and pier paddle. The order of each component is usually different at each event and organized to share the paddleboards among competitors.

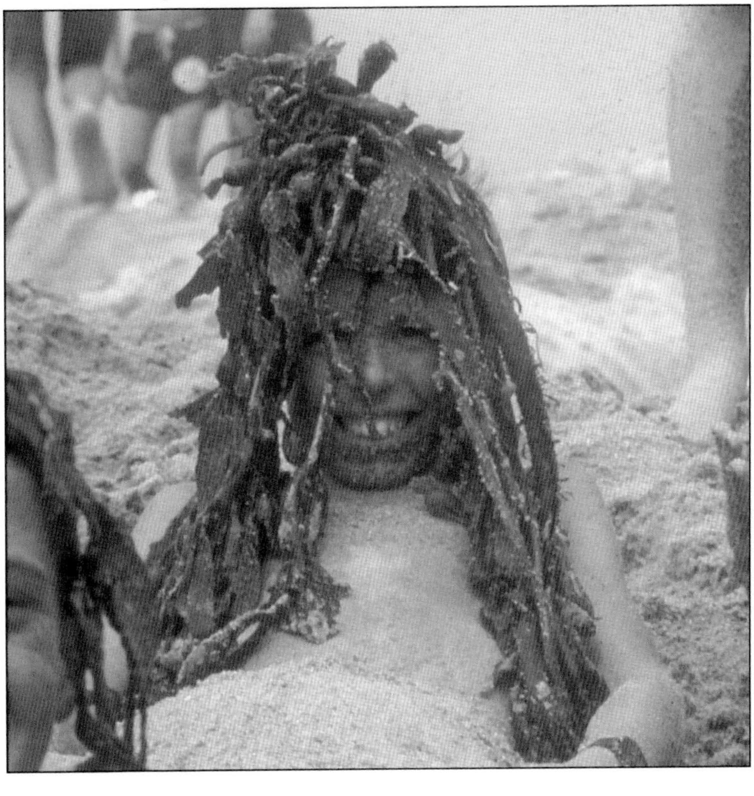

Junior lifeguards may just have a little too much fun at the beach. This little one got the chance to cover himself in sand and kelp during a break or just after doing an "Iguana." After jumping in the water, junior lifeguards take turns crawling down a long, dug-out trench while friends pile sand on top.

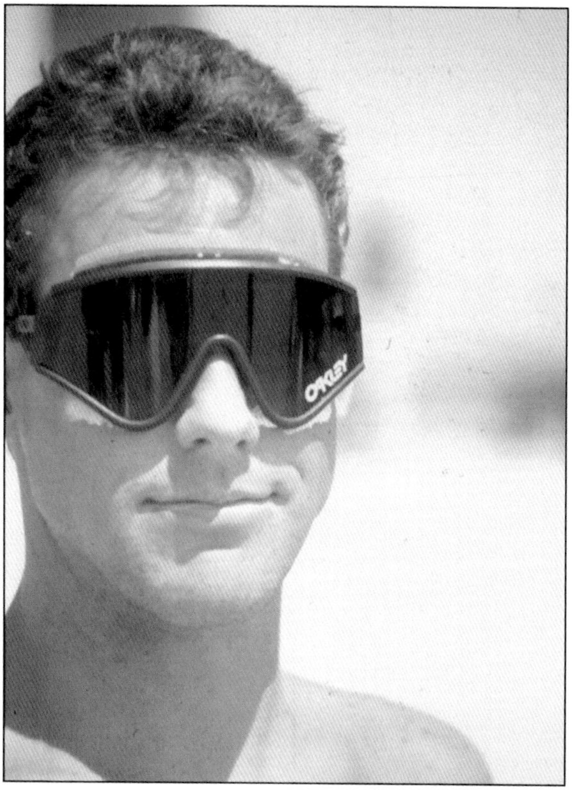

Junior lifeguard "C" instructor Tom Gallagher on occasion ran to work from his home in Long Beach, kept his junior lifeguards busy all day, and then ran back home from Huntington. Within the international triathlon community, in 1988, Gallagher was ranked the seventh best in the world. Gallagher, Gordon Duff, and Andy (Miller) Bray were all past winners of the infamous state beach run-swim-run Megacolossus.

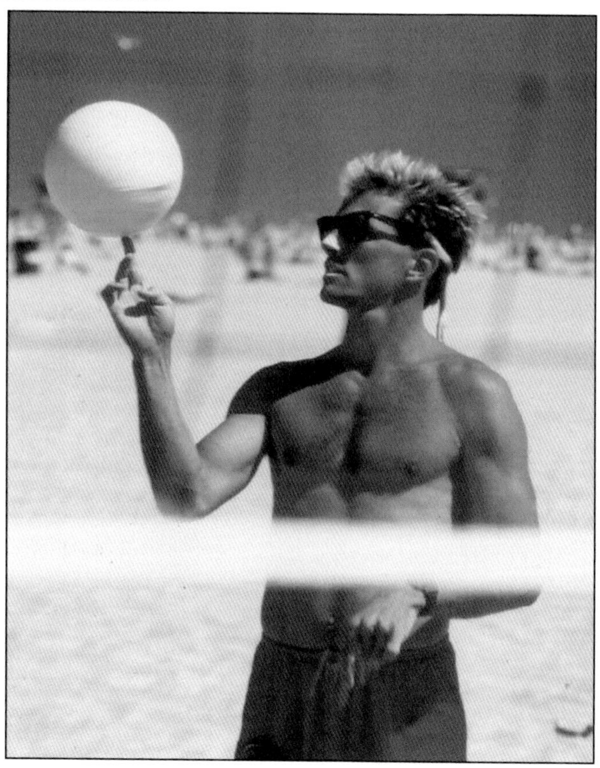

Junior lifeguard "A" and later captains instructor Gordon MacDuff, seen here in this 1989 photograph, rarely missed the traditional instructor volleyball game during lunch break. As a junior lifeguard, Gordon completed the longest Ray Bray run-swim-run from Point Conception to Huntington Beach. He is also a three-time national lifeguard winner of the three-kilometer beach run, three-time consecutive winner of the Catalina Marathon, and three time competitor in the Hawaiian Ironman.

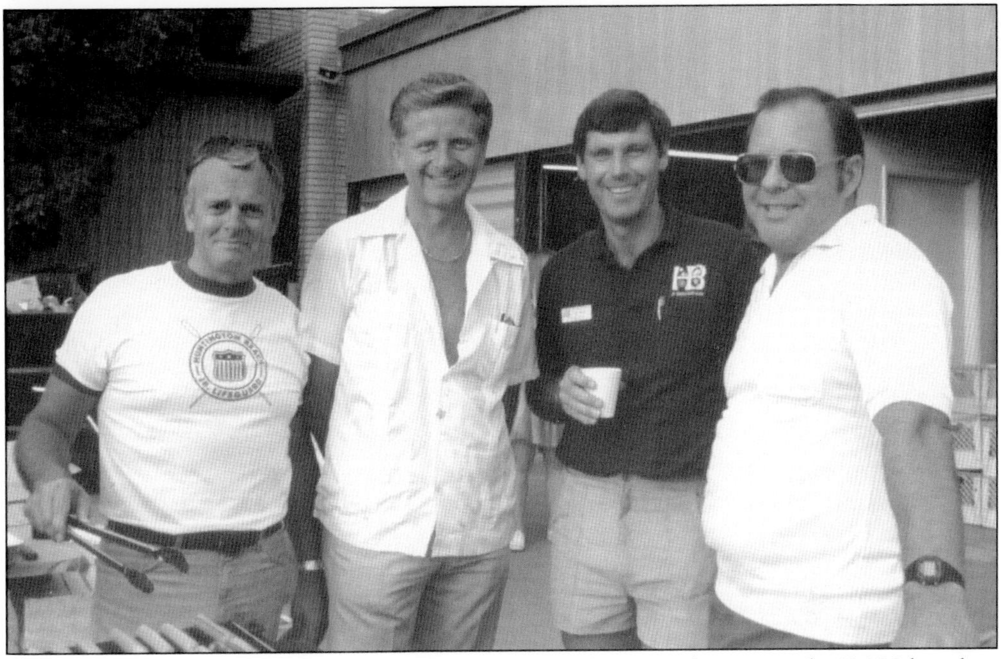

The annual junior lifeguard hot dog barbecue is more than a tradition; nearly 10,000 hot dogs are cooked each summer. The now 1,000-strong youth group enjoys the event with family and friends. Seen here working the grill in 1983 are, from left to right, Max Bowman, city councilman Don MacAllister, Dave Simcox, and Doug D'Arnall.

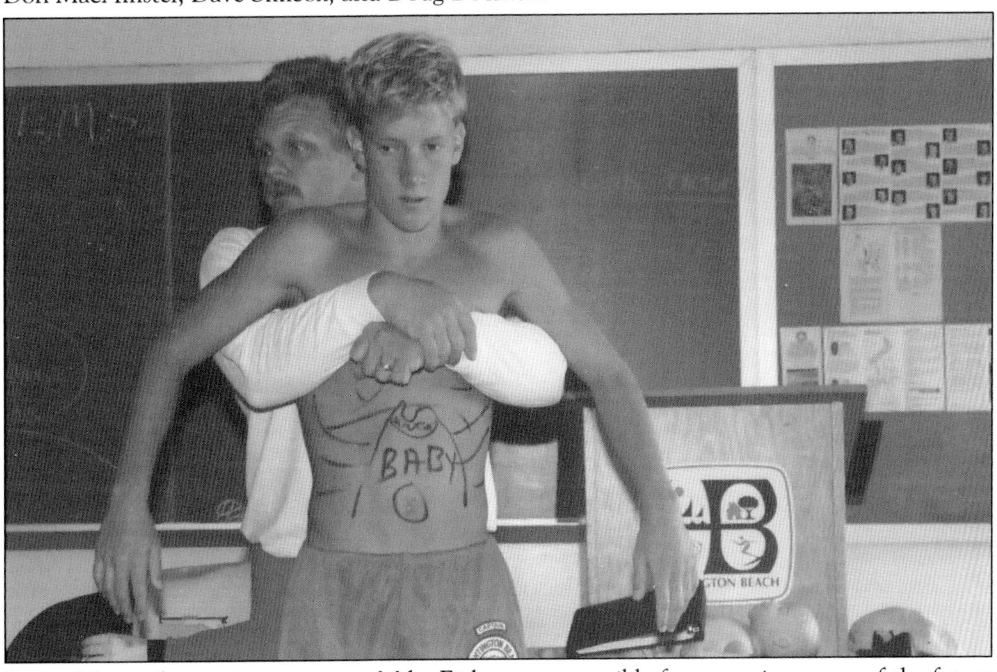

Junior lifeguard captains instructor Mike Eich was responsible for preparing many of the future Huntington Beach lifeguards. He also continues to instruct for the lifeguard cadet school each year in the spring. In this 1992 photograph, Eich demonstrates the relief of an obstructed airway with a willing and "pregnant" captain and later lifeguard Dave Prior.

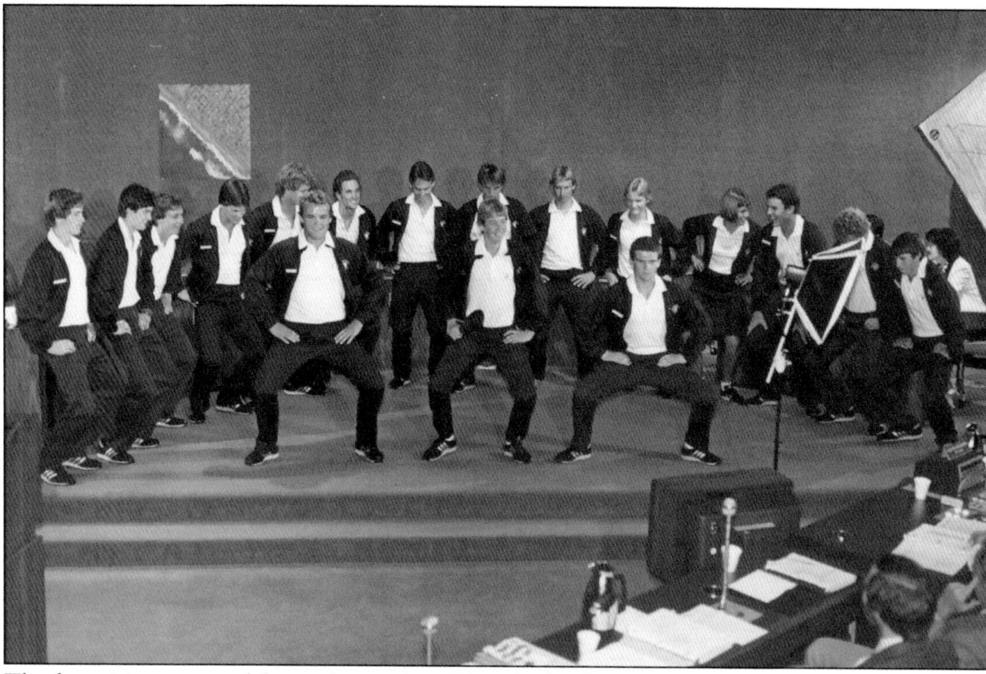

The first visiting junior lifeguard team from New Zealand in 1983 performs the traditional Maori "Haka" in the Huntington Beach city council chambers. The tradition of this exchange program, with the kiwis visiting every other year and the Huntington Beach junior lifeguards visiting New Zealand, continues today.

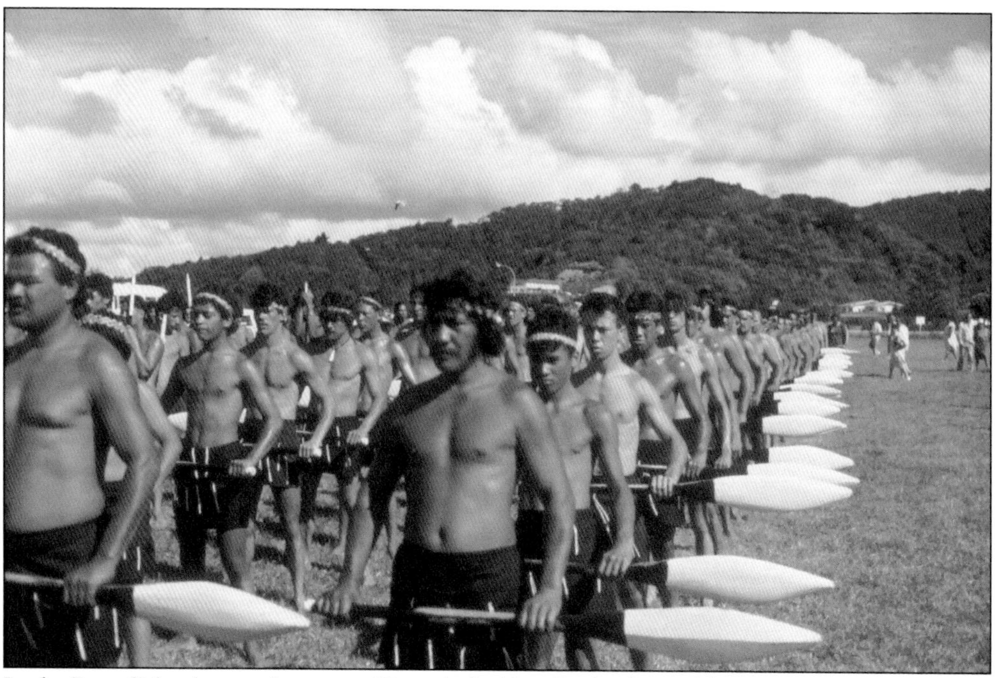

In the Bay of Islands near the town of Russel, the New Zealanders celebrate their national holiday Waitangi Day in 1986. The cultural and international travel experience the junior lifeguards obtain is priceless.

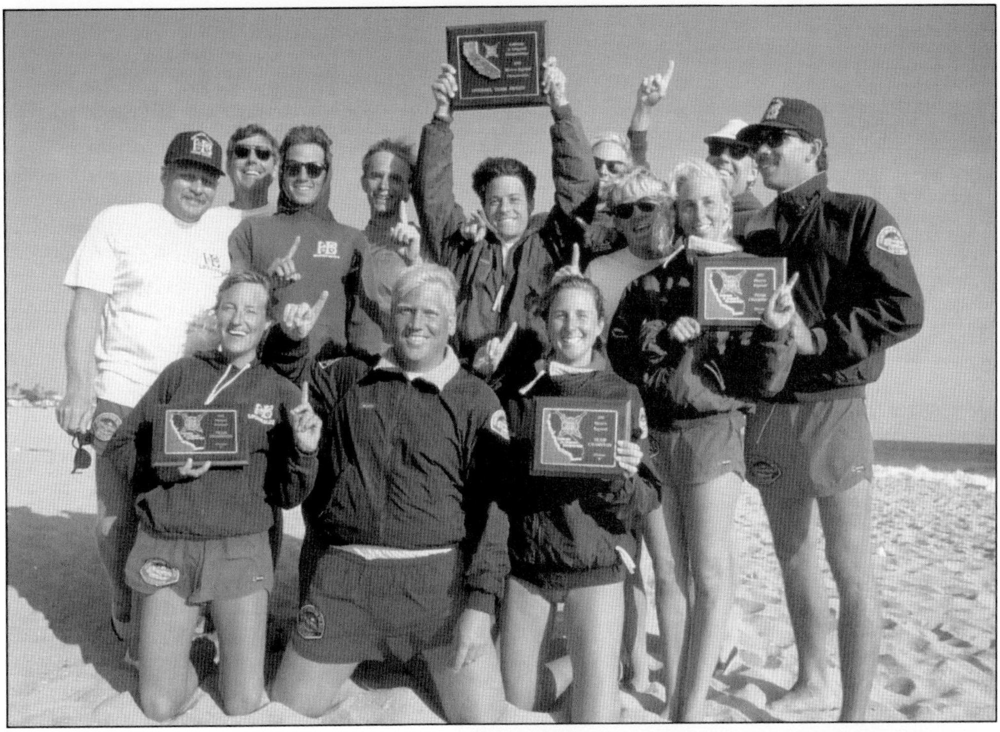

The California Surf Life Saving Junior Lifeguard Championships each summer sees teams participate from Santa Cruz to Imperial Beach. Here, in 1991, the Huntington City instructors display their awards and include, from left to right, the following: (first row) Karen Crow, Dave Wilson, and Morgan Marklinger; (second row) Jay Duebler, Jeanene Bryant, Tom Denny, and Matt Whitmore; (third row) Mike Eich, Dave Simcox, Jason Huffman, Charlie Bush, Brendan Carroll, and unidentified.

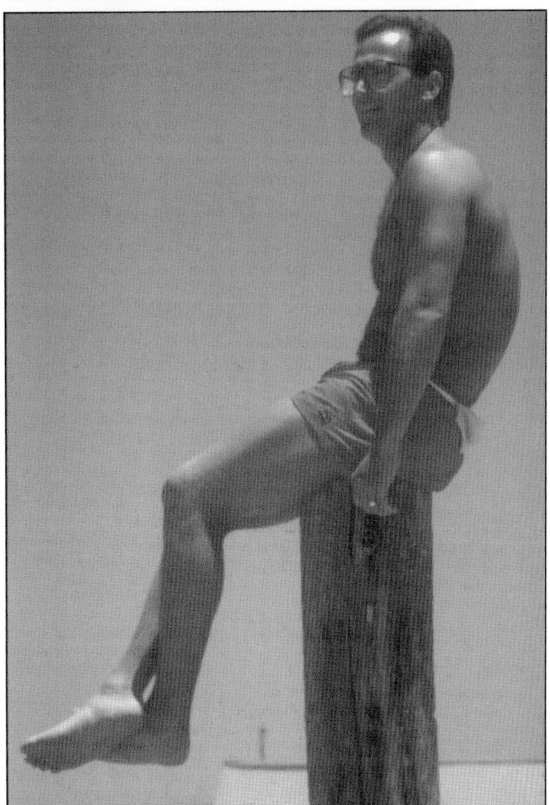

Junior lifeguard "A" instructor Andy Bray in 1985 surveys from on high the land of junior lifeguards. In 1995, Andy changed his last name to that of the man who raised him, Raymond Bray. Andy is an All-American swimmer who has won several annual Huntington Beach pier swims and competed in the World Championship Open Water 25 kilometer in 2003. Two of Andy's three children were Huntington Beach Lifeguards in 2007, Elisabeth and Kenneth Bray.

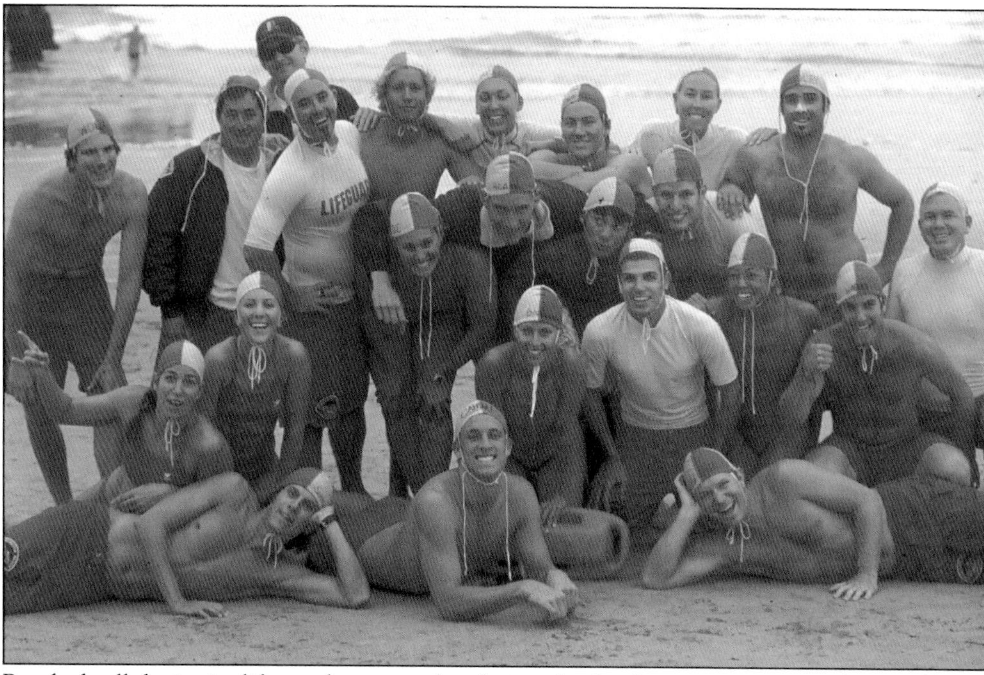

Rarely do all the junior lifeguards get together during the day for an event, except for possibly the two-mile beach run. Even rarer is this 2004 junior lifeguard instructor group photograph next to the pier with them acting a little silly after what are called "All Ins."

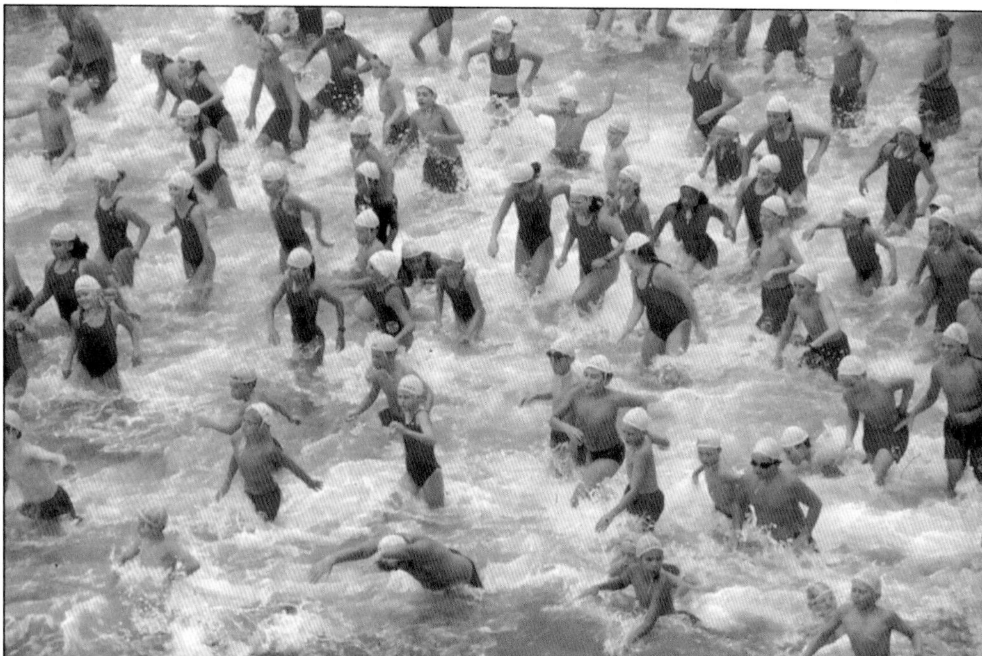

In 2007, the junior lifeguard "C" group, wearing their yellow beanies, could be seen from the pier entering the water on the west or north side. When a large group of junior lifeguards enter the water like this, it is called a "mass pier swim" and even the territorial surfers move aside. An event like this is a great sight to see.

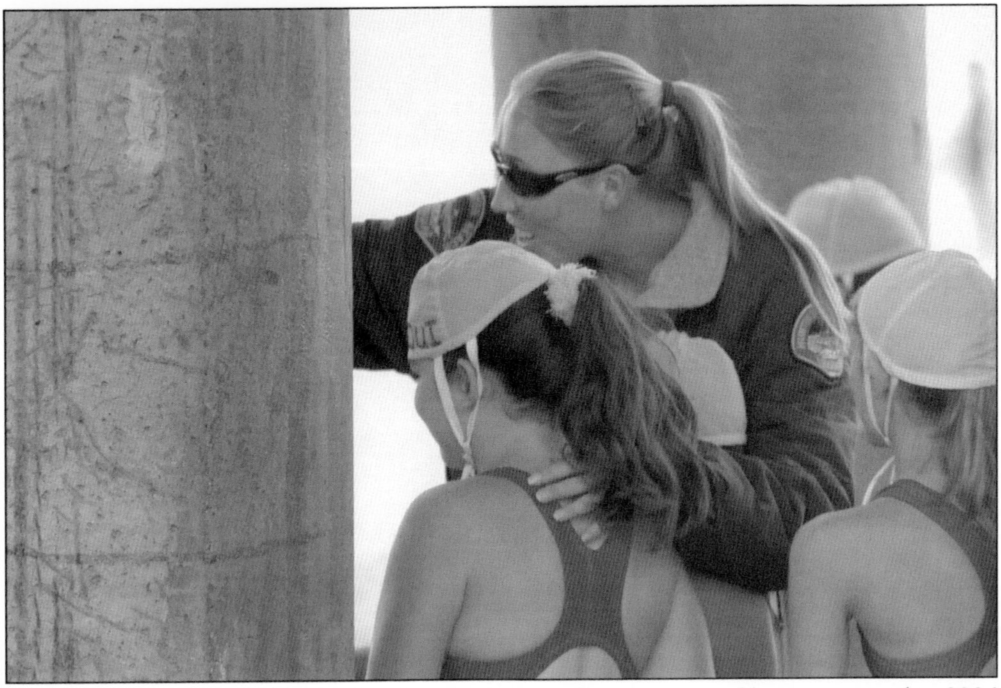

Junior lifeguard "C" instructor Brooke Flemming talks to a part of her group in this 2006 photograph. Pier orientation and safety is an integral part of the program and begins at the pier pilings on dry sand.

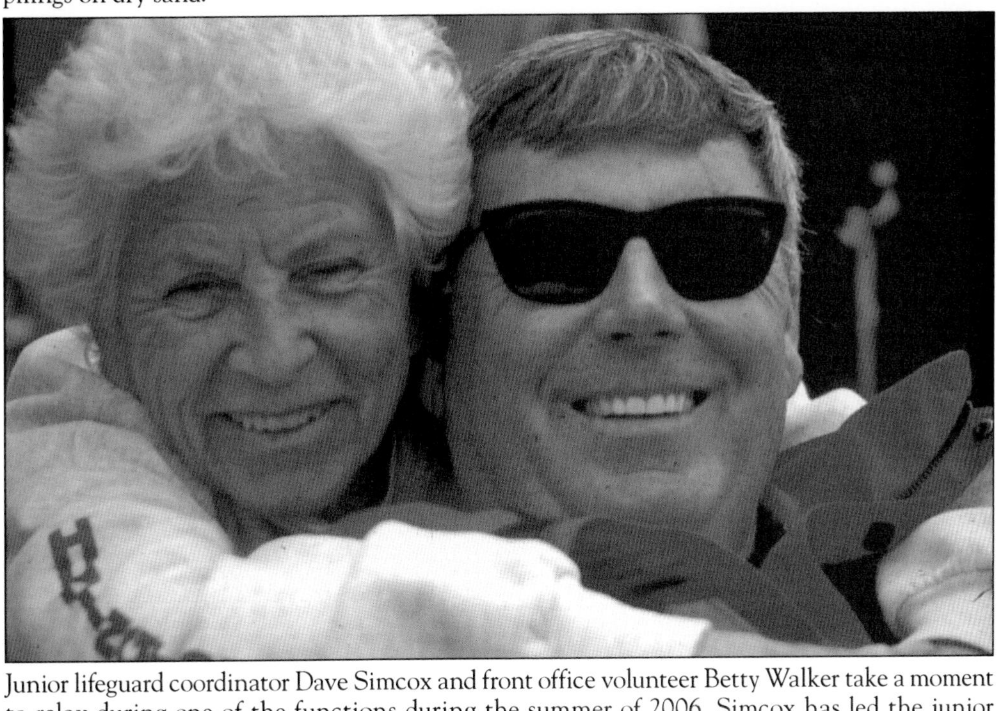

Junior lifeguard coordinator Dave Simcox and front office volunteer Betty Walker take a moment to relax during one of the functions during the summer of 2006. Simcox has led the junior lifeguards, the city's premier youth program, since 1976 and has received several awards starting back in 1980 at the Chamber of Commerce Public Safety Awards.

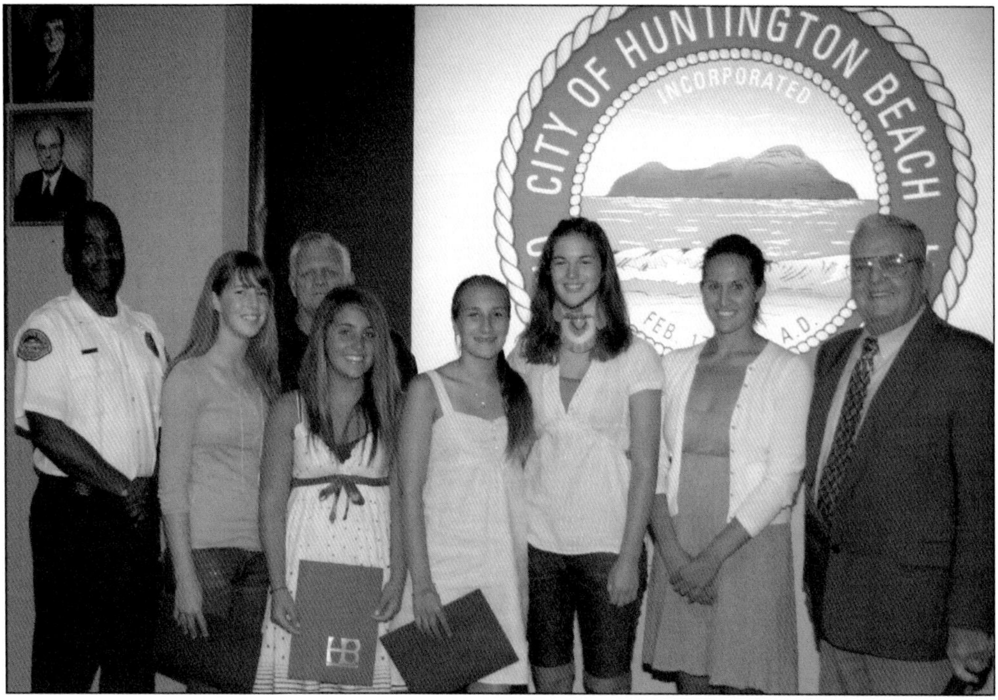

Three Huntington Beach junior lifeguards saved their best friend's life and received the Good Samaritan Award from the chamber of commerce. They were also recognized by the City of Huntington Beach and the California Surf Life Saving Association. Devyn Bisson injured her cervical spine while surfing and benefited from her friends' use of the training skills recently taught by their instructor Kristina Eich. Pictured are, from left to right, marine safety chief Kyle Lindo, Paige Bisson, Mike Eich, Carley Zylstra, Kyle Cucinotti, Devyn Bisson, Kristina Eich, and Mayor Gil Coerper.

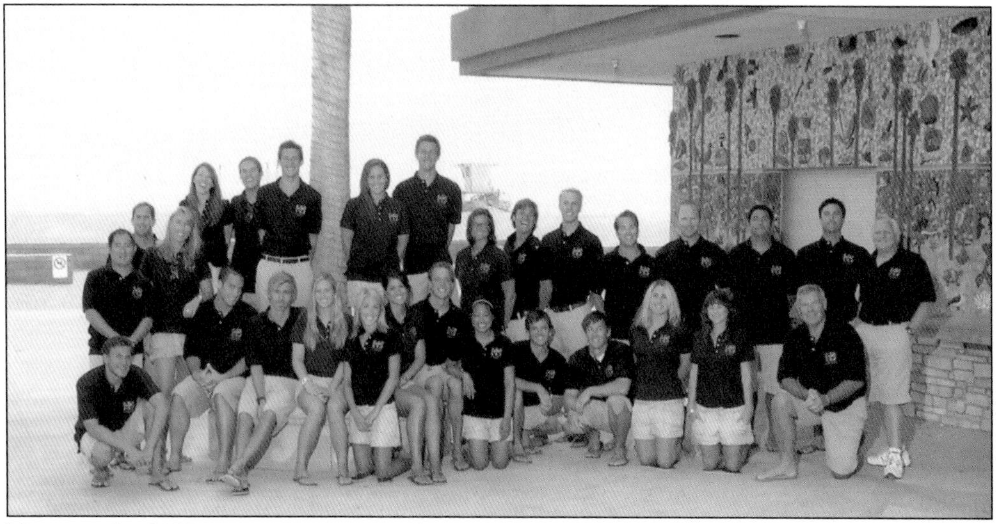

Here are the 2007 instructors next to the new Huntington Beach Marine Safety Educational Center, the home of the junior lifeguards. They can be contacted by phone at (714) 374-1501, on the Internet at www.juniorguard.com, or by mail at P.O. Box 190, Huntington Beach, CA, 92648.

Six

Surf City USA® and Beyond 2000-2007

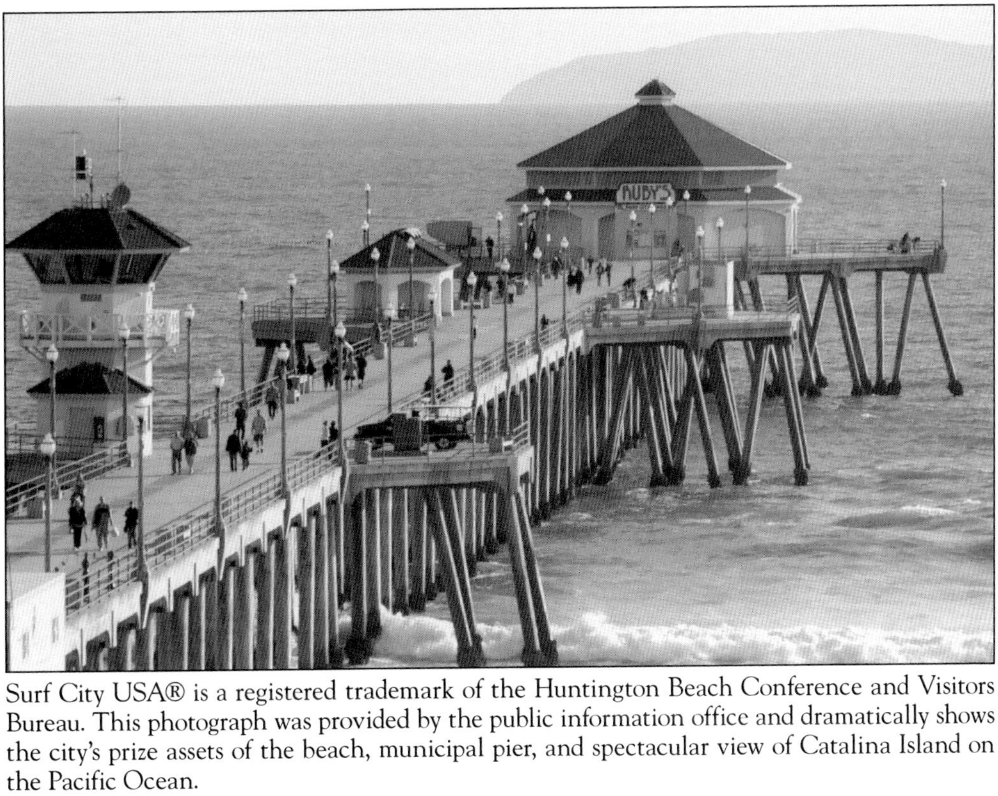

Surf City USA® is a registered trademark of the Huntington Beach Conference and Visitors Bureau. This photograph was provided by the public information office and dramatically shows the city's prize assets of the beach, municipal pier, and spectacular view of Catalina Island on the Pacific Ocean.

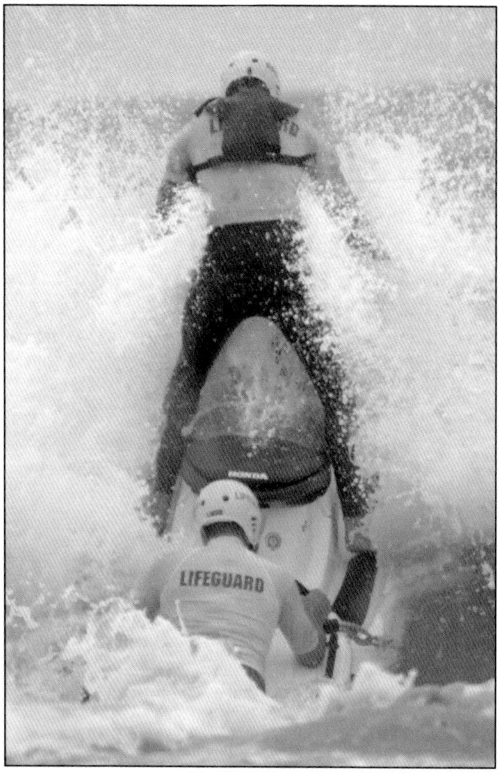

The Personal Water Craft (PWC) became an integral part of the marine safety operation in the early 1990s. In this 2002 photograph, marine safety officer Eric Ching operates, with a lifeguard on the rescue sled, a Honda-sponsored PWC, four-cylinder, 746-pound AquaTrax.

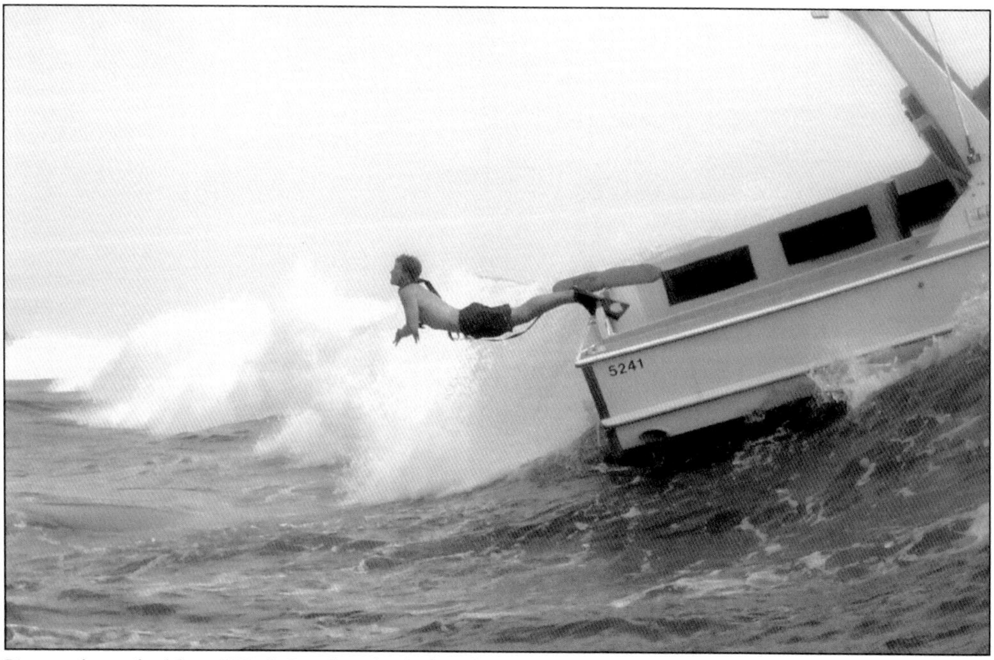

Rescue boat deckhand Kirk Sandvig had already gotten the "go!" and leapt off the stern of *Sentinel* 5240 in this 2003 photograph. A deckhand will beat a beach lifeguard to the rescue nearly every time. Given the right surf conditions, *Sentinel* 5240 is a critical asset to the marine safety operation and for preventing the loss of life.

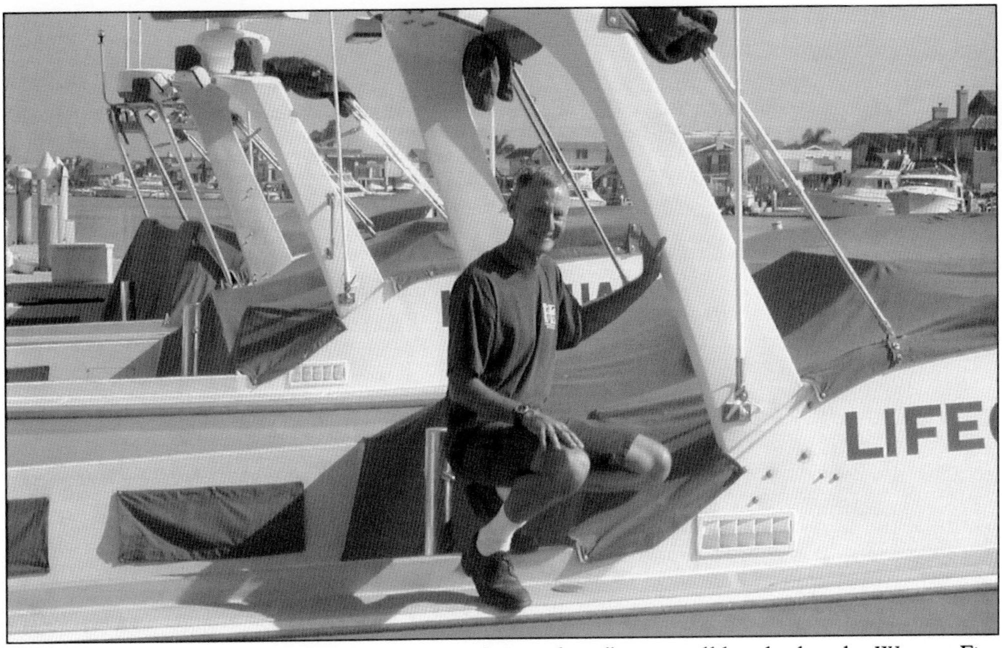

The *Sentinel*, *Sentinel II* and *III*, and the retired *Guardian* fleet are all berthed at the Warner Fire Station lifeguard rescue boat dock. Here, in 2003, the keeper of the fleet, Carl Pearce, proudly stands at the dock.

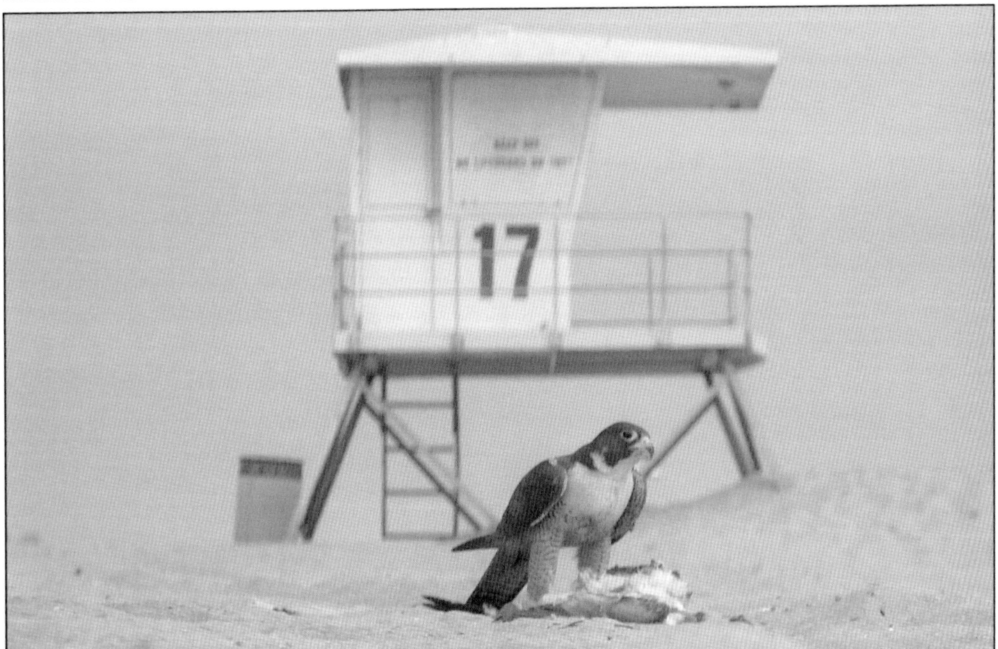

The wildlife encounters for lifeguards are typically injured or sick sea lions, pelicans, grebes, and seagulls. Laguna Beach Friends of the Sea Lion will pick up seals and rehabilitate them. Others can be transported in the lifeguard truck to the Wetlands and Wildlife Care Center of Orange County on PCH and Newland Street. In 2002, this falcon stopped to feast in view of the lifeguard on patrol.

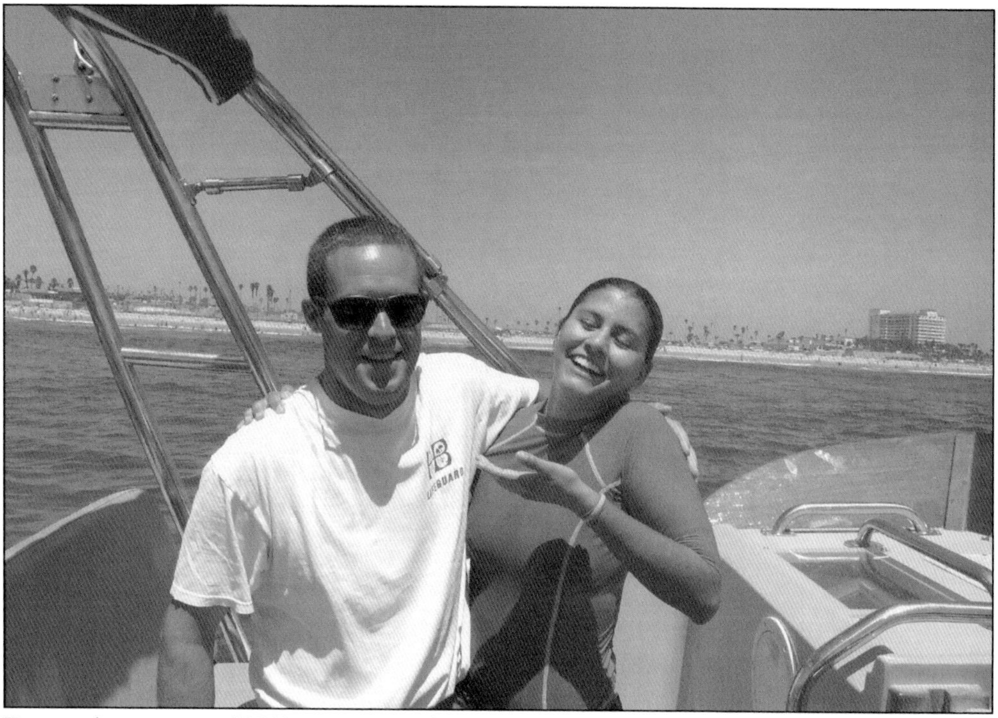

During the summer of 2002, rescue vessel 5240 was seen south of the pier waiting for the next rescue call. Here deckhand Scott Magnuson welcomes lifeguard Lindsey Ortega, who swam out from shore during her break at dispatch.

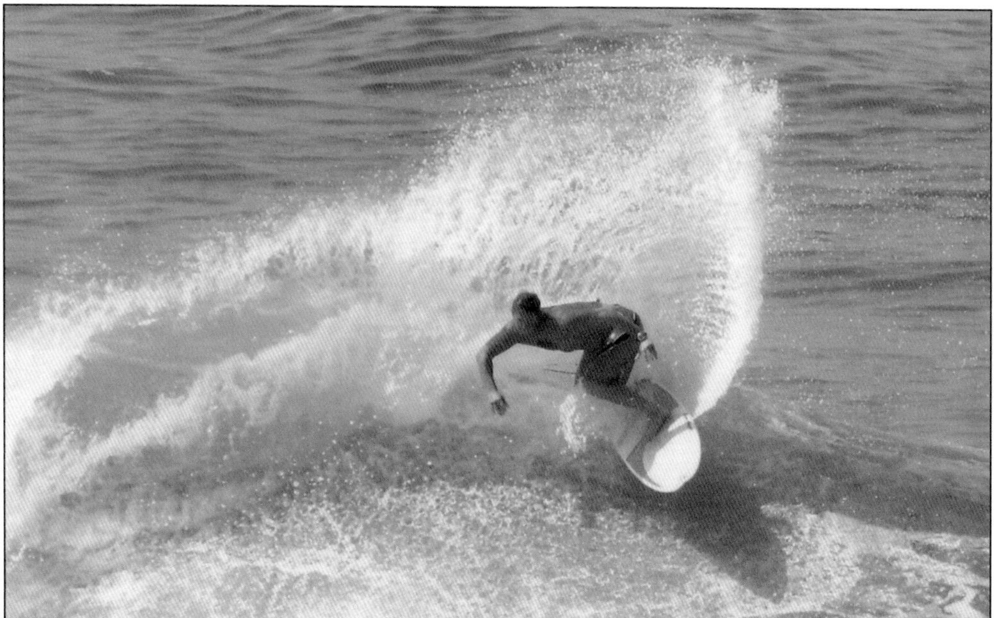

Greg Eisele was a lifeguard north of Durban, South Africa, and the 1993 national surf champion. While working as a lifeguard in Huntington, Eisele also was the overall winner and "Super Heat" champion in the Huntington Beach City summer surf contest from 2000 to 2003.

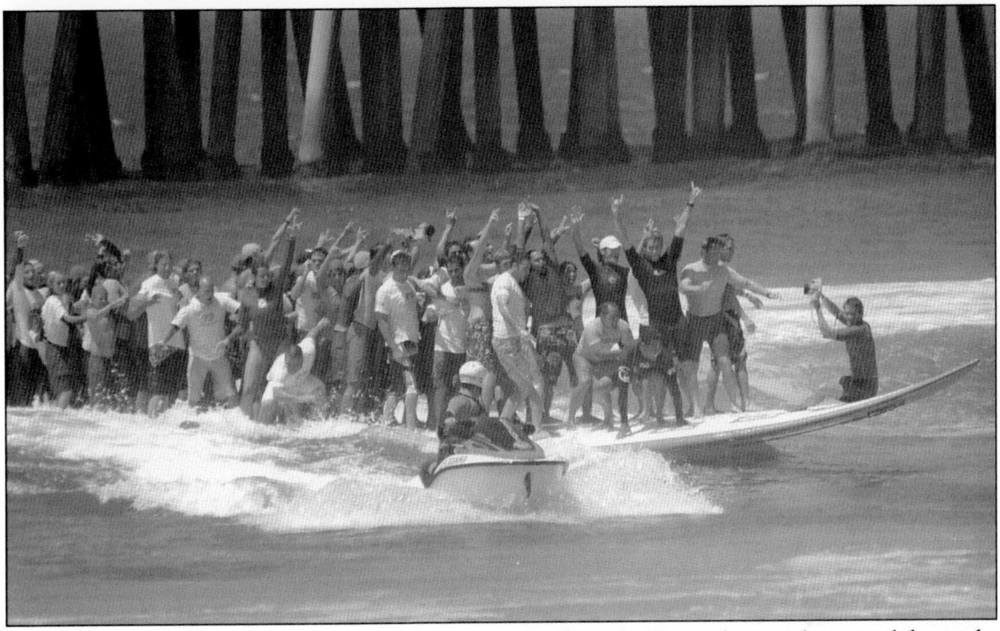

A Guinness World Record Longest Surfboard was made with 60 people, mostly junior lifeguards, lifeguards, and local surfers, during the 2005 U.S. Open of Surfing. The Nev Hyman, 1,200-pound surfboard (without 60 people) was towed in by marine safety officer Matt Karl. All three giant fins snapped off in the shore break.

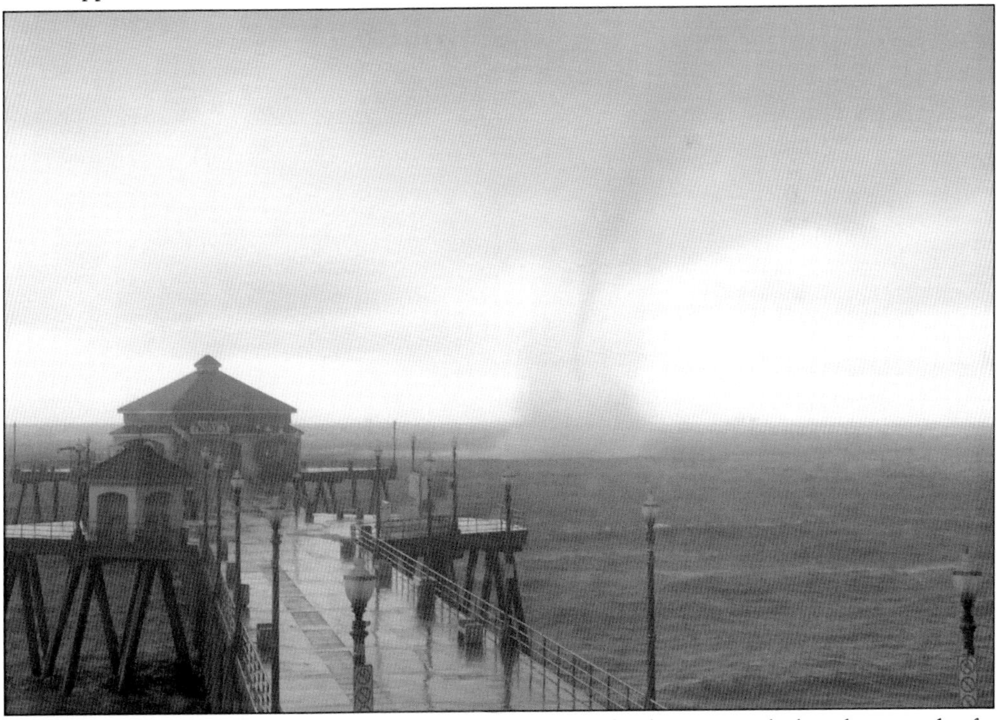

On February 19, 2005, at 7:35 a.m., marine safety officer Claude Panis took this photograph of a waterspout approaching the pier from Tower Zero. The photograph became so popular that he obtained a copyright for it and offers signed reproductions.

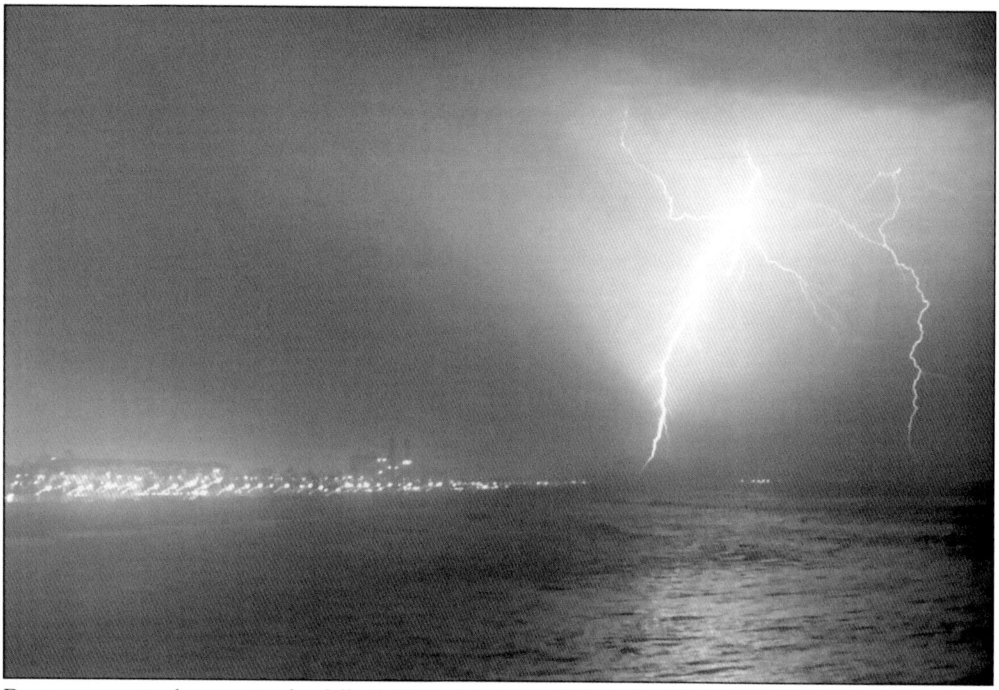

During a tropical storm in the fall of 2006, this incredible bolt of lightning was captured by off-duty lifeguard Eric Rex from the pier. Looking south, the power plant and the Hyatt Regency Huntington Beach Resort and Spa are in view.

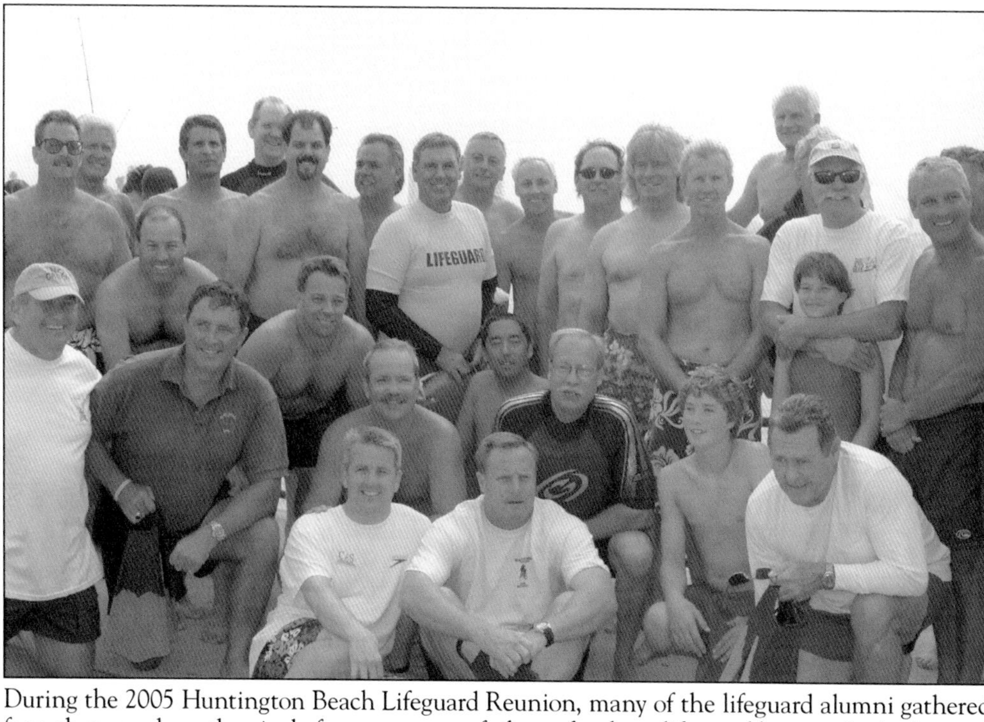

During the 2005 Huntington Beach Lifeguard Reunion, many of the lifeguard alumni gathered for a photograph on the pier before a moment of silence for those lifeguard heroes who had passed before. Immediately after were the infamous last-day pier jumps and visits to *Sentinel* 5240.

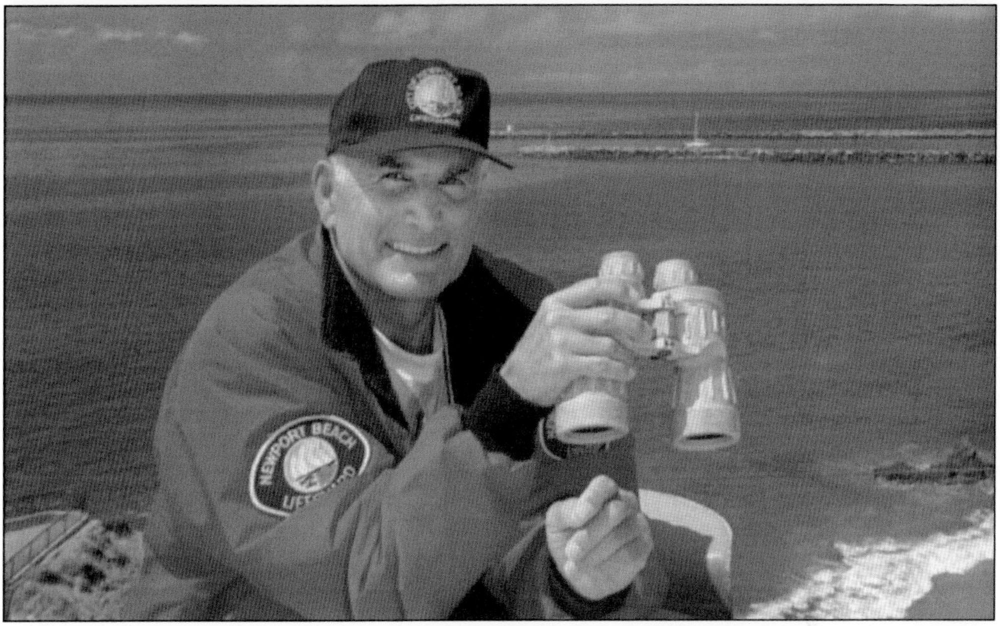

Buddy Belshe, a legendary lifeguard, retired in 2007 after 47 years at Newport and 10 years at Huntington Beach. His parents, Gene and Johnie, are pictured with Bud Higgins on the first page of this book. He was the Orange Coast College's Athlete of the Year in 1955 and part of the leadership of the National Surf Lifesaving Association in 1964. Pictured here, in 2002, Belshe has the Newport Harbor entrance in view.

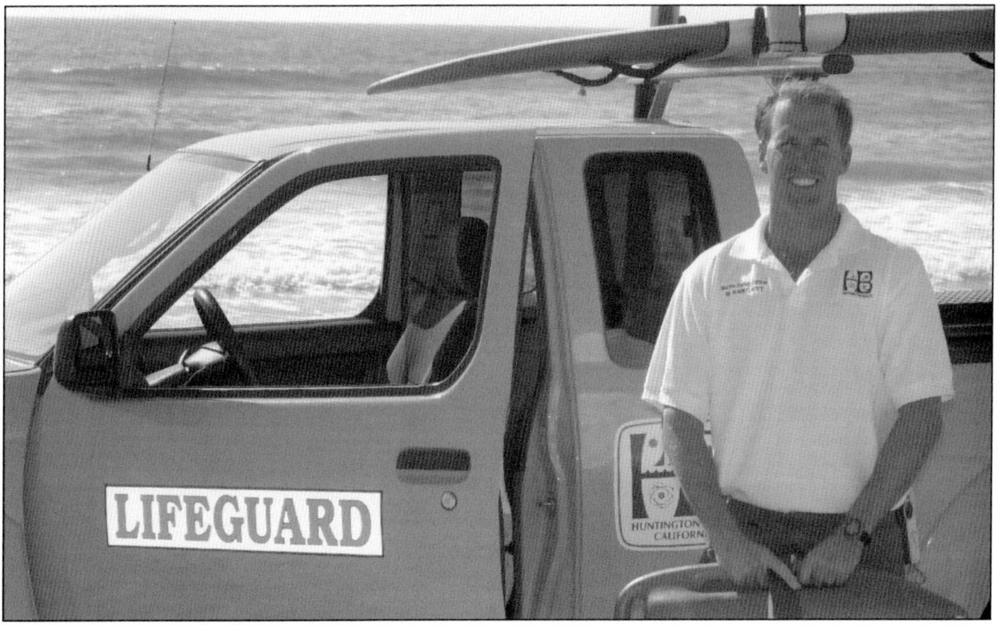

In October 2005, Mike Bartlett received the Award of Valor at the Huntington Beach Chamber of Commerce Public Safety Awards. Near the area of Tower No. 14, Bartlett rescued three swimmers in a large rip current. A lifeguard in Tower Zero later reported, "They certainly would have drowned." Bartlett is also the past president of the HBSLSA and the current editor of the *American Lifeguard Magazine*.

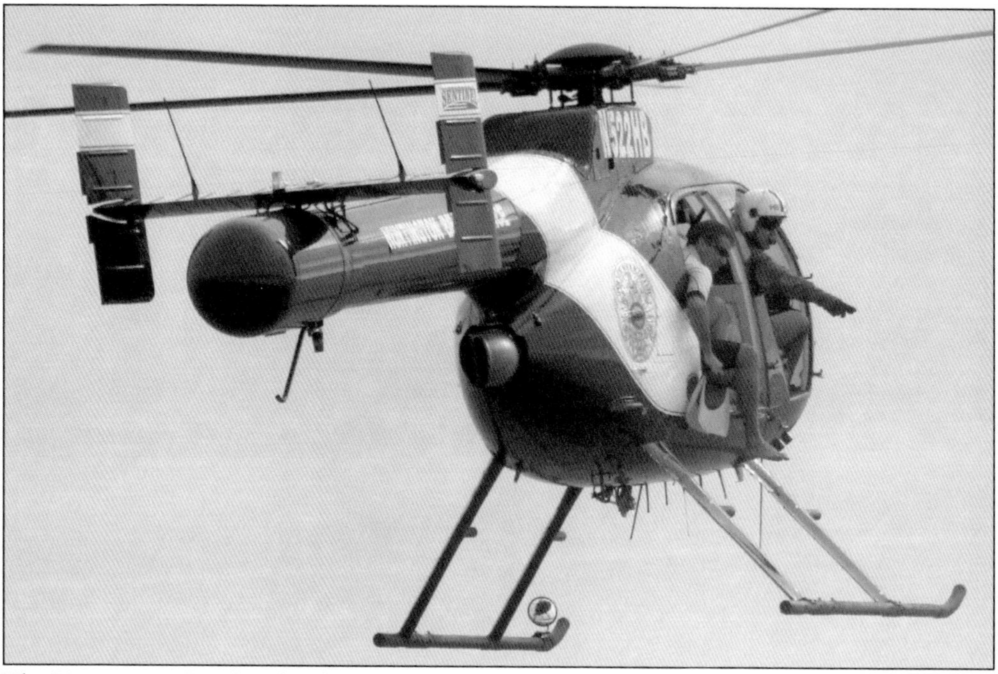

The Huntington Beach police helicopter *HB1* during a 2007 "Code-X" has marine safety officer Matt Karl on board searching the surf line. A Code-X is the search for a presumed drowning victim. *HB1* can quickly deploy the lifeguard directly to the victim when and if the victim becomes visible by air, versus lifeguards on the beach and in the water.

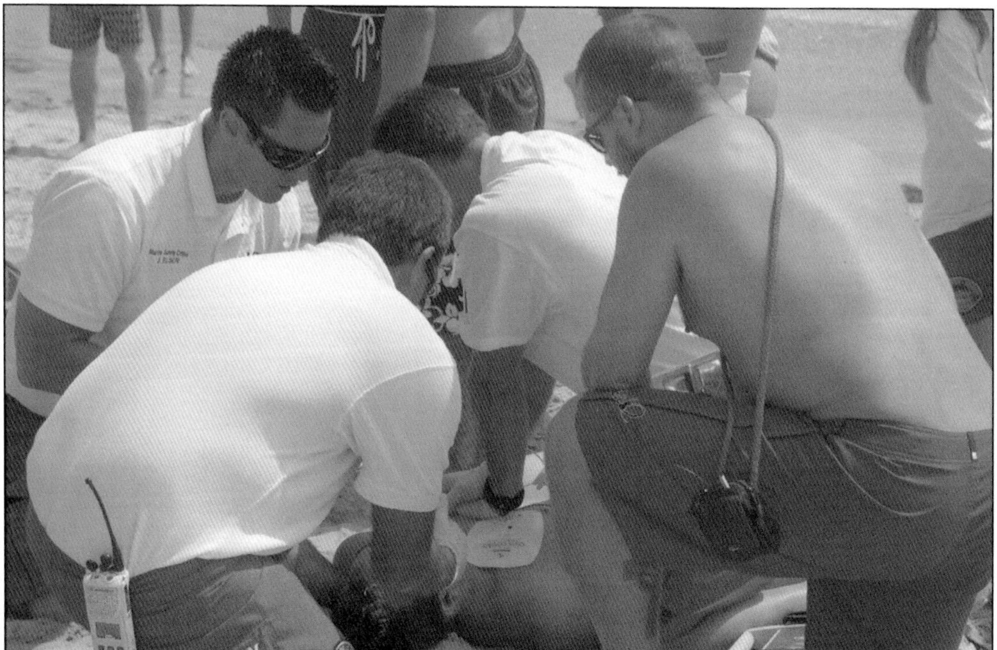

Lifeguards, CPR, and the Automated External Defibrillator (AED) saved this teenager's life near Tower No. 1 in the summer of 2007. On scene are marine safety officers John Elser (left, sunglasses), Matt Karl (radio on waist), lifeguard Tim Stewart (administering CPR), and Troy Rulmyer.

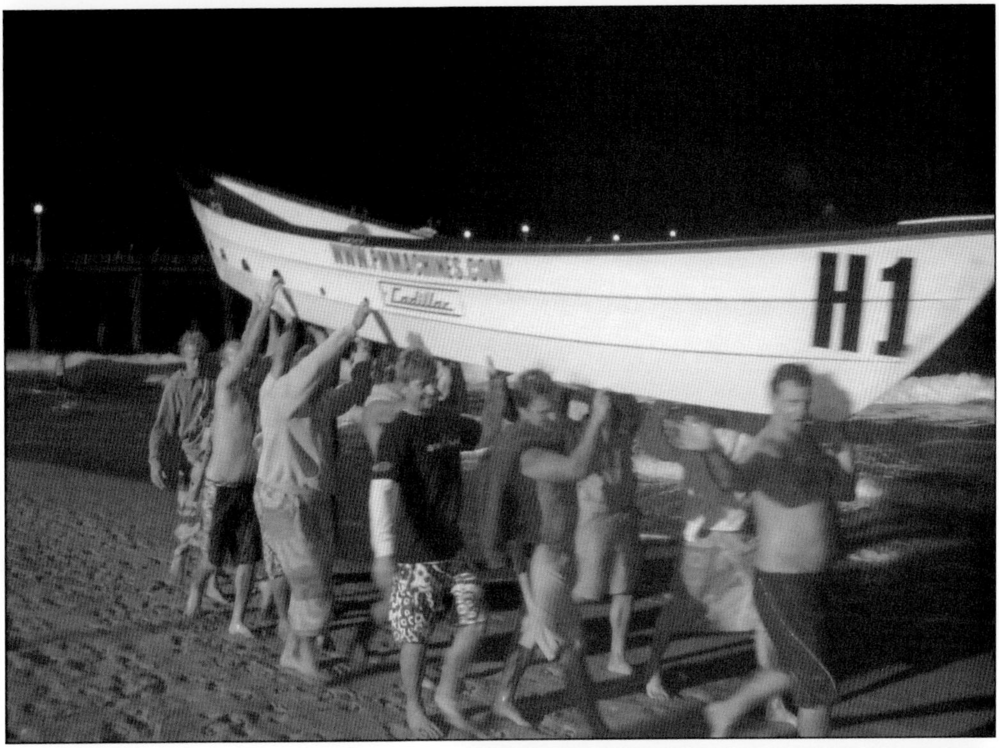

The 2006 Huntington City Beach team carry their lifeguard dory *H1* off the beach at the prestigious Los Angeles County Lifeguard Taplin relays. The annual 16-person team event includes 4 swimmers, 4 paddlers and 4 two-person dory crews. The Taplin is held at night under the bright spotlights placed on the beach and pier.

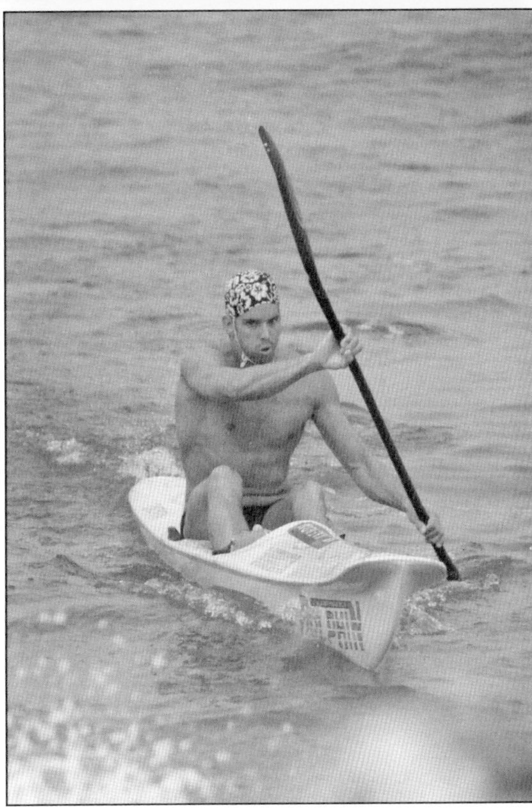

Lifeguard and junior lifeguard instructor Blaine Morgan, on the surfski during the iron man competition in 2005, competes for Huntington Beach, L.A. County, and the California State Parks. Blaine is a NCAA All-American swimmer and twice a U.S. Olympic swim trialist. He is a USLA Lifeguard Nationals 21-time champion and a four-time, top point winner. Morgan is also the two-time winner and record holder of the 200-meter swim with obstacles at the World Lifesaving Championships.

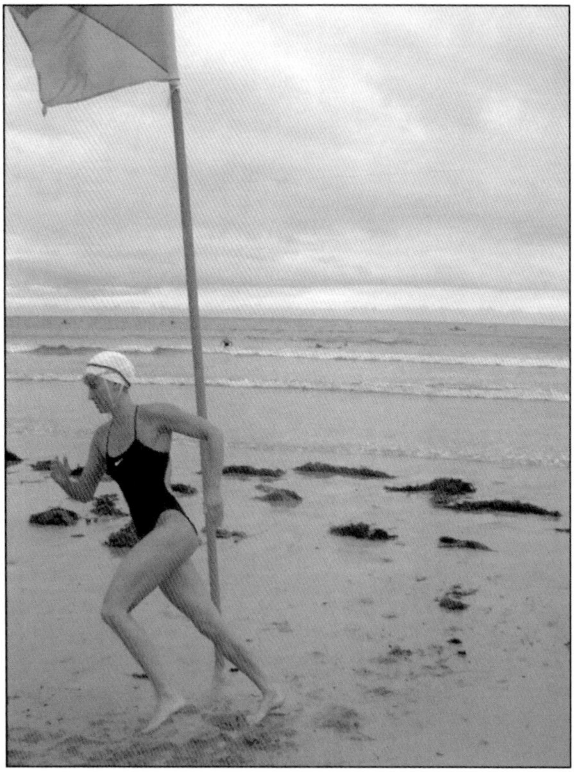

Pictured here in Australia, Micha Burden competed on the Weiland Shield Team with the Los Angeles County lifeguards. Burden was the 2006 Huntington Beach Pier Swim women's division record holder, a 2002 and 2004 All-American swimmer, and a two-time USLA team member of the World Lifesaving Championships. She is currently training for the 2008 Beijing Olympics in the 10-kilometer, open water, swim event.

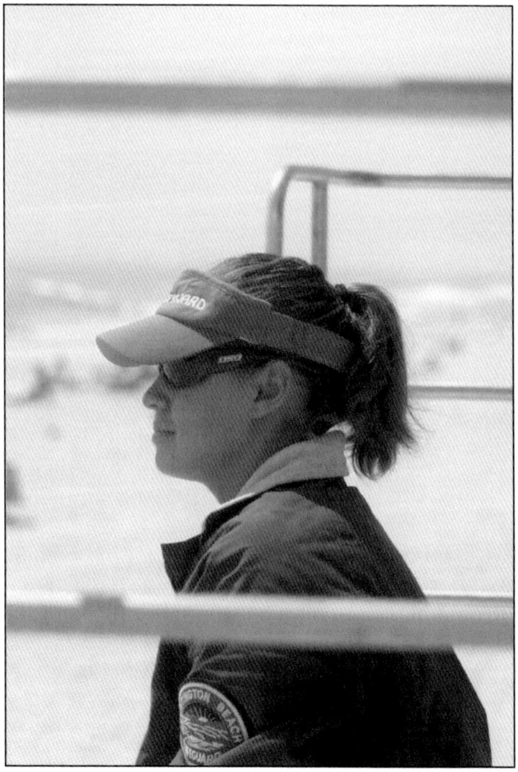

Aubry Panis finds herself in the unique position of working on the beach with her father, marine safety officer Claude Panis. She is a faster swimmer than him, much faster. In 2007, Aubry set a new record of 9:46 in the 2007 Huntington Beach Pier Swim women's division. She was a freshman All-American swimmer at University of California, San Diego.

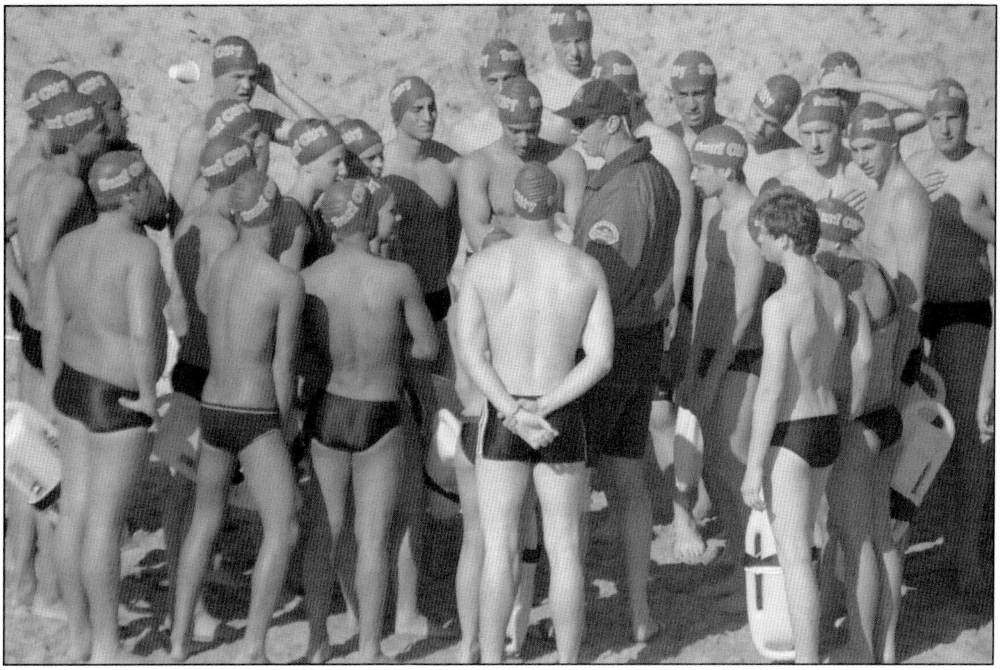

Lifeguard cadet school, sometimes referred to as "rookie school," is gathered here in 2003 next to the west side of the pier. Lt. Greg Crow, charged with the responsibility of marine safety training, briefs the young cadets with their next assignment. The group may expect a rigorous pier orientation or another timed swim "around the pier," a phrase cadets are used to hearing.

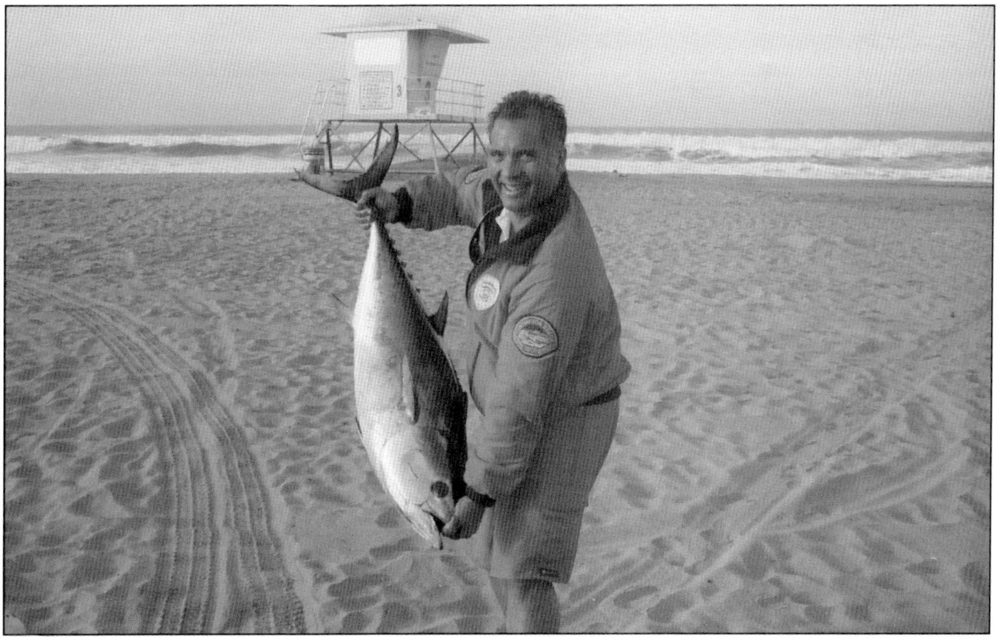

During a routine patrol on April 12, 2007, about 6:35 a.m., between Towers Nos. 3 and 5, marine safety officer Claude Panis saw what he thought to be a baby dolphin very close to shore. He quickly turned from rescuer to hunter and wrestled this 34-pound yellowfin tuna into the Nissan lifeguard truck. Panis and the tuna made the *Western Outdoor News*.

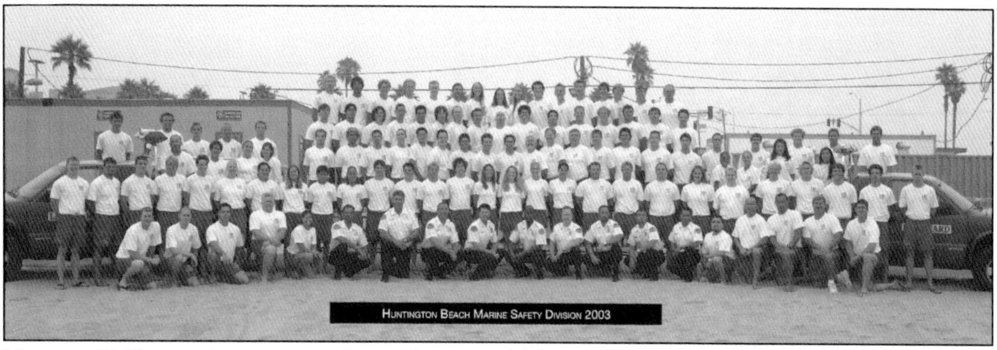

Here, in 2003, are the marine safety officers and lifeguards in front of the temporary lifeguard headquarters, better remembered as the "compound." On April 24, 2003, the old 8,000-square-foot Vincent G. Moorhouse Lifeguard Headquarters, the fourth headquarters structure in the city's history, was demolished. The building no longer met the departmental needs, including having adequate facilities for more female lifeguards and emergency equipment storage.

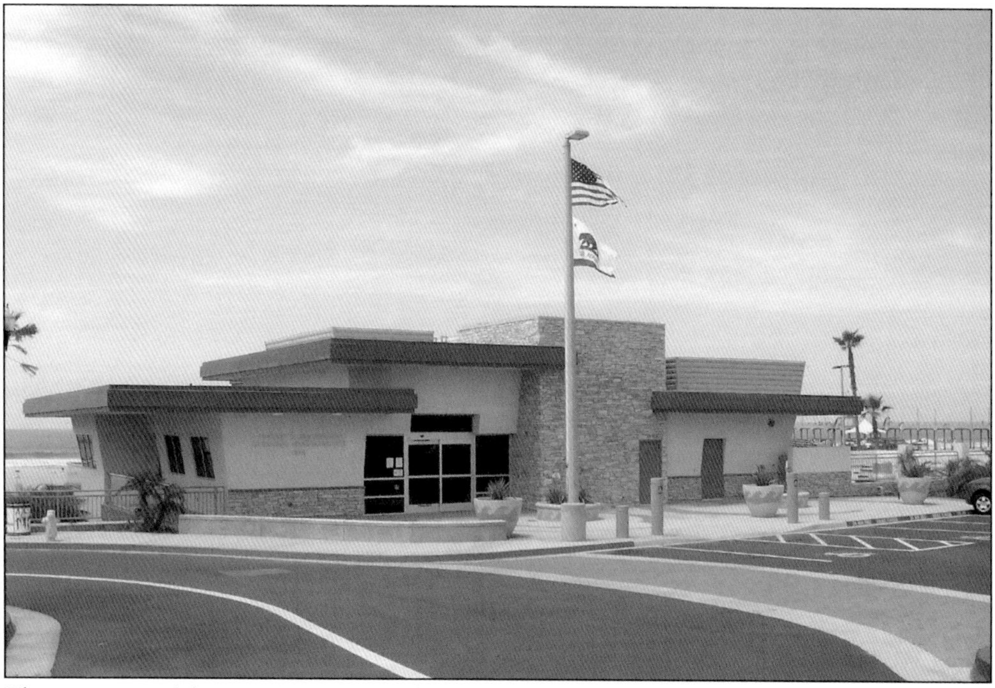

The new, state-of-the-art, 12,000-square-foot Vincent G. Moorhouse Marine Safety Headquarters, located at 103 Pacific Coast Highway, became operational on April 19, 2005. The new building is in the same location and virtually the same footprint as the old one. For emergencies call 911, for business call (714) 536-5281, and for a surf report call (714) 536-9303. The headquarters also has a Web site, www.ci.huntington-beach.ca.us, with a pier webcam.

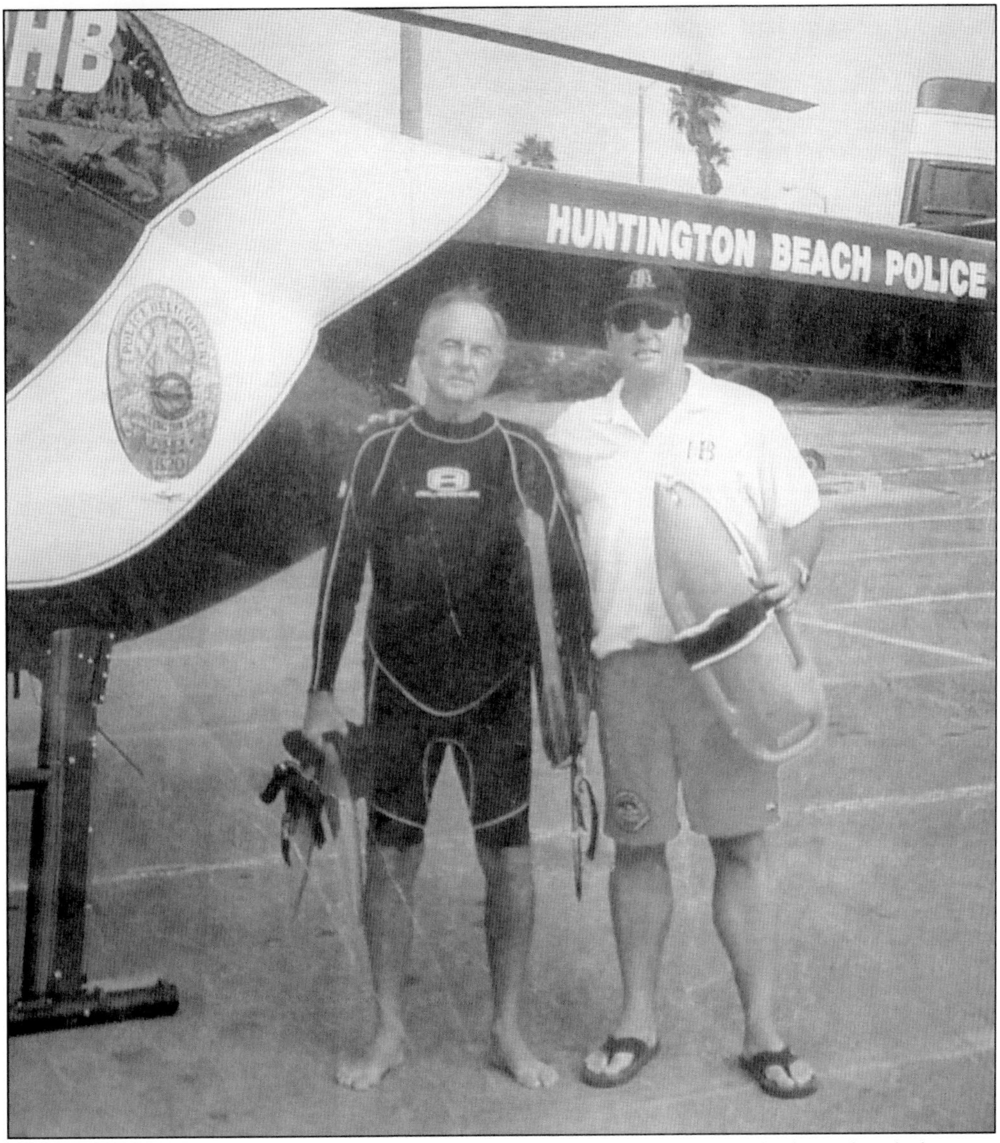

Here, with the author (right) in 2003 during marine safety training with the police helicopter *HB1*, lifeguard alumni Harlo LeBard (1944) stopped by after a surf session. Born in Switzerland and raised in Huntington Beach, Kai Weisser was a Huntington Beach junior lifeguard with his younger sister Ellen and brother Bjorn. After graduating from Edison High School in 1977, he started his lifeguard career in 1979, was appointed marine safety officer in 1987, a rescue boat operator in 1990, and graduated from Cal State Fullerton in 1985 and later the University of Phoenix with a master's degree in organizational management in 1997. Weisser had the distinct privilege of participating in educational lifeguard exchanges to New Zealand in 1986 and South Africa in 1990. In 1988 and 1989, he organized the California Surf Life Saving Championships in Huntington Beach with Mike Gifford and Herb White, and a separate lifeguard test match—California versus New Zealand—which aired on ESPN. Weisser also served as president of the Huntington Beach Surf Life Saving and the Marine Safety Officers Associations and in several elected positions with the California Surf Life Saving Association. Weisser retired in 2006 and lives in Mesa Verde, Costa Mesa, with his wife, Tara, and children Lauren and Nolan.

Consistent with our mission to preserve history on a local level, this book was printed in South Carolina on American-made paper and manufactured entirely in the United States. Products carrying the accredited Forest Stewardship Council (FSC) label are printed on 100 percent FSC-certified paper.

MADE IN THE USA